T0354985

Living A Principled Life

Uncovering 80 Universal Principles of
Life That Can Change You

Richard C. Matteson

authorHOUSE

AuthorHouse™
1663 Liberty Drive
Bloomington, IN 47403
www.authorhouse.com
Phone: 833-262-8899

Published by AuthorHouse 11/16/2021

ISBN: 978-1-6655-4336-1 (sc)
ISBN: 978-1-6655-4337-8 (e)

Library of Congress Control Number: 2021922656

Print information available on the last page.

Living A Principled Life Areas

➤ **Character:** A description of the internal qualities of a good person which could be identified as moral strength or fortitude. It is defined as the way someone thinks, feels, and behaves. It is a set of moral principles that are shared by all good people.

➤ **Conduct:** The manner in which a person behaves, especially on a particular occasion or in a particular context. The conduct principles of life shared are those that are positive.

➤ **Confidence:** A certainty or belief in one's own abilities and an assurance that you can do something well and succeed at many things. It can be illustrated by the words self-confidence or boldness.

➤ **Community:** A group of people with diverse characteristics who are linked by social ties, share common perspectives, and engage in joint action in geographical locations or settings.

Living A Principled Life

Principles of Character - Area One

Principles of Conduct - Area Two

Principles of Confidence - Area Three

Principles of Community - Area Four

Living A Principled Life
Foreword

Principles to live life by seem to have changed with the times and are so riddled with man's opinion that they are no longer the principles of God. What we have turned them into are simply clichés to be put on a poster and sold for decoration.

This book returns us to God's principles for living and asks questions for introspection that will help you gain a greater understanding of God's Word so that you can apply it and grow in wisdom, not just knowledge.

This is not a book to read and set back on the shelf, but a book to repeatedly frequent and put into practice the principles God's Word reveals. As you gain a greater understanding of each one, the questions Richard asks will help you reflect on what you do and how you live. You will grow in your understanding and get better at the application of God's Word.

Richard has been a pastor, father, friend, mentor, and most importantly a student of God's Word for decades now. In wanting to help his children daily, he began writing, Today's Word, which simply shared what he was learning from his daily quiet time. He then wrote down a quick question or two that would help his children apply God's Word daily. I was one of the many additional people that benefited from it and as it grew, more and more told Richard, this needs to be a book.

Richard's observation and listening skills are second to none. God has uniquely equipped him to see the unobvious! His help in coaching men for decades and bringing them back into alignment with God's Word, has brought to light that it is easy to miss a principle which God's Word was teaching.

He has a unique way to exegetically bring to light what they missed or share a new understanding about a problem or situation, and always pointed it back to God's Word, not just an opinion, or what he might do.

In doing this, he helps you broaden your understanding of God's Word and the ability to apply it and live it out. Knowing the Bible is one thing, but we want wisdom to go along with that knowledge. To grow in wisdom means having the ability to apply it so that our lives reflect it as real, show its' importance to us, and most of all, know that God changed our heart because of it.

What you have before you is the result of years of refinement for a quick and easy daily read of principles you can live out in your life. Asking yourself the questions at the end of each essay gives the Holy Spirit space to show you how He wants you to refine, grow and change. This helps you as you go into the mission field; our families, our jobs, and our neighborhoods, and shine the light of Jesus to a world that desperately needs it.

Most men, active in their Christian walk and involved in their church, can look back on their life and point to a godly man who impacted their life and invested in them. Many would say, "If it had not been for that person, I would not be the man I am today. I'm plugged in and active in church, serving others, and most importantly, pouring into other men, so they can develop their walk with Christ." Richard is just such a man and has done a wonderful job of pouring into others.

Tone cannot be determined by the written word, so my prayer is that when you read this book, you will hear the voice of the one who invested in you or the tender voice of a loving, caring parent or grandparent who genuinely cared and wanted the best for you. They came alongside you to help you see what God, through His Spirit, was trying to show you and where He was trying to grow you. I pray you listen with your heart as well as your ears knowing the sincere voice of grace calling not for condemnation but for change so that we might become who God has called us to be.

I have been a beneficiary of this investment by Richard, as a mentor and friend. I hope that as you read, you will realize his desire to see God work in you because of a clearer understanding of the principles of God and your desire to apply them.

The principles are biblical and needed, and the essay questions are specifically designed for self-introspection, and the cultivation of the ground of your heart, so that God's Word can take root, grow and produce a life lived in service to Jesus.

In coaching men for more than two decades, his help of others has always been anchored in the Bible with the desire that others find the help, guidance, and truth that they need to live life fuller. My opinion could be helpful, too, but God's Word is the unchangeable truth that provides exactly what we need.

Mike Manrose,
Found and owner TXKM Holdings
President Creteworks LLC

Introduction

Why I am writing this book.

Words carry meanings, describe situations and influence thought and activity. That's why having a full understanding of the right language can help you direct your life forward successfully, or, if it is the wrong language, direct your life toward destruction.

Every educational discipline, industry, profession, and religion has its' own list of words, letters, and abbreviations meant to describe and clarify it. FBI, USAF, Rev., Renaissance, Art Deco, baptism, born again, integrity, EMT, RN, to name just a few. Other examples below:

Educational Disciplines	Professions	Religions
Mathematics Language	Teacher's Language	Pastor Language
Science Language	Engineer's language	Prayer Language
History Language	EMT Language	Practices Language
Art Language	Military Language	Theology Language
Music Language	Farmer Language	Morality Language

This book can help individuals, families, groups, churches, and businesses learn the words that identify principles of life, a language that has true value and when understood aids in people's maturity. Communication occurs when someone says one word and you immediately can visualize a situation that pictures that word in your mind. It then gives you a clearer understanding of what the other person is expressing, even more than she could explain in several paragraphs.

When you say the name of one of these principles to yourself or others, it means you know the name of the action happening, or you recognize the principle when you see it in the attitudes or actions of those around you. They are of inestimable value if daily kept accessible, however, are valueless if just received as vague thoughts that quickly disappear.

I chose to call them principles and categorize them in the areas of character, conduct, confidence, and community. They are rules without cracks, essential qualities, and the way people can live a more dedicated life to themselves, to others and to God.

They free people to operate their life so that they are not causing intentional hurt to others. To experience this freedom, they need to be inculcated and maintained in the forefront of your mind. That happens best when you continue to expand your understanding of them, identify them in attitudes or actions of yourself and others, and depend on them in your life.

These principles guide you to and through a fulfilled life and away from natural inclinations. A principled life cannot be over-rated. It is a key element aiding a believer to perpetual growth.

Today's world has lost sight of these principles that guided us for centuries. We have also lost sight of the Bible, where the roots of these principles are anchored. We will renew that connection through using many biblical stories of individuals that thrived when these principles of life were followed, but declined when they were discarded.

Living a principled life is acting on a stated body of moral truth which helps you recognize the difference between right and wrong. It is based on a given set of principles that guide you towards holistic living in all the areas of your life and can become a perpetual resource for you as you look for the right words to fill your life with the right actions. Enjoy it and the maturity you will gain because you integrated these principles into your life.

What you need to know before you read and use this book.

These essays on principles of life are not the end all concerning them. They are a starting point of recognition which can, through further study by the reader, bring you to a more complete understanding of each principle and its application to your life.

Neither are these the only principles available in the Bible. More principles are available through regular study of it by you.

These 80 principles of life, captured from the Bible, are not just for believers, they are principles incorporated into the universe that God created; a part of His creation. So, they are applicable to the billions living on the earth, including all ethnicities, nations, tribes, ages, and genders.

You will notice, for the most part, that we have not given you specific applications to "try." What we trust is that the questions asked at the end of each essay, with the Holy Spirit's help, will cause you to find the answers that will work best in your context. In other words, a good question may have several answers depending on the person, family, church, or business reading the book.

Passing over the questions at the end of each essay is a mistake. The intent of them is to help you inculcate the principle into your life. That is hard to do if you don't use the questions as a catalyst for brainstorming and conversations.

We have chosen to capitalize the pronouns when they are being used for God. This is probably a writing no no, but we want to respect God in this way throughout the book.

Here are some brainstorming ideas that might be helpful to you in how you could use the information in this book:

- As a bedtime story for some ages of children – plenty of stories in the essays to share.
- As a dessert after dinner to create discussion.
- As a point of reflection for your own life and your movement forward.
- Find the principle that has specific application to a problem you are currently experiencing to give you more help in solving it.
- As a series, or several series at church for student classes.
- The community principles could be a pulpit series.
- The community principles could be a small group series.
- The community principles could be a series for an adult class creating more discussion and less preaching in class rooms.
- Use them at the beginning of a contest. Read the essay with emotion. Then have a member review for everyone the most important elements of the principle.
- Establish a church class to review all the principles.
- Create a series to read and have a student or adult do a search of the Bible to find various stories that support the principle you are discussing together.
- Discuss a principle on a date.

Final thoughts:

These essays are not all in the same format. We used a variety of formats for the information and stories to keep the reader fresh but all do convey the truth of the word.

The NLT (New Living Translation) is the translation we are predominantly using. If another translation is used it will be identified as such.

We hope that your journey will be one of realization, decision making, and growing in maturity, and that your life will be filled with these principles and their positive results.

Living A Principled Life
Character Area

Character is moral strength, fortitude, and a description of the internal qualities of a good person. It is defined as the way someone thinks, feels, and behaves. Or a set of moral qualities that are shared by all good people.

Blameless Principle

It is hard to fathom a blameless life because it seems we often make mistakes in words and actions. I remember a day I stood before a friend, acknowledged my wrong, and asked them to forgive me for what I had done to them. They said, "Yes," and I walked away with a clear conscience. That was a hard day but a good day because it removed a hurt from a friend and a blot from my life.

A clear conscience has a lot to do with blamelessness. Joseph's brothers were eaten up with guilt because of what they had done to him. At the age of seventeen, he was sold by his brothers into slavery and taken to Egypt to be sold again. It was a long hard road for Joseph for the next thirteen years but at just the right time, God stepped in and Joseph found himself in charge of all of Egypt. He was praised for his forethought and Egypt's abundance brought his brothers to him, although they didn't know it was him because they believed their own lie, that he was dead. Their family in Canaan was low on food and they came to buy more in Egypt. Reconciliation did happen and they fell at his feet, the guilt had been so heavy for them. Joseph forgave and blessing abounded in all their lives.

To become blameless and find personal relationships restored from a wrong doing is satisfying in and of itself, we just have to bust through the pride barrier present in our flesh that holds us back from real freedom. Meeting this challenge changes the trajectory of our life and places us back under the blessing of God.

This is a worthy goal that all should strive for, even long for, as we

1

bounce off others on the pool table of life. The question is, are we leaving bruises or blessings? Do people enjoy being around us because it is peaceful, or do they hide from us because it's uncomfortable?

To be blameless means to have no one that is accusing you of an intentional wrong and to be of such an internal state that you are not blaming yourself for hurting any other person unintentionally. It relates to the way God sees us, blameless before Him, which is not accomplished of our own accord but is the result of our connection to Jesus Christ through faith.

Blameless people are sprinkled throughout the Old Testament.

- God did a great work through Noah "a righteous man, blameless among the people of his time" and one who walked with God (Genesis 6:9).
- Abraham was challenged by God to "walk before me and be blameless" (Genesis 17:1).
- Moses told the people of Israel that they "must be blameless before the Lord your God" (Deuteronomy 18:13).
- In Psalm 101, David sought after a life that could be seen outwardly and understood internally as blameless. Psalm 51 is David's description of the pain he felt in his sin against God, Bathsheba, and her husband Uriah. Finally, his spirit was broken and his fellowship with God restored through confession.
- Solomon promised that "the blameless will be rescued from harm" (Proverbs 28:18a). This could happen either by their protection in life or by their death.

The New Testament also accents a blameless life.

- The Church will be presented to Jesus "without stain or wrinkle or any other blemish, but holy and blameless" (Ephesians 5:27).

- Paul prayed for the Thessalonian church that Christ might "strengthen your hearts so that you will be blameless and holy in the presence of our God and Father when our Lord Jesus Christ comes" (1 Thessalonians 3:13).

- Paul urged the Philippians to overflow with love and keep on growing in knowledge and understanding because he wanted them "to understand what really matters, so that you may live pure and blameless lives until the day of Christ's return" (Philippians 1:10). And, he encouraged them to "do everything without complaining or arguing, so that no one can criticize you" (2:14-15a).

- Peter encouraged the saints to "make every effort to be found spotless, blameless, and at peace with Him [God]" (2 Peter 3:14).

- It was made a guideline for elders in the church to be "holy and blameless" (1 Thessalonians 2:10).

- 144,000 witnesses in Revelation 14:5 will be "found blameless," therefore able to do the work of God during the Tribulation years.

There is another who fits this description, Jesus Christ. He died, taking on our past, present, and future sins in his blameless state. "He had done no wrong and had never deceived anyone" (Isaiah 53:9). Recognizing Jesus as Savior and Lord allows us to take on his blamelessness. Paul understood the importance of us being like this, "he chose us in Him…to be holy and blameless in his sight" (Ephesians 1:4).

What are we finding here? It is important to be blameless; to rid ourselves of a guilty conscience and to have a clean heart so that we can please God and also be a testimony of Christ living in and out from us.

Let's go back to David's words in Psalm 101. They suggest some actions that make a blameless life possible. First, David was connected to God. On his mind was God's love and justice all day long and God was the focus of David's praise (vs. 1).

Second, he carefully examined his life and made decisions that would lead him through each day blameless. He could hold his head up high if

God surprised him with a visit because he had hidden nothing from Him. Inside his home, in his secret place, he walked with a blameless heart and set no vile thing before his eyes (vss. 2-3).

Third, he lived in opposition to faithless men and they could find no blame to put on him. He pushed away from these people and their ideas and made conscious decisions to stay far from them. He silenced slanderers and arrogant people and separated himself from them (vss. 4-5).

Finally, he gathered around him faithful and blameless people as companions. Those who deceived and spoke lies, he dispatched from his presence and kept up the daily fight against such people (vss. 6-8).

This aided David to live a blameless life. It was not easy or an intermittent action but the perpetual and intentional action of his heart to honor God, protect himself, and live among like-minded people.

Here's one more thing to consider. Solomon stated, "The righteous man leads a blameless life; blessed are his children after him" (Proverbs 20:7). His righteousness leads to personal actions and responses to others that are blameless and never the cause of their problems. Plus, there is a trickledown effect of blessing received by his children because of his blameless life. The nourishment of the branches is drawn from the roots of the tree.

Key Takeaway: To live a blameless life requires intentionality and integrity. In Paul's final words to the church at Thessalonica he said, "may your whole spirit and soul and body be kept blameless until our Lord Jesus Christ comes again" (1 Thess. 5:23).

Applications:
Consider which area of your life is not blameless and which of the four actions of Psalm 101 you need to focus on so that you can have a blameless life.

How could you as a parent teach your children about having a clear conscience to receive the benefit of being blameless?

What could your church do to instruct its attendees about the benefit of blamelessness?

How could this be integrated into your business?

Diligence Principle

Who do you know that lives a life of diligence? I'm not talking about a person who is periodically diligent, but a person who is perpetually engaged in diligence, doing work that benefits them and others. Take a minute to reflect on a person who might meet this criterion.

Diligence is understood as steadfastness; a continual "nose to the grindstone" type effort. It draws from its taproot of persistence, which we will talk about later, and is focused less on emotion and more on mental determination.

A diligent person is one characterized by steady, earnest, and energetic effort. They allow no dust to settle on them and are routinely doing what is necessary to succeed in family and work, in school and even in leisure. They give the proper attention and care expected or required in regards to everything they do.

Solomon said, "the desires of the diligent are fully satisfied" (Proverbs 13:4b). There are rewards for their diligence, they are confident, satisfied and trusted by being such a person and cause others to respect them and be happy to work alongside them.

The woman of Proverbs 31 is such a woman. She is capable, trusted, energetic, strong and dignified; a hard worker busy about objectives determined to be necessary, a helper of the poor, and a weaver of clothing for her family. Besides this, King Lemuel viewed here as one who gave instructions with kindness, never demanding but always leading by example. "She gets up before dawn to prepare breakfast for her household and plans the day's work for her servant girls. She goes to inspect a field, knows what she is looking for, and when she finds it, buys it. She makes sure her dealings are profitable; her lamp burns late into the night" (31:25). She is an example of diligence to the max and nothing will stop her from fulfilling her dream of a fed, clothed, protected, honored, and blessed family.

Solomon spoke of the diligence necessary to keep family wealth secure when he said, "Be sure you know the condition of your flocks, give careful attention to your herds; for riches do not endure forever, and a crown is not secure for all generations" (Proverbs 27:23). We know that to own large plots of land and grow grains, fruits and vegetables, plus maintain many animals would require much effort.

Diligence that Solomon spoke of has always been needed. In the agrarian age of farming, in the industrial age of factories rather than fields, and in the information age of high tech where people even work from home. Diligence is never out of style.

Whatever your livelihood, you must understand and give careful attention to diligence. You should not delay when you feel or know you need to act. It takes continual learning and perseverance, in spite of circumstances, to make a living. Diligence, industry and personal attention to your work is paramount if you are to succeed. There is no room to coast if you want to develop your own business, or even if you desire to advance in the business that employs you.

The ant examples the practice of diligence. The ant "has no commander, no overseer or ruler, yet it stores its provisions in summer and gathers its food at harvest" (Proverbs 6:7-8). This simple but famous creature has the foresight to store up supplies during the summer to carry the colony through the winter when food sources will not be available. They respond with industry to search for food, bite off the ends of grain to prevent germination, and store it away for future meals. They need no hierarchy to tell them what to do, they respond with faithfulness to how God created them and what daily objective He gave them.

An advancing army needs to practice diligence, too. Facing the estimated cost of victory they press forward, past barriers and obstacles not allowing those to deter them. They anticipate the twists and turns to a battle, rejoice at incremental advancement, and find solace in victory.

The diligent person anticipates the "what ifs" of life, is faithful in work, and thoughtful in their every action. Diligence is focused on meeting needs and overcoming work's daily monotony by envisioning the satisfaction of the completed task.

Essential to our daily routine, diligence accomplishes necessary tasks, and helps us gain trust from others. It speaks loudly to who you are, what you love and where you are going.

Key Takeaway: Diligence means to be steady, earnest, and energetic in effort and to persist until you accomplish everything undertaken. The Apostle John challenged all of us to "be diligent so that you receive your full reward" (2 John 1:8).

Applications:

On a scale of 1-5, with 1 representing laziness and 5 denoting as perpetual busyness, what number best represents your level of diligence? What can you do to increase your diligence?

How can you illustrate diligence to your family?

What would be two ways to expand your church's or business's understanding of diligence?

Faith Unshakeable Principle

Although it is seldom thought about in this way, you exhibit general faith daily. Sitting down into a chair suggests faith that the chair will hold you. Driving a car requires believing that car can take you where you want to go. Drinking water from your tap reveals faith in the government that purifies the water of anything dangerous to your health. Passing under a green light, you have faith that the car at the intersection under a red light will stay stopped. This is a general use of the word faith, but today we are writing of a more specific faith.

It is described by the writer of Hebrews as "the confidence that what we hope for will actually happen; it gives us assurance about things we cannot see" (Hebrews 11:1). It is holding tightly to something unseen in the belief that it is worthy to acknowledge and rest your life on.

It is called unshakeable by Paul as he writes to Timothy and compares the instruction of false teachers, which led to meaningless speculations about myths and spiritual pedigrees which don't help people live a life of faith, and his instruction's purpose "that all believers would be filled with love that comes from a pure heart, a clear conscience, and genuine faith" (1 Timothy 1:5). This was and still is a faith that is real, genuine, sincere and as previously said, unshakeable.

Let's use an acrostic, F.A.I.T.H., to get a better understanding of faith.

The "F" is for forsaking. It means to give up or abandon. We have an old life that was sinful and now by faith in Christ the indwelling Holy Spirit has given us the power to forsake that life and live a new life given to us at the time of our salvation. Abandon means to walk away from, which we can do because "God has given us all we need for living a godly life" (2 Peter 1:3). We have the Holy Spirit within us and the church around us. We have the Word of God to speak to us and the new nature to help us live out what God says. All that we need. Spiritual power, direction from the Word, a new nature that moves toward God, and a body of believers to encourage and challenge us. We are not just walking away from something; we are walking towards something. We are forsaking to accept a new life.

The "A" is for all. "All means all and that's all all means!" said a good friend of mine. We cannot live around the edges and skirt giving all. It must be complete, wholehearted devotion to God.

The Israelites coming out of Egypt struggled with being wholehearted to God after 400 years in a place with many gods. Their life was focused on meeting their physical needs, everything was tangible. But when they exited, "All of them ate the same spiritual food, and all of them drank the same spiritual water. For they drank from the spiritual rock that traveled with them, and that rock was Christ" (1 Corinthians 10:4). They came out to a life of faith in God for their daily provisions and lived on the basis of the spiritual rather than the physical. Sure, it was a huge change but it portrays the way we must live our lives today.

The "I" is for you, the same as it is in pride. It is not a life lived by proxy; it is one lived in person. We still are the ones who have to live by faith. The writer of Hebrews spoke about others who lived by faith included the following:

- Abel offered an acceptable sacrifice to God as the second son of Adam and Eve. It was evidence that he was a righteous man (Genesis 4:4).
- Enoch pleased God by the way he lived his life "walking in close fellowship with God" for three-hundred years (Genesis 5:21-24), and we know that it is "impossible to please God without faith" (Hebrews 11:6).

- Noah had to build a big boat that he would need by faith in God's word that a flood was coming. He received the righteousness that comes by faith because he believed God (Genesis 6:9, 14, 17; &:13, 20-21).

- Abraham had to believe by faith that God would give him a physical son by Sarah and not his nephew Lot, or Eliezer his servant, or Hagar's child Ishmael. God promised his son, Isaac, would be born and that came true by faith and then Abraham's faith would deepen when he took his son, Isaac, up on the mountain to sacrifice. God spared Isaac as Abraham acted on his faith (Genesis 15:1-6).

- Sarah also believed by faith she would have a son. It took her a while to get there but she finally understood she could not through Hagar manipulate the birth of her "own" son. She had to believe in God's proper provision, a son of her own (Genesis 18:1-15).

- Hebrews 11 shares many other stories of people that experienced the faith journey, some to great heights, but also, some to painful lows, but all were identified as walking by faith.

The "T" is for trust. Trust is a firm belief in the reliability of some person or thing. That reliable person is God in whom we have a confident expectation. He has promised much and has delivered on it every day. To trust is to give the benefit of the doubt to. He is the one we place our confidence in and He has shown Himself to be worthy of trust.

The "H" is for Him. The Father, the Son, and the Holy Spirit: God the Father planned all, God the Son gave all, and God the Spirit indwells all believers. He is the creator, sustainer, encourager and lover of us. He is the source responsible for everything.

And so, we understand faith better as Forsaking All I Trust Him. This is a daily, even hourly activity that is supported by the Holy Spirit living within us. It is a conscious releasing of our hands on the wheel of our life and letting God do the driving.

It demands a walk that is wholeheartedly engaged.

Key Takeaway: "Stand firm in the faith" (1 Corinthians 16:13). "We live by believing and not by seeing" (2 Corinthians 5:7).

Applications:

How are you living by faith in your spiritual, physical, emotional/mental, relational/social, financial, vocational and family life?

How could you exhibit more faith as a family?

What would emphasize this life of faith at your church?

Faithful Principle

Most of us have attended at least one funeral in the last ten years. How would you like to attend 603,548 funerals over a period of 38 years? That would be 15,883 per year and 1,324 per month and 44 per day. More than difficult, it would be impossible and you would have no time to live a normal life.

A year after Israel's departure from Egypt, the Lord spoke to Moses while the nation was still staying at Sinai and told him to "record the names of all the warriors by their clans and families. List all the men twenty years old or older who are able to go to war" (Numbers 1:2).

God was preparing Israel as a large military force. He had already directed them to create all the elements of worship to Him, designed the Tabernacle tent, and set aside the tribe of Levi to direct their worship. Further, God had given instructions to establish a legal system of judges for their fledgling government. Now they needed a standing army to protect them from enemies in their future.

After another year, they were camped in the wilderness of Paran, close to the Promise Land. From this place, Moses sent out twelve spies to travel forty days through the Promise Land and answer the questions Moses suggested to them. Then they returned to the camp for show and tell. They presented the bounty and spoke descriptively of the land, however ten of these spies also reported that there were many giants and walled cities to conquer. Too much, they decided, for the infant nation to handle. Only Joshua and Caleb, of the twelve, said it was possible to conquer the inhabitants. That's a one to five ratio of good news to bad news. The predominance of negative scenarios incited the people to think about stoning Joshua and Caleb and voting in new leadership that would return them to Egypt. Quite a negative domino effect from ten unfaithful spies. Can you imagine them all passing under the hand of Pharaoh once again?

At that, God told Moses to turn around and head into the wilderness because disbelief and unfaithful people were going to get disciplined. All the men of this army would never see the Promise Land, but died in the desert because of their lack of faithfulness to God's direction. It was funeral time, every day. All 603,548 died, except Caleb and Joshua, the two positive, faithful, and faith-filled spies would, thirty-eight years later, enter and enjoyed the Promise Land.

Faithful is defined as having fidelity and dependability, being reliable and loyal. Luke captured Jesus' story about a shrewd manager of an estate, knowing he was about to get fired for wasting his employer's money, called in all the debts owed to his wealthy owner. He adjusted the debts so that he would have friends to rely on when he no longer had a job. Jesus' point of clarity was that "If you are faithful in little things, you will be faithful in large ones. But if you are dishonest in little things, you won't be honest with greater responsibilities" (Luke 16:10).

The parable suggests that being faithful where you are now is necessary to ever obtain expanded responsibilities and the added benefits they provide. Being faithful implies consistency, highlights diligence of the heart, and penetrates every area of your life.

There are three specific focuses of being faithful. One, there is a need to be faithful to yourself. Who you are and how you act? Are you a person with healthy and high standards, uplifting desires and dreams? What do people say about you when you are not in front of them? It not only deals with being respected, but also having a good reputation for being faithful.

Two, you need to be faithful to others. Securing good friends depends on your ability to be faithful to them. That may mean keeping things they share in confidence. Or, being there for them when they need you. It may even mean confronting them when they are wrong or about to make a big mistake. A friend is a terrible thing to waste, so learning how to be faithful to others makes you a better and more reliable friend.

Third, is the need to be faithful to God. This means seeing Christ in a proper perspective. To illustrate, if you've visited your local Art Museum and saw a five by seven-inch picture surrounded by a two-foot-wide frame, you would be drawn to the frame first, not the picture. What you should desire in your life is for others to see Jesus in you, not you. The psalmist reveals that the name of God is at stake in your life (Ps. 23:3), so to reflect God as your creator and Lord is to be faithful to Him. What does your attire, attitudes, actions and words advertise about you to the world? Is it easy to recognize that you are faithful to God?

If you establish faithful patterns, however small you may think they are, then that bit of being faithful will spread itself into other areas of your life. Being responsible in doing small things will enhance your ability to be responsible in doing large things, like the verse above suggested.

Take a quick review of your life. Where do you find yourself not faithful? Now, don't just review the big things in your life, look at the small things too, which could include little rules, small money, and little actions. Many quote the thought-to-destiny phrase as an illustration of the process to either faithfulness or unfaithfulness in your life: "Sow a thought, reap an action; sow an action, reap a habit; sow a habit, reap a character; sow a character, reap a lifestyle; and sow a lifestyle, reap a destiny."[1]

Being faithful will produce actions in line with the thought-to-destiny process that will lead to good in your life. Studying the faithful people lives below can help you see why they were faithful and possibly learn new ways for you to become faithful:

- Moses was faithful as a servant (Heb. 3:5)
- Abraham was faithful (Rom. 4:20)
- Paul promoted Timothy as "beloved and faithful" (1 Cor. 4:17)

- Tychicus was a "faithful helper" who served with Paul (Eph. 6:21; Col. 4:7)
- Epaphras was "Christ's faithful servant" (Col. 1:7; 4:12-13)
- Onesimus, a slave, was "useful" to Paul (Col. 4:9; Philemon 10-11)
- Silas was also a "faithful brother" to Peter (1 Pet. 5:12)
- Paul emphasized the need to be faithful when you manage things (1 Cor. 4:2)
- Most of all, God is faithful (1 Cor. 1:9; 10:13; 1 Thess. 5:24; 1 John 1:9)

Also, to help you see how you could be more faithful, here are some of the activities of a faithful person:

- Faithful person conceals matters others share with them (Prov. 11:13)
- Faithful actions towards others (Acts 16:15)
- Faithful messengers refresh those who send them (Prov. 25:13)
- Faithful is a fruit produces by the Spirit in us (Gal. 5:22)

There is much to consider about being faithful. We do much better in being faithful when we depend on the Holy Spirit to help us. You might want to read over this principle again to let it sink into your soul. If you determine that this is a principle you are going to practice daily, then include the Spirit in your plan to carry it out and learn more about how powerful being faithful can be to your life.

Key Takeaway: Being faithful is a priority for a believer. It starts with faithfulness to yourself, expands to being faithful with your neighbors, and most of all being faithful to God in your daily thoughts and activities, for He has been faithful to you.

Applications:

In what ways have you been faithful to yourself, others and to God?

What other stories of faithfulness are you aware of in the Bible?

What would be necessary for church attendees to understand and start living out faithfulness?

Godly Principle

Godly is not a static state of being but a perpetual process of centering your life on God. Its meaning is the convergence of devotion to God and right conduct through His Spirit. The secret of the godly life is Jesus Christ's walk while on earth which was the example we can follow but obviously never live up to. Individuals are identified as godly because their lives exhibit attributes that can be seen in God.

Often the word godliness is used in Scripture and the difference between godly and godliness is that godly refers to the person and godliness relates to actions of the godly. We can be deceived into thinking that doing the actions that are godly are what we need to be godly, but God indicates that being godly does not find its origins in actions but rather in an inner life connected to God. Therefore, godly is the internal state expressing itself by godliness in good attitudes and actions.

Twenty-eight times over the course of three chapters, 10-12, in Solomon's book of Proverbs this word, godly, is used. The words of the godly are noted as "a life-giving fountain" (10:11), and "sterling silver" (10:20). Godliness is the cause that is "making a nation great" (14:34), and a "whole city celebrates when the godly succeed," plus "upright citizens are good for a city and make it prosper" (11:10-11). This reminds of the response to Esther and Mordecai when they defeated evil Haman by amending the proclamation, he had convinced King Xerxes to sign, that permitted people to murder all the Jews in the kingdom. Under Mordecai's new proclamation, Jews were given the authority to unite and defend themselves in that persecution and that brought joy and eventual victory. And it was noted in the passage that, "the people of Susa celebrated the new decree" (Esther 7:15), which validates statements above.

Further, Solomon said, "the hopes of the godly will be granted" (10:24), "will result in happiness" (10:28), "and the godly are rescued from trouble" (11:8). On a more personal note, related to godly people, Solomon saw that they "care for their animals" (12:10), "care for the rights of the poor" (29:7) and "encourage many" (10:21).

The Apostle Paul sent Timothy, his young disciple, to churches that needed a leader. Paul knew that Timothy was a good man and could be a good leader if he could understand the challenge presented to him. Paul charged him to, "Train yourself to be godly" (1 Timothy 4:7), for this would offer benefit for his present life and the life to come.

The word "train" is properly translated "exercise" and is in the present active tense, means to continually or perpetually train. It also is an imperative command to Timothy. He is to "exercise" in the proper way, regularly and continually. Paul located the places in which he was to be godly, "in what you say, in the way you live, in your love, your faith, and your purity" (4:12).

First, Paul wanted Timothy's words to be godly. Words are powerful, they can hurt, and they can encourage. Timothy was to make his words useful to others and to himself. This would take a lifetime of training his tongue to be positive rather than negative.

Second, he wanted the behavior of Timothy to be an example. That would mean others could look at his daily actions and see godliness exhibited not selfishness. He wanted his actions to align with his words.

Third, he was to be godly in love, making it about God's agape love flowing through him and out to others, not seeking admiration or love for himself. That would require the continual evaluation of his motives.

Fourth, he challenged Timothy to be godly in his faith. Living out belief was the goal; belief in what God has done, what He is doing now, and will do in the future. Others would ask, "does he believe what he is saying, do his actions complement his belief, does he transcend the physical life with his spiritual beliefs?" His faith would be an important lesson for those around him.

And fifth, he encouraged Timothy to live a pure life. This has a moral emphasis to it, but certainly includes his motive's purity, and also his actions and attitudes.

These five areas of challenge for Timothy are good challenges for us even today. Are we godly in our words, our daily activities, the love we show, the faith we believe, and the moral purity of our life? Training yourself to be godly is a perpetual work that takes routine "exercise" to accomplish.

This may all be new to you, so let me offer twelve simple traits of a godly person identified for us in Psalm 112:1-10. This suggests places for us to begin training, if not already happening.

- Obedient - 1b
- Generous - 4b, 5a, 9a
- Compassionate - 4c
- Righteous - 4d
- Fair - 5
- Fearless - 1, 6-7a, 8b
- Trust God - 7b
- Confident - 7b, 8a
- Victorious - 8c
- Remembered - 3b, 6b, 9b
- Influential - vs. 9c
- Honored - vs. 9d

What's really interesting about the list is the response the writer expected from those who were not godly but wicked, he said, "The wicked will see this and be infuriated. They will grind their teeth in anger; they will slink away, their hopes thwarted" (112:10).

The godly person is perpetually training themselves in the ways of God. It helps to have someone, as in Paul and Timothy, who holds you accountable for all the areas of your life. And in all that to understand that "godliness with contentment is great gain" (1 Timothy 6:6) and that "God has given us everything we need for living a godly life" (2 Peter 1:3). So, it is up to us, and the Spirit of God, to live godly and radiate godliness in our attitudes, actions, and motives.

Key Takeaway: The life of the godly is full of light and joy, but it is a never-ending challenge that requires intention, accountability, and personal reflection concerning our motives. The goal is to be like God and be conformed to the image of Christ.

Applications:

In what ways can you expand the godly life which is beginning to bud in you?

How can you teach your children, though words, experiences, and example to be godly individually and as a family?

What would be one way your church or business could example godliness both inside and outside those walls?

Honesty Principle

"Honesty is the best policy"[2] is a proverb attributed to Edwin Sandys who was an English politician in the House of Commons in England from 1589-1626 A.D. and a senior official at the Virginia Company responsible for the founding of Jamestown, Virginia.

If it's the best policy, can there be too much honesty? You've probably heard a friend say something like "that person is just too honest!" They are referring to someone they felt didn't know when to not say something that hurts, embarrasses, or inflames the person receiving it.

The television series, *The Good Doctor*, stars Freddie Highmore working in a hospital surgical unit as Shaun Murphy a young autistic and savant syndrome surgical resident who continually finds himself being too honest with patients. A part of his disease makes him brief and to the point. So, for him, honesty is not always the best policy, the better option would be to say things accompanied by more compassion.

William Shakespear described honesty as an attribute people leave behind when he wrote, "No legacy is so rich as honesty."[3] Various scholars have explained his line in scene 5 as being about a legacy of honesty one gains from previous role models, such as teacher, parent or pastor/priest that taught by their lives and words how to present an honest and truthful character, noting it to be more powerful than any other existing trait.

Honesty is an overarching moral word that describes attributes such as truthfulness, straightforwardness, and trustworthiness. It "guides good people" and the godly are directed by it (Prov. 11:3, 5). It requires an absence of lying, cheating, and false statements.

A return to honesty is experienced by King David in Psalm 32. This along with Psalm 51 share a view of the process David went through in coming to grips with his murder of Uriah and adultery with his wife, Bathsheba. After his confession in front of the prophet Nathan, Psalm 32 is David's expression of the joy of being free of guilt. "What joy for those whose record the Lord has cleared of guilt, whose lives are lived in complete honesty" (Psalm 32:2).

The psalm reveals the hand of God on him so severely that his body wasted away, he groaned all day long and his strength evaporated like water in the summer heat. This was a dire time for the king which resulted in his confession that brought about genuine joy.

Solomon said, "An honest answer is like a kiss of friendship" (Prov. 24:26). Or as some translate, "like a kiss on the lips." What he is suggesting is that you gain the hearts of people by being honest much more than by being sympathetic and favorable to them.

May each of us be able to say what the Apostle Paul said to the Thessalonians, "You yourselves are our witnesses—and so is God—that we were devout and honest and faultless toward all of you believers" (1 Thess. 2:10). Honesty is developed in community, by believers who have integrity and the desire to pass it on to the next generation.

Key Takeaway: Honesty is the best policy to be accompanied, when needed, by compassion. It is something you can leave as a powerful legacy to those who lived around you. It guides godly people and is the best recipe to the growth of a body of loyal friends.

Applications:
Take some time to review your level of honesty with others. Where could you have been more honest?

As a parent, honesty is important to impart to your children as a legacy from you. How will you do this?

Honorable Principle

Why is a judge called "Your Honor?" An honorable judge is one who possesses high moral principles with intentions to operate inside the law, as well as, be impartial to both the prosecution and the defendant. Its synonyms include honest, moral, ethical, principled, and righteous. So a judge is addressed as "Your Honor" to give him/her due respect for the mandate they possess to apply the law correctly.

The desire of every righteous leader is to be honorable. The writer of the book of Hebrews was familiar with his audience when he wrote to the readers. Although Hebrew's writing style has some of the characteristics of Paul, the Apostle, most commentators are hesitant to say he was the writer.

Whoever it was, this special writer said in the closing verses to his readers, "Pray for us, for our conscience is clear and we want to live honorably in everything we do. And especially pray that I will be able to come back to you soon" (Hebrews 13:18). These two things, a clear conscience and a desire to live honorably in everything he did, were the basis of him being honorable both today and in the future.

His clear conscience came from a sense of doing his duty, and no hurt was left unaddressed. He was living in fellowship with the Spirit of God, so his conscience would be sensitive to any impurity in his life. And he was the kind of person that dealt with it quickly, re-entering a state of free to approach God without reservation, offering acceptable service and worship.

This was further understood to come out of a deep desire to live honorably in the future. He set his goal to not allow anything, perceived as or actually evil, to take place in his life. Said another way, above all, in his dealings with these believers, and everyone else beyond them, his actions were governed by heartfelt devotion and godly sincerity, enabled by God's grace, not by his will or any worldly acquired acumen.

An honorable life attests to credible conduct and denotes a reputation that is untarnished or soiled. The word integrity can also characterize it. It means to be guided by a keen sense of duty and ethical conduct, which should be the baseline for every believer.

Hidden amongst a list of "other" descendants of Judah, after David, Solomon, and Jehoiachin's lineages were revealed, was a man named Jabez. These lists give us little about the activities of the next generation, but two verses about Jabez are the exception.

The writer said, "There was a man named Jabez who was more honorable than any of his brothers. His mother named him Jabez because his birth had been so painful. He was the one who prayed to the God of Israel, 'Oh, that you would bless me and expand my territory! Please be with me in all that I do, and keep me from all trouble and pain!'" And God granted him his request" (1 Chron. 4:9-10).

Usually, a child was named according to the circumstances at his birth. Esau was a hairy child and that is what Esau means, hairy. Jabez's name sounds like a Hebrew word meaning "distress" or "pain." How would you like to live with that kind of burdensome name? Certainly he felt handicapped by his name, but decided not to accept life as named, "with pain," but instead called on an available resource, God, to change his future. He asked to be blessed, have his territory expanded, for God to be with him, and to keep him from trouble and pain. God provided all he asked for. Jabez enjoyed a social position of respect and honor, rather than one of a looser, by accessing that which was outside his situation to request blessing and remove the burden of his name. He was honorable.

We should all want to be identified as honorable persons, doing what would qualify us for that designation. That would mean we honor our word and follow it up with proper actions. Paul told the Romans to "do things in such a way that everyone can see you are honorable" (Rom. 12:17b), meaning live a transparent life. The Apostle James echoed Paul, "If you are wise and understand God's ways, prove it by living an honorable life, doing good works with the humility that comes from wisdom" (James 3:13).

In writing the second time to the church at Corinth, the Apostle Paul stressed the importance in his life of being honorable because of who he represented. He wrote, "We are careful to be honorable before the Lord, but we also want everyone else to see that we are honorable" (2 Corinthians 8:21).

He clarified the steps he was taking to ensure that a large offering in his possession was properly received by the church at Jerusalem, without being mishandled. God and others called him honorable, because of the way he guarded the large offering to its proper use. The views of others, that he was honorable, agreed with Paul's internal belief and his effort to be so.

Peter gives us a further reason for an honorable life as one that "should silence those ignorant people who make foolish accusations against you" (1 Peter 3:15). A life could be so honorable that its very review by others would cause them to cease their criticism.

To Timothy, Paul suggested another reason for being honorable. He said, "If you keep yourself pure, you will be a special utensil for honorable use. Your life will be clean, and you will be ready for the Master to use you for every good work" (2 Tim. 2:21).

Peter wrote a caution to believers, he encouraged them to, "Be careful to live properly among your unbelieving neighbors. Then even if they accuse you of doing wrong, they will see your honorable behavior, and they will give honor to God when he judges the world" (1 Peter 2:12).

What we learned through the life of the writer of Hebrews was that being honorable starts with a clear conscience and extends to the desire to live a daily life with integrity. Jabez showed us it is honorable to not accept life as given to you, but to be more than expected by the world. Paul and James said it was good to do works with humility that were honorable.

Other bonuses of an honorable life would be the ceasing of foolish accusations against you, being used as a special utensil in the hands of God, and allowing unbelievers to see the honorableness of your life and be drawn to God as a result.

Key Takeaway: Acting in an honorable manner helps us to make and keep friends. When your word can be trusted, and your actions follow suit, trust is built, and friendships grow and last. It destroys accusations and brings peace.

Applications:
How do your actions back up your honorable words?

As parents, you want to be honorable in front of your children and also be seen as honorable by them. What could you do to help this take place?

How are your congregation and its leaders honorable?

Humility Principle

King Nebuchadnezzar of Babylon walked on the roof of his palace and exclaimed, "By my own power, I have built this beautiful city as my royal residence to display my majestic splendor. While these words were still in his mouth, a voice called down from heaven, 'O King Nebuchadnezzar, this message is for you! You are no longer ruler of this kingdom. You will be driven from human society. You will live in the fields with the wild animals, and you will eat grass like a crow. Seven periods of time will pass while you live this way, until you learn that the Most High rules over the kingdoms of the world and gives them to anyone He chooses" (Daniel 4:30-32). You can continue to read this story in the book of Daniel and see that it came true and did last for seven years, then, the king's sanity was restored by God and you can see his response to God after that amazing discipline (4:34-37).

Solomon said it well, "Pride ends in humiliation, while humility brings honor" (Proverbs 29:23). Jesus said, "Those who exalt themselves will be humbled, and those who humble themselves will be exalted" (Matthew 23:12). This is better translated, "the lowly in spirit shall lay hold on honor."

Mordecai, one of the Jews in captivity, sat at the gate of King Xerxes of the Medes and Persians and did not bow down or show respect to Haman, a vicious enemy with a high government position, when he passed. Haman despised him and delighted to plot his death along with all the Jewish people in this kingdom of 127 provinces. It is a sorted tale in Esther 7-8 of the workings of the plan of God these two people experienced.

Pride often is exhibited in those with high position, extreme talent, or with any supposed superiority over others but the humble eventually are honored. "I will bless those who have humble and contrite hearts, who tremble at my word. But those who choose their own ways—delighting in their detestable sins—will not have their offerings accepted" (Isaiah 66:2b-3a).

Honor was eventually proclaimed to the humble Mordecai while Haman, when confronted with the truth of his evil actions, was taken out from the dinner table of King Xerxes and Queen Esther and hanged on the gallows originally constructed for Mordecai's death. This verse says it all, "You [God] rescue the humble, but you humiliate the proud" (Psalm 18:27).

From Adam's son, Cain, forward, God has dealt with prideful people and if they would not humble themselves, then they were crushed under His mighty hand. It maybe didn't happen immediately, but always ended with God's judgment being carried out on them.

Humility is the crown of humans and true greatness, fashioned and jeweled by the hand of God. Self-abasing confessions of great men in God's eyes were like these:

- Abraham, the father of the Jewish nation said, "I am but dust and ashes" (Genesis 18:27).
- Job, a contemporary of Abraham, at the end of all his suffering said, "I take back everything I said, and I sit in dust and ashes to show my repentance" (Job 42:6).
- Jacob, whose name was changed to Israel said, "I am not worthy of all the unfailing love and faithfulness you have shown to me, your servant" (Genesis 32:10).
- Paul, the Apostle, born out of due time, said, "I am the worst [sinner] of them all (1 Timothy 1:15).

The glory of God shines out from within the humble and they divert the glory they might receive to God, praising Him for what He has done. Their real glory eclipses all pomp and circumstance and any pride in "achievements and possessions" (1 John 2:16). Joseph and Daniel when low and then elevated to high positions, exampled the truth of this. They declared God as pre-eminent and themselves as lowly servants.

Honor will come to those who are humble in "due time" (Job 22:29). Peter certainly spoke from his own experience about the principle of humility when he said to the leaders of churches, "so humble yourselves under the mighty power of God, and at the right time He will lift you up in honor" (1 Peter 5:6).

Here are some other verses that you might study to enhance your view of humility:

- Paul said to "show true humility to everyone" (Titus 3:9).
- For honor to be rightly dealt with first requires humility, "humility precedes honor" (Proverbs 15:33; 18:12).
- And a sobering statement from the psalmist, "though the Lord is great, He cares for the humble, but He keeps His distance from the proud" (Psalm 138:6).

Let us understand that "what this world honors is detestable in the sight of God (Luke 16:15). Let God praise you and not men, for He sees the deepest part of your heart, and you will hear a welcome like this one spoken to Mary, "Greetings, favored woman! The Lord is with you" (Luke 1:28). Jesus exampled this attitude of humility and "therefore, God elevated him to the place of highest honor" (Philippians 2:9a). If you can understand this, then your life will be better and blessed by God.

Key Takeaway: Humility is not something you can fake. Ego shows up without you being aware. Humility only happens when you are constantly aware of your frail humanity and in awe of God's divinity and all that it implies.

Applications:

Honestly evaluate your heart and consider how you can better example humility.

What safeguards could you establish to make sure you are not trying to be humble now, so that you will be honored later?

How have you as a parent exhibited true humility when your children were around?

How could humility be taught and more readily experienced in your church?

Integrity Principle

Integrity is an essential for a life that stands before the Lord. "The Lord detests people with crooked hearts, but He delights in those with integrity" (Proverbs 11:20). The word integrity means "without wax." It references a pot that was not cracked.

In early days, clay pots were fashioned and sold in the market places. Each pot was inspected but once in a while a store owner would see a crack in a pot and push some wax into it, then rub pot dust into and over it so the crack would disappear. When a smart person came to buy a pot, she would hold it so the sun would shine down into the mouth of the pot. If the pot had integrity there would be no glowing spots reflecting the sun's rays through the wax on the outside of the pot, but if it did, well, that was not the pot to buy because it would not last long in its usage before failing.

King David had some good words about integrity. "I have acted with integrity; I have trusted in the Lord without wavering. Put me on trial, Lord, and cross-examine me. Test my motives and my heart. For I am always aware of your unfailing love, and I have lived according to your truth" (Psalm 26:1-3).

David exampled right living with God and even more proved his integrity by not spending time with liars or going along with hypocrites. He hated gatherings of evil doers and he refused to join in with the wicked. It sounds a lot like the first psalm where the righteous person does not "follow the advice of the wicked, or stand around with sinners, or join in with mockers" (Psalm 1:1). This verse reveals the downward progression of a bad friend that starts with a little advice, then mingling with wicked people, and finally sitting at their table and eating with them.

David believed that his associations, language, and desire to worship God activated a blameless behavior and identified him as having integrity or being "without wax." He also said, "my integrity and honesty protect me, for I put my hope in you" (Psalm 25:21). David was confident that if tested or God looked at his heart motives it would reveal his steadfastness toward God.

He was aware of God's love always. God was in the forefront of his thoughts throughout the day or night. There was an outside standard that David lived up to. That standard was God's truth about him, his kingship, and his deeds. Living according to God's truth kept him from living situationally and excusing his behavior.

Integrity demands a daily dose of honesty about yourself, your actions, and your thoughts. It requires singlemindedness, wholeheartedness. The heart, mind and will all have to be headed in the same direction and that direction has to be blanketed with the truth. That is how you immunize yourself against the virus of dishonesty. It is easy to speak a "white lie" but soon after it will become black as night. Truth is like light, once it is turned on it reveals all that surrounds it. Solomon knew it as a cornerstone to the building of anything lasting. He also knew that it was the best way to keep yourself safe and that's why he said, "People with integrity walk safely" (Proverbs 10:9).

Integrity has to reach into every crevice in your heart and every area of your behavior. It is good to decide in advance how you will act based on your integrity. It can be a baseline for self-evaluation that will keep you strong, directed, and without blame. The word itself means sound, whole, and complete. It is used to identify the state of a building, bridge, company, family, and speaks of wholeness, quality and strength.

When I was hired by a church as their Singles Pastor, after about two weeks at the church the Senior Pastor called me into his office and told me to find an accountability partner. Seriously but sadly, I was forty-one years old and had never been challenged in this way.

I asked him what the purpose of such a person was and he explained it was to make sure you have integrity and accountability. I asked one of the Deacons to meet with me regularly and I provided him a short list of important and private questions I wanted him to ask me at every meeting. The time I spent over a meal and discussing my life with him became very precious to me. I have sought an accountability partner in my life ever since then.

The concept of accountability stems from a genuine desire to maintain a high level of personal righteousness, integrity, and perpetuate the three ideals of purity of life, unity of purpose and evangelistic zeal in your life.

Our challenge is living a life of integrity in every area of our life. That is hard. Selfishness, stubbornness and sin's beckoning call are always there to entice us from the right way. Even unbelief slips into the corner of our mind and causes us to waiver. Living with integrity is a faith and works journey and God is our resource and strength for it. He is the rock you can stand on above the beck and call of the world.

Key Takeaway: Integrity in a life, or in a building or any metal structure, means that it is strong, safe, and dependable. It is valuable and essential if we are to live a life pleasing to God. The godly person will walk with integrity because he has a unified core, soul and spirit, that is in agreement with God.

Applications:

David had three check points in his life. How would you answer them?

- Who are the people that you associate with? (Make a list)
- How free are you from wicked people?
- When and how do you worship God?

Every parent wants their children to act correct, so, how could you encourage them to have another person, beside mom and dad, meet with them to help them protect their integrity?

What could your church implement to teach integrity and accountability to its attenders?

Loyalty Principle

Stories of loyalty are heartwarming and inspiring showing us what can happen when two people decide to be loyal to each other. Mountains are climbed, rivers are forded, money is spent, and sometimes the ultimate price is paid for carrying out their loyalty to their friend.

Jonathan was the son of King Saul and friend of David from the time of his defeat of Goliath. King Saul wanted Jonathan to follow him on the throne and was dead set against David gaining that prize. So, the last years of his rule he searched for David to kill him.

Jonathan knew that David was the better choice for king and in a field far away from the palace after a long discussion said to David, "May you treat me with the faithful love of the Lord as long as I live. But if I die, treat my family with this faithful love, even when the Lord destroys all your enemies from the face of the earth" (1 Sam. 20:14-15). They made a pact there and Jonathan asked David to reaffirm his vow of friendship, which he did.

When Jonathan became convinced by his father's words and actions that he did want to kill David, he met with David one last time. At that meeting he said, "Go in peace, for we have sworn loyalty to each other in the Lord's name. The Lord is the witness of a bond between us and our children forever" (20:42).

Not long after, Jonathan, his two brothers, and his father were killed by the invading Philistines on Mount Gilboa. "The Philistines closed in on

Saul and his sons, and they killed three of his sons—Jonathan, Abinadab, and Malkishua" (31:2) and Saul was the last to die.

David was anointed the King of Judah (2 Sam. 2:4) and then after a brief civil war with most of the other tribes, they too anointed him King of all Israel (5:3). Time passed as David defended the nation against the Philistines and other nations testing his strength as the new king. Then, one day David asked, "Is anyone in Saul's family still alive—anyone to whom I can show kindness for Jonathan's sake" (9:1). Obviously, David remembered his vow with Jonathan and was seeking to fulfill it.

One of Saul's servants, Ziba, was brought to David to answer that question and he told David that a son of Jonathan was still alive, Mephibosheth. David had him brought to a friend's home and said to him, "I intend to show kindness to you because of my promise to your father, Jonathan. I will give you all the property that once belonged to your grandfather Saul, and you will eat here with me at the king's table" (9:7). So, David was loyal to his promise to Jonathan although no one would have ever known about their promise if he had not said anything about it.

The other compelling story of loyalty is that of Ruth, a Moabitess, who had married into a family from the tribe of Judah. Elimelech and Noami with their two boys, Mahlon and Kilion, had left Judah during a severe famine and lived in Moab. Through the ten years of their sojourn there, both sons married Moabitess. Then Elimelech and the young married boys died, too, leaving Naomi and two daughters-in-law to fend for themselves.

Naomi decided to go back to Bethlehem and begged the girls to stay in Moab where they could find new husbands. But Ruth clung tightly to Naomi, and said, "Wherever you go, I will go; wherever you live, I will live. Wherever you die, I will die, and there I will be buried. May the Lord punish me severely if I allow anything but death to separate us" (Ruth 1:16).

Ruth was a hard worker, toiled in fields to gain small portions of grain, and was rewarded well for all her efforts. Boaz noticed her and told her to only glean in his fields as a protection for her. He later became Naomi's family redeemer purchasing all the lands of her dead husband and boys and took Ruth as his wife. She bore Obed as their first son; his child was Jesse who was David's father.

Loyalty and kindness are conjoined twins. They are the weapons we wield to overcome reproach. These actions are God-like because it is Him who first was loyal and kind to us.

Solomon wrote, "Loyalty makes a person attractive" (Prov. 19:22a). It draws people to us. It is as expensive as the most expensive proof of love. Who can measure that gift or even pay it back? It reveals a compassionate heart. It shows on the outside what is being felt on the inside. Even those who live in poverty speak of loyalty as more valued than presents.

Here is the truth, many will say they are loyal friends, as Peter did, but who can find a person that is truly loyal? Loyalty to God will be tested by temptation. Loyalty to authority is not an option. And, loyalty to believers will involve sacrifice. The challenge to us is to "never let loyalty and kindness leave you! Tie them around your neck as a reminder. Write them deep within your heart" (3:3).

Key Takeaway: Loyalty is closely knit with kindness and its best is shown by those who trust in God. The loyalty of David to his friend lived in his heart long after Jonathan's death. A new generation was able to enjoy its fruit. Ruth made a decisive choice to be loyal to Naomi and God blessed her for it. She became one of the four unique mothers mentioned in the line of Jesus: Tamar mother of Perez, Rahab mother of Boaz, Ruth mother of Obed, and Bathsheba mother of Solomon (Matt. 1:3-6).

Applications:

How have you been loyal to Christ and God the Father?

Parents, loyalty is a powerful instrument of love, how could you teach it to your children?

What would loyalty look like in your church attenders?

Persistence Principle

Ever experienced the persistence of a child or student? They have focused their eyes on something, a toy, a visit to the zoo, or a driver's license and they shamelessly keep asking about it. It is irritating but their persistence pays off eventually.

Jesus always gave his disciples more than they asked for. Luke shares the story of them coming to him after he was finished praying and asking him to "teach us to pray" (Luke 11:1). Jesus shares the simple prayer which today is called The Lord's Prayer. In a sense he said, pray to God the Father expressing His holiness and desire for the coming of Kingdom, then pray for daily food and that daily sins will be forgiven. Commit to forgive others who sin against us and help us not to yield to temptation.

But in the verses that follow his example prayer he taught them to be persistent. He shares the story of a man who goes to his neighbor at midnight to ask for three loaves of bread. The neighbor is in bed and not ready to fulfill the request. He tells the friend to go away emptyhanded. But the friend keeps knocking and eventually his persistence pays off as his neighbor gives him the bread.

Jesus states the following after this story, "So I tell you, keep on asking, and you will receive what you ask for. Keep on seeking, and you will find. Keep on knocking, and the door will be opened to you. For everyone who asks, receives. Everyone who seeks, finds. And to everyone who knocks, the door will be opened" (Luke 11:9-10).

Asking implies humility and actual need. It presupposes that God can provide and wants to be involved in your life. Seeking is asking plus acting. It implies earnest petitioning, but also active endeavoring to obtain what is needed. To illustrate, you should pray for a deep knowledge of the Bible but should also be reading and studying it. Finally, knocking is asking plus acting plus persevering. All these three are imperatives and in the present tense which means they all command you to continue to do them.

Persistence is as essential to prayer as it is to anything that you do in your life. If you don't ask, how can you receive? If you don't seek, how can you ever find? And, if you don't knock, how can the door ever be opened? The lesson of Jesus is not only to pray but to ask, seek, and knock, for no success happens unless you do.

He told the disciples another story about persistence later. There was a judge who didn't fear God or care about people. A widow came to him repeatedly, saying, "Give me justice in this dispute with my enemy. The judge ignored her for a while, but finally he said to himself, 'I don't fear God or care about people, but this woman is driving me crazy. I'm going to see that she gets justice, because she is wearing me out with her constant requests'" (Luke 18:1-8). Jesus' point, "So don't you think God will surely give justice to his chosen people who cry out to him day and night? I tell you, he will grant justice to them quickly!'" (18:7-8).

What a joy to be persistent in prayer and see an answer to that prayer, not always exactly what you wanted but certainly an answer from God. The very word ASK has the elements within it, A-ask, S-seek, K-knock. Have you been persistent in prayer? Sometimes you may ask but then stop, then go further and seek, but stop there. Persistence is the continual pushing forward until the doors are opened. Keep that in mind when you pray.

Key Takeaway: Persistence is a repeated coming to someone and sharing your need. It assumes it is a real need and not just a want. You don't voice it once but often always in a state of respect. God knows before you ask, but people don't, so let your persistence be evident.

Applications:

How could you be more persistent in your requests to God and people?

How could you teach your children to be persistent with people but also in prayer?

How could persistence be encouraged in the prayers of your church members?

Purity Principle

We are continually told that "there is good in every person," that we have to look for it, and believe that people are good at their core. Although that may be the opinion of some, that does not align with God's view, because Jeremiah said under God's inspiration, "The human heart is the most deceitful of all things, and desperately wicked. Who really knows how bad it is" (Jeremiah 17:9)?

The heart, not the muscle but the interior of our being, is composed of the mind, emotion and will, and is identified as deceitful (Proverbs 6:14; 26:24), scheming (Proverbs 6:18), perverse (Proverbs 11:20; 17:20; Psalm 101:4), evil (Proverbs 26:23), destructive (Psalm 5:9), slanderous (Psalm 41:6), and cunning (Psalm 64:6). Wow! That is saying a lot about the sin within each of us.

It is one thing to label it, but is there other proof of these accusations? Yes. After the fall of Adam and Eve, God said they couldn't stay in the Garden of Eden, so they were ushered out. Years later Cain, their oldest son, murdered Abel their second son. They were brothers with the same parents and it happened within a comparatively short period of time. How could animosity gain such preeminence so quickly?

More time passes, and Noah is engaged by God to build the ark to house animals and eight human beings. The rest of animals and humans die in the worldwide flood because "God saw that the earth had become corrupt and was filled with violence, for everyone on earth was corrupt" (Genesis 6:11-12). No one was excluded except the eight that were saved.

Later after hundreds of years of slavery, the people of Israel exited Egypt, and given the Ten Commandments, directing them in their actions toward God, parents and neighbors. These Commandments were given because of the negative nature of what humans do. People were just not good at the core.

Then Jesus enters the world, lives among men, and dies on a cross having done no evil. He is good to the core, because He is God to the core. He becomes God's perfect and sufficient sacrifice for the sins of everyone, and provides a way for humans again to have a heart that could be called upright. Several other words describe the heart saved from its own sin: pure (Proverbs 22:11; Psalm 24:4; 32:11; 73:1, 13), clean (Proverbs 20:9; Psalm 51:10); true and right (Psalm 7:10; 11:2; 97:11), honest (Psalm 36:10), and virtuous (Psalm 94:15).

In these verses, purity of heart is tied to gracious speech and pure hands. The person with a pure heart thinks carefully before speaking. Attitudes and actions are present that lean toward God and not away from Him. A "light shines on the godly, and joy [shines] on those whose hearts are right" (Psalm 97:11). The way of these people is bright and joyful. How has this change happened? It is all because Christ exchanged His nature for our sinful nature, and brought us a new nature that can be and do all the above with a purity of heart when in relationship with God.

To be pure is to have a heart that has been cleansed; made new by God. Its motives and actions are pure from evil. A pure heart says, "You have taken away my clothes of mourning and clothed me with joy, that I might sing praises to you and not be silent" (Psalm 30:11-12). The godly sing for joy to the Lord, whether they can carry a tune is not important. So let singing burst forth from your heart!

Key Takeaway: Understanding that we are not good, and all need a Savior, leads us to understand the price God paid to give us a pure heart which is possible because of God's grace and mercy.

Applications:

What is the state of your heart?

Parents, how are you helping your children understand what is a pure heart?

What would be the most effective way for a church to share this truth about purity with their congregation?

Resilience Principle

Resilience is the ability to recover strength and spirit quickly. Some might call it bouncing back and others might characterize it as failing forward, meaning there is always something you can learn from failing and if you learn it, you can move forward quicker.

In the physical area, we might be close to exhaustion and can't do anything more until we get water and electrolytes back in our system, along with rest, to replenish our depleted supplies. That was the experience of Elijah near Mout Sinai after he was threatened by Queen Jezebel.

In the emotional area, we need community and comfort along with a touch of hope to move us toward healing and reset. Understanding that there is a grief cycle and noting where we are on it can put us on the path to recover.

In the mental area we can burn out with no margin in our life to fall back on. Time away, evaluation of priorities, and confidence in your own resilience can have a positive effect on how long it will take to get back to normal.

In the spiritual area, resting and trusting in God, praying regularly about everything, yielding our life to the Spirit who resides within us will help us find renewal. We may be tired in the battle and don't know how weak we really are. Identifying our present downward slide, confessing sin, seeking forgiveness and choosing to move forward all help us in resilience.

In the family and financial there are bumps in the road always, but resilience does not let that deter us from moving forward, it just means we may have a long road ahead. Resilience in these two areas does not mean you will get immediately back to a good place. Some things take more time and effort, the key is to not be frustrated with the pace.

When we experience tough times whether they be physical, emotional, mental, financial, familial or spiritual, it can be helpful to reflect on our past performance to see what actions helped us recover and how long it might take to bounce back.

A perfect illustration of resilience would take us to the Apostle Peter. It seemed like he was always sticking his foot in his mouth around Jesus but always able to move forward.

At a critical point in Jesus' ministry, he began to tell his disciples plainly that he needed to go to Jerusalem and that he was about to suffer many terrible things at the hands of the Sanhedrin. He would be killed but would raise from the dead on the third day after.

Simon "took him aside and began to reprimand him for saying such things. 'Heaven forbid, Lord,' he said. 'This will never happen to you'" (Matthew 16:22). You have to believe Peter the fisherman had missed a lot of key statements that Jesus said in the past. Jesus turned to Peter and said, "Get away from me Satan! You are a dangerous trap to me. You are seeing things merely from a human point of view, not from God's" (Matthew 16:23).

This must have been a disappointing moment for Peter but six days later Jesus took him, James, and John up a high mountain where he was transfigured before them, plus Moses and Elijah appeared to talk with Jesus. Peter said, "Lord, it's wonderful for us to be here! If you want, I'll make three shelters as memorials—one for you, one for Moses, and one for Elijah" (17:4). Peter's idea was shut down by God the Father affirming His Son's actions from a cloud. The three disciples were terrified, fell face down on the ground and there was no more talk about building shelters.

Then, on the night before his crucifixion, at the Last Supper, Peter declares to Jesus that "Lord, I am ready to go to prison with you and even to die with you" (Luke 22:33). In return, he hears Jesus tell him he will deny three times that he even knew him. Another blow to Peter. And, he does deny Jesus three times the very next night and as the rooster crows, from inside the building, Jesus "turned and looked at Peter...and Peter left the courtyard, weeping bitterly" (22:61). This had to be the deepest discouragement Peter has ever experienced. Is he done with Jesus? We don't see any record of the next several days until resurrection Sunday.

Jesus is resurrected Sunday morning, meets with Mary Magdalene who comes immediately to the house of John where Peter was. They run to the tomb to see it open and Jesus gone. That night the disciples are together meeting behind locked doors and Jesus appears. Then eight days later in another disciple meeting, Jesus appears again specifically for Thomas. Several days later Jesus appears to seven of the disciples that were out fishing. He provides a meal and has a private discussion with Peter. He asked him three times if he loved Jesus, possibly to counter the three denials, and tells Peter how he will die. Another powerful moment.

For forty days Jesus appeared to the apostles several times. Then he commanded them to stay in Jerusalem until Father God sent the Holy Spirit. They obeyed and we see after those days concluded that it is resilient Peter who was the standard bearer for Christ speaking to all the people gathered for the Pentecost festival and three-thousand believed in Jesus as their Messiah.

Paul's resilience is legendary. The litany of the circumstances where Paul was crushed, overwhelmed beyond his ability to endure, with the eminent possibility of death near at hand were many. He was pressed on all sides by trouble, "perplexed, but not driven to despair we are hunted down, but never abandoned by God. We get knocked down, but we are not destroyed" (2 Corinthians 4:8-9). More of his experiences are detailed in 2 Corinthians 6:4-5. All the time, he had his eyes on Jesus, and though living in time and space, made due with whatever happened, proud to suffer for Christ, and looking forward to seeing him when he died.

Resilience does not focus on our lack or who did what to whom, rather it immediately seeks to find the way out with the confidence that God wants us up again so that our testimony can help and comfort others.

Here are some ways that might strengthen our resilience muscles before they are needed:

- Assume that bad times will come and plan in the good times the way through for the bad times.
- Recognize God walking beside us. He is not hiding, walk with Him.
- Develop your prayer life, pray longer, include fasting if medically possible.
- Be of comfort to others in their journey through life.
- Decide not to wallow in the mud or else you might get stuck.
- Journal the positive events of your life so that you can read them in the tough times.
- What would you add here specifically for you? _____

The deepest reason the godly are resilient is stated in a passage in the psalm, "For they are transplanted to the Lord's own house. They flourish in the courts of our God" (Psalm 92:13). Because we are God's children, our resilience can be empowered by God and our path can be lit with His light. The closer we are to God the more we can grow.

Resilience recognizes that God does not cause failure in humans but neither does He waste it. Consider this as you come back from hurts and sorrows to help you push towards growth. Resilience is when we allow God's hand to guide us in the way He wants us to go even if it's not the way we want to go. It is keeping an eye out for His mercy, compassion and direction.

Key Takeaway: Resilience is characteristic of people who refuse to stay in the hard times but choose to move through them and find the greener pastures on the far side. We can have it in every area of our life and we can us it to be of help to others so in need of it. One of the best things to do to have resilience when you need it is to journal today, the good and the bad of it, to be reviewed when we experience it again.

Applications:

How have you seen resilience happen in your life over that last two decades?

What are some ways you can help your children be resilient?

How can your church learn from resilient attendees so that they can better help those who are not there yet?

Responsible Principle

Jesus told the story of a nobleman called away to a distant empire to be crowned king of his country. However, before he left, he brought together ten servants, gave them each one pound of silver, and told them to "invest this for me while I am gone" (Luke 19:13).

When he returned as king, he met with the ten servants to see what kind of profits they achieved. The first invested the one pound of silver and increased it by ten times. The second invested it and gained five times the original amount. But, the third servant had only hidden it to keep it safe, knowing that the nobleman was a stern man with high expectations. Nothing was said about the other seven servants, Jesus only needed the three responses given to complete the illustration.

The first two were rewarded with the responsibility of governing ten cities and five cities respectively. The third servant's silver was taken from him and given to the one who already had ten. He pleaded with the master that the other man already had ten pounds, but the new king's reply was, "To those who use well what they are given, even more will be given, but from those who do nothing, even what little they have will be taken away" (19:26).

Obviously, the nobleman knew he would be crowned king with a kingdom, so this strategy was imposed to find responsible and obedient servants whom he could lift to even higher positions and help him rule his kingdom well.

Responsible people learn how to live independently, with everything dependent on them doing what is legal and profitable to be successful in all kinds of ventures. They know how to commit responsibly to requests of help from others. They are seen as devoted, driven, and destined to be in larger roles because of their responses in more limited roles.

Often times, new opportunities of responsibility come to them because trust and wisdom were testified to about them by their friends and associates in previous jobs, on a board, at church or in a civic area. It was not overnight that they were lifted up, but it came after many years of consistent, persistent and faithful work.

Being responsible also connects to our attitude. A responsible person is operating out of devotion to themselves, others and God, rather than out of duty or dread for whomever. These last two produce a façade of devotion but a heart that is far from committed, it is just enduring. They are fearful and dread-filled and that does not lead to permanent and positive outcomes.

An attitude of humility maintained in the midst of their actions is another reason for their upward movement. This prevented them from pride of position, knowing that they were put there at the request of others who extended trust to them and expected them to be responsible in their new job.

In a different way, there are authority sources which require responsible actions from all of us. We need to pay our taxes, obey the law, live with the Ten Commandments in mind, understand the laws of business, and more. We have to be aware of these responsibilities and with our acknowledgement fulfill our commitments, for that will make us responsible adults.

There is one more person that we need to be responsible to, the Holy Spirit. He lives in us and can be grieved by our sinful acts or quenched by us not listening or obeying his promptings. He is not there to watch you but to grow you into a mature dedicated servant of God. He is responsible to the Lord Jesus Christ and the Father to carry this out.

It is not just people who face being responsible, we have many examples of it in the animal kingdom. All kinds of animals exhibit responsible behaviors. A beaver builds a dam to live in it protected from his foes. A lion brings home food for his family. An eagle builds its nest high on a mountain to protect its eaglets until they are pushed out of the nest and have plenty of room to learn how to fly, on the fly. Every creature is fulfilling their responsible role in the whole of creation. That's what make this world a beautiful place.

Key Takeaway: Being a responsible person with all its attributes and with what is presently in front of you, at whatever level you are now, can eventually lead to obtaining a position of greater responsibility. Responsibility grows to those who actively engage with it.

Applications:

What presently are you responsible for? Make a list and then ask, "Where and how could I be more responsible?"

In your family, how are you teaching and exampling responsibility?

How could your church or business best teach responsibility to people?

Self-Control Principle

Samson was head-strong and selfish. He wanted things right away and had no patience. As one of the judges in the book of Judges, he performed miraculous feats, destroyed personal property of his enemies, killed thousands of Philistines and eventually broke Israel's bondage to this pesky and militant people.

However, his inclination to give into his passions led him to an engagement to be married to a Philistine. But when that didn't work out, he lived with a prostitute and after that fell in love with a woman, Delilah, who would become complicit in his demise by charming him into revealing the secret of his great strength. He was angry, arrogant, revengeful, and disrespectful of his parents. He was not an example of a self-controlled person.

Self-control is the ability to control your flesh when it desires to respond to input from the five physical senses and old mental tracks. It is a reactive response to hold onto control as it seems to get away from you rather than being proactive and prepared inside for circumstances and people. That would be more about the principle of discipline which we will talk about in the confidence area later.

Self-control has to exert itself to deal with hurt, bitterness, temporal things and moral impurity, just to name a few. The challenge is that the flesh desires satisfaction now, so that's when self-control must be engaged.

It is interesting that Paul addressed this action when writing to Titus about the characteristics of an elder and older men. He put stipulations on anyone who would desire the position of elder, saying, "he must not be arrogant or quick-tempered; he must not be a heavy drinker, violent, or dishonest with money" (Titus 1:7b). No room here for men without self-control as they minister to a congregation. And, he told Titus to "teach the older men to exercised self-control, to be worthy of respect, and to live wisely" (2:2). As they got older, the challenge for the aged men on the isle was to be examples, fit for the next generation to imitate. Paul wanted the older men in the church on the island of Crete to not be disrespected because of out-of-control actions.

Peter listed self-control as a part in the maturing of a believer, saying, "supplement your faith with a generous provision of moral excellence, and moral excellence with knowledge, and knowledge with self-control, and self-control with patient endurance, and patient endurance with godliness, and godliness with brotherly affection, and brotherly affection with love for everyone" (2 Peter 1:5-7). Notice what is before self-control, knowledge, and what is after self-control, patient endurance. Knowledge brings awareness of situations where self-control would have to be implemented and patient endurance is not just enduring through grit but being patient in that endurance, not mad, impetuous or anxious. Self-control is third in the seven important growing actions which build on each other and make you "more productive and useful...in your knowledge of our Lord Jesus Christ" (1:8).

God knew we would need help in this on-going struggle of self-control, that's why He said when we enter heaven we would finally be at rest. But, not to just have rest in heaven, a part of His plan was to give us the indwelling Holy Spirit to help us with life in earth situations. Notice that self-control is a part of the fruit of the Spirit listed in Galatians 5:22-23, just after sixteen examples of people out-of-control. It comes last in the listing: love, joy, peace, patience, kindness, goodness, faithfulness, gentleness, and self-control. It too is a positive action, although we might think of it as a "no" rather than a "yes," because we are empowered by the

Spirit rather than by our own will power to keep us from responding in our flesh and creates a stellar testimony among believers and the rest of the world.

As he said, "there is no law against these things" (5:23b). There is no reason to make a law against any of them. They are the making of a well-rounded believer, submissive to the Spirit's work in their life with no law needed to boundary them in. Self-control is the on-going development in the mastery of our own desires and impulses and necessary to victory in our lives.

Felix, the governor of Judah, made his court in Caesarea on the coast of the Mediterranean Sea. At the end of Paul's life, in Jerusalem attacked by false accusations from members of the Sanhedrin, he requested his trial be Roman because of his citizenship. That meant he would appear before Felix in Caesarea for a hearing. When it began, all sorts of false accusations were again bantered by the Jewish leaders, but Paul debated their truth and explained all the actions they assumed the worst of.

Felix and wife Drusilla wanted to hear Paul talk about his faith so they brought him out from jail during the two years Paul was imprisoned there. His message when he appeared before them had three points; righteousness only came when sin was addressed, self-control in life was essential; and judgment was coming for all.

This was an interesting message when you think of who he was talking to. Felix was a greedy and cruel ruler, eager to get whatever he could at no cost to him and Drusilla was a Jewess whose great-grandfather was Herod, the one who tried to kill Jesus as a baby, and just to be sure, instructed his men to kill all the two-year-old and below male children in Bethlehem. Her grandfather was Herod Antipas who killed John the baptizer, and her father was King Herod Agrippa who, according to Acts 12:2, killed the Apostle James, brother of John.

Further, when Paul spoke of self-control, that really struck a chord with the couple because she had divorced her husband to become the third wife of Felix. They were the epitome of a lack of self-control, both self-centered and controlling everyone else was more important to them than controlling themselves. Judgment was the final point Paul raised and it wasn't long before Felix was frightened because of guilt because he received Paul's message loud and clear, so, sent Paul away.

All this said, we understand how important self-control is to each one of us and how we do not need to face our issues alone, for God already planned to help us in this battle against the flesh through the Holy Spirit. It is most important to know the why, when, where, and what about self-control. Why are we needing it to happen in our life? To help in keeping us righteous. When will self-control be an issue? Anytime and when you least expect it. Where? Could be anywhere, at home, work, church, in the car, in a store, no telling where else. And, what would it be like? It can come in any form and may try to convince you of your own rightness in being out-of-control.

Be prepared.

Key Takeaway: Self-control is essential in your ongoing battle against your own fleshy desires and impulses, and is necessary to victory in your life.

Application:

- Where do you lack self-control and why with all the power available to you?
- How could you help your family understand and prepare for lack of control times?
- What would be a good way to teach self-control to a church group?

Trustworthy Principle

All of us like a hero and love to see him at work. There are some created every year but not widely known. It would be nice to hear a hero story every day, they seem to always be popping up and are so encouraging. We can find many in the Old Testament books during the time of Abraham saving Lot, Moses' leading the Israelites out of Egypt, Joshua leading them into the Promise Land, during the Judges period which would include Gideon and Samson, and then many of the prophets that close out the Old Testament.

King Josiah was a hero. He ascended to the throne of the Southern Kingdom of Judah just before their time of 70 years of captivity became a reality. His great-grandfather, Hezekiah, was also a great king who influenced the Kingdom of Judah in a great time of revival. But Manasseh, who followed his father, Hezekiah, was the most wicked king of all and his son, Amon, was wicked like his father and executed by his own household servants.

Which brings us to Josiah, who began to reign after Amon's death, as an eight-year old under the protective hand of the priests and elders of Judah. His first independent action as king was declared at the age of twenty-six, eighteen years into his reign. He ordered the restoration of the Temple. But that all started in his heart as a sixteen-year-old when he began a purging of false worship from Judah. You can read about that in 1 Chronicles 22-23. Idol worship was pervasive, ugly, and took many forms as kings of Judah brought more and more of it into their nation and ignored the God of their fathers. Josiah was meant for this time.

Some of those unsung heroes we talked about earlier are found and placed in very prestigious positions by him. King Josiah needed men to direct the work of restoration and called on Shaphan, the grandson of Meshullam and the court secretary to appoint some trustworthy men.

He told him, "Go to Hilkiah the high priest and have him count the money the gatekeepers have collected from the people at the Lord's Temple. Entrust this to the men assigned to supervise the Temple's restoration. Then they can use it to pay workers to repair the Temple of the Lord. They will need to hire carpenters, builders, and masons. Also have them buy the timber and finished stone needed to repair the Temple. But don't require the construction supervisors to keep account of the money they receive, for they are honest and trustworthy men" (2 Chron. 22:4-7).

These men would have large sums of money at their disposal, and they were not being watched in their jobs. They hired workers, purchased materials, and supervised the construction process. The amount they receive had already been counted by the high priest, so it was known how much was available to them, but the high priest and King Josiah trusted them completely, so much so that they didn't require them to even make an accounting...just get the job done.

Think about the enormous amount of money needed. Think about how easy it would be to slip some of those funds into their pockets knowing they didn't need to account for them. Yet, these men were trustworthy and honest, using all the funds to accomplish the high task they were given. They had a reputation of trust, were dedicated to the Temple rebuild, and did not have sticky fingers. Certainly, they were paid for the job they were doing, but their pure hearts kept them from dishonestly full pockets. That is a trustworthy group of general contractors.

Later in Israel's history, Daniel, a teenager taken in the captivity to Babylon, was rewarded for being able to interpret King Nebuchadnezzer's dream. He was still there when the kingdom changed hands and King Belshazzar, during a celebration, saw a hand writing on the wall. He sent for Daniel, and he came with the interpretation which was strong against the king. For it, Daniel was dressed in purple robes, a gold chain was hung around his neck, and he was proclaimed the third highest ruler in the kingdom. That night Belshazzar was killed, and Darius the Mede took over the kingdom.

This king chose Daniel and two others as administrators to supervise the high officers and protect the king's interests. He proved himself more capable than the others and the king made plans to place him over the entire empire. "Then the other administrators and high officers began searching for some fault in the way Daniel was handling government affairs, but they couldn't find anything to criticize or condemn. He was faithful, always responsible, and completely trustworthy" (Daniel 6:4). So, they convinced the King to enact a new law, then used it against Daniel, so that he ended up in the Lion's den. The next day he was removed from there and his accusers were thrown in for a lion's hardy meal.

Is being trustworthy worth it? Daniel is a good example that it is always good to be trustworthy.

Another group of men, four supervisors for the Temple storerooms and even their assistant, were considered trustworthy to make honest distributions to their fellow Levites from the storerooms of the Temple. It was said of them, "these men had an excellent reputation [trustworthy] (Nehemiah 13:13).

Further, Solomon in his book of Proverbs gave examples of the results of a trustworthy person when he said, "they will get a rich reward" (Prov. 28:20); "they can keep a confidence" (Prov. 11:13b); and "trustworthy messengers refresh like snow in summer; they revive the spirit of their employer" (Prov 25:13).

You don't have to be a general contractor, a priest, or a high official of state to be trustworthy. However it is important to build it into your life one decision at a time and during any position of responsibility, starting at home, being seen by others in the classroom, and at your jobs as you expand into a profession. It doesn't matter at what level you are, what matters is the state of your heart and your ability to be continually worthy of the trust of others.

Here are some suggestions to help you be trustworthy:

- Allow God full reign in your life.
- Recognize how dangerous the love of money is to your life.
- Keep yourself accountable to someone else.
- Practice confidentiality in your relationships.
- Be trustworthy when not in charge and when your circumstances aren't necessarily being good to you.
- Consciously add "trustworthy" to the group of words that describe you.
- Ask yourself the question often, "Am I worthy of being trusted?"

Key Takeaway: Being a person who is trustworthy expands your possibilities and brings benefit to your life as well as the lives of others.

Applications:
How could you personally develop your ability to be trustworthy?

What would be a good way to develop trustworthiness within your family?

How could your church or business expand trustworthiness among its members or teams?

Wholehearted Principle

Upon completing the Tabernacle in the wilderness and receiving the Ten Commandments, the people of Israel set out toward the Promise Land. They camped in the Desert of Paran and Moses, at the Lord's prompting, sent out twelve men to explore the land of Canaan. Among them were Joshua and Caleb.

After 40 days surveying the land, the twelve spies returned and reported. They all affirmed that it flowed with milk and honey, but ten expressed deep concern because the people of the land were powerful and the cities were large and fortified. They spread a bad report and expressed their disbelief that they could conquer what they now called, the giants in the land. They said, "We seemed like grasshoppers in our own eyes, and we looked the same to them" (Numbers 13:33). They were discouraged by their circumstances.

Only two, Caleb and Joshua, spoke positively about going up into the land and conquering its inhabitants. Their confidence was in the Lord who led them out of Egypt and for two years since had continued to lead them. They were confident He would give them the Promised Land.

It was this sequence of events that led the Lord to make the people of Israel wander for thirty-eight more years in the desert, during which every man who was twenty years old and above would die, because they believed the report of the ten spies. But Caleb and Joshua had a "different spirit and followed wholeheartedly" (Numbers 14:24, 30). As Moses began the book of Deuteronomy he reflected on this event and said that Caleb "will see it, and I will give him and his descendants the land he set his feet on, because he followed the Lord wholeheartedly" (Deut. 1:36).

When Caleb approached Joshua after seven years of battle in the land of Canaan in which the Lord gave Israel the victory, he reminded him of the report with the spies and said, "I, however, followed the Lord my God wholeheartedly" (Joshua 14:8). Joshua agreed and blessed Caleb with Hebron as his inheritance, "because he followed the Lord, the God of Israel, wholeheartedly" (14:14). Caleb had a "different spirit" within him (Joshua 14:24). It was not an unbelieving, despairing spirit or a proud and rebellious spirit but rather an obedient and believing spirit of trust; an unwavering fidelity of heart.

The text uses one word for wholeheartedly and English words that parallel it are "complete, come to an end, consecrated, dedicated, and making full." To be wholehearted is to be completely given over to one direction.

King Hezekiah's turning back to God was a wonderful story of a leader leading and his people following. "In everything that he [Hezekiah, King of Judah] undertook in the service of God's Temple and in obedience to the law and the commands, he sought his God and worked wholeheartedly. And so he prospered" (2 Chronicles 31:21).

The most descriptive word used to explain the state of his soul toward God was the word "wholeheartedly." It was like the three actions of full commitment in marriage: leave, cleave, and become one flesh. Wholeheartedness or an undivided heart toward God requires leaving your old ways, cleaving to God in faith and trust, and becoming more like Christ each day through your increasing sensitivity to the Holy Spirit living within you. It suggests a completeness of heart with regard to mind, emotion and will, all being aligned to support each other and move in the same direction. It does not suggest that you will never sin again, but it does suggest that through confession your state of being wholehearted can be renewed and you can move forward.

This is not a light word but a heavy word of total commitment to God. It started in the heart and flowed out into actions and words that expressed the pureness of a heart dedicated to God.

What would it look like to have a heart [mind, emotions, and will] that was fully dedicated to one direction? We see this in a limited way in a dedicated athlete or a soldier or master of industry. But can you be this way, too, in your spirituality? Yes.

A wholehearted heart is the opposite of a divided heart. James 1:8 speaks of a "double-minded man" and says he is "unstable in all his ways." To be wholehearted is to incorporate God into your life; your desires and your vision. It is to run from sin and seek God's face daily. This is a life of joy and peace, since you are not then one who waivers.

Key Takeaway: Living wholeheartedly leaves no room for wavering, fear or doubt, only complete faith and belief in God; what He has done, what He is doing, and what He will do.

Applications:

What do you need to release/confess to God that is not aligned with a wholehearted life?

What would it take for your family to live wholeheartedly?

How could this principle be promoted and taught in your church?

Living A Principled Life
Conduct Area

Conduct is our behavior; the way we act. It has a direct relationship to our character.

Bond-Servant Principle

Slavery has always been a part of the world system. Servants have been acquired by purchase, by capture, by birth, into slavery, as prisoners of war, to pay off a debt with the servitude of a family member, and individuals selling themselves because they were poor.

Jewish law allowed slavery with restrictions. While they were slaves, could not be treated harshly, nor sent away empty handed at their release. Hebrews considered them part of the family, with right to the sabbath rest, and allowed to have possessions.

Every seventh and fiftieth year, which was a sabbatical and jubilee years, slaves had to be given their freedom, and were to have their ancestral land restored to them and be provided with goods sufficient to make a new start.

On the other hand, outside of Israel, slaves were treated as property; beaten, considered in less humane situations with their masters, and very rarely released of their service, unless a large price was paid.

When a Roman Commander would win a battle over a city or tribe, he would parade chained captives walking behind his chariot, as the Roman crowds would cheer his victory. This was what Paul was referring to when he wrote to the Corinthian Christians, "But thank God! He has made us His captives and continues to lead us along in Christ's triumphal procession. Now He uses us to spread the knowledge of Christ everywhere, like a sweet perfume" (2 Corinthians 2:14). It is not a life of disappointment to be led behind Christ, rather a privilege of being there at all and understanding the eternal nature of your relationship with him, as a bond-servant.

There are several words used related to slaves. Using the word "slave" meant a person who was owned by and absolutely subject to a master, as by capture, by purchase, by birth from owned slaves, or as payment for a debt. The slave was not willingly involved; he was there by force, or dominance.

A "servant" was not necessarily a slave, just as a "hired worker" was not necessarily one either. Some of these hired workers were highly skilled and trusted administrators. Then there were those who were referred to as "bond-servant," a Greek term which has to do with willingness; one who had elected to remain with their master. He had struck an agreement with his master and now he was more than just a servant; he was an honorable, trustworthy person whom the master loved. He became so by having his ear lobe pierced at a door post, which showed evidence, as did his ear lobe, of his choice to willingly remain.

This was a commitment for life; a no turning back decision. The master would accept him, love him, give him food and a place to live. He was considered part of the master's family with rights.

This is our status as believers. We are bond-servants of Jesus Christ. We have not paid the price; he has paid it for us. He is our Lord and Master. Peter, Epaphras, Paul, James, and Timothy all refer to themselves as this type of servant. These are some of the benefits that accrue from a bond-servant relationship:

- Freedom (living within boundaries that free us)
- Purpose (give us hope, daily actions focused on Him)
- Protection (never to be separated from God)
- Insurance (never leave you nor forsake you)
- Sincere Love (cross love, enough for Jesus to die for us)
- Peace (the peace with God through salvation and the peace of God daily)
- Belonging (adopted into a new family)

Paul wrote to his friend, Philemon, a believer in the Colosse church. He had owned a slave named Onesimus, who had fled from his master, Philemon. We are not given the reason for his disappearance. God brought that slave across the path of Paul, who led him to Christ. Paul writes to Philemon to tell him of the change of heart in Onesimus, and that he is sending him back to Philemon with a letter asking him to forgive him for his waywardness, and to treat him like a brother in Christ.

Paul does not demand the reconciliation of Philemon, but does recognize that "Onesimus hasn't been of much use to you in the past, but now he is very useful to both of us" (Philemon vs. 11). Paul is not going to force his will on Philemon to forgive Onesimus because he wants that to be the willing choice of his brother in Christ. There is no second chapter in this book that shows us how this situation turned out, but we know that three believers, with clean hearts, could make a peaceable end of it. Think of this, Onesimus left as a slave of Philemon, but returned as a bond-servant of Christ.

There are other stories in the Bible that speak of believers in slavery. Joseph's brothers received twenty pieces of silver for him, but the benefit was the reconciliation of Jacob's family, and the unmistakable moving of God to protect the family that would turn into a nation. Daniel and his three friends, Hananiah, Mishael, and Azariah were taken as captives to Babylon and had great influence in high places. And we think of Mordecai and Esther, who were used to take down Haman and his plot to destroy all Israelites.

Being a bond-servant to God always produces good things. It spreads the good news and examples a different kind of life that all desire in their hearts. In the end, it doesn't matter what their status was; they all served the Lord God and He provided for them in their servanthood.

Key Takeaway: Understanding servanthood helps us put our lives in perspective. We do not know the future, nor the length of our life, but we do know the God who does and we believe in the one and only Savior,

Jesus Christ the Lord. Bond-servant to a good master is better than being in charge of your own life.

Applications:

Where are you on the whole idea of becoming a bond-servant to Jesus Christ?

How can you model servanthood to the Lord and share the benefits of it to your family?

What could your church do to help people understand that a life given over to Christ in servanthood is freer than a life lived without him?

Compassion Principle

"O to be like Thee! blessed Redeemer,

This is my constant longing and prayer;

Gladly I'll forfeit all of earth's treasures,

Jesus, Thy perfect likeness to wear.

O to be like Thee! Full of compassion,

Loving, forgiving, tender and kind,

Helping the helpless, cheering the fainting,

Seeking the wand'ring sinner to find."[4]

These two verses of the hymn, O to be Like Thee! says it all. It tells us that Jesus is the model to follow and the image or likeness to put on. But before Jesus Christ showed us, through his life on earth, all that compassion could be, God the Father illustrated it in His work with the Israelites.

A verse written in the Old Testament and repeated in the New Testament is God the Father saying, "I will make all my goodness pass before you, and I will call out my name, Yahweh, before you. For I will show mercy to anyone I choose, and I will show compassion to anyone I choose" (Exodus 33:19) and (Romans 9:15).

God the Father showed compassion on His people during the wilderness years and during the Judges era that followed when the Israelites were cycling through both rebellion and repentance experiences. This verse also suggests that God will not exhibit His compassion until the proper time, which is also mentioned in Deuteronomy 32:26 where He said, "Indeed, the Lord will give justice [or show compassion] to His people, and He will change His mind about His servants, when He sees their strength is gone and no one is left, slave or free." Because they were His children, sometimes God was moved to have compassion on them, increase their numbers, and restore their fortunes because of His promised oath to their forefathers.

Then Jesus was born on earth and became our model for compassion. "Moved with compassion, Jesus reached out and touched him [man with leprosy]. 'I am willing,' he [Jesus] said. 'Be healed!'" (Mark 1:41). Jesus was filled with compassion for people in three different areas of their existence. He was filled with compassion by their spiritual lostness when he saw huge crowds of people wandering and exhausted in their search for rest (Matthew 9:36).

He was filled with compassion by their hunger and pain from disease and their desire to be fed and healed (Matthew 14:14; 15:32). And he was filled with compassion when he saw those who had lost a loved one in death by resurrecting several, including a widow's son and Lazarus, the brother to Mary and Martha (Luke 7:13; John 11:42-43). He touched blinded eyes, healed crippled legs, and allowed power to flow out of him and heal a woman with a persistent disease.

He was not worried about his reputation, the Jewish rulers, or the Roman army but had compassion on people because "they were like sheep without a shepherd. So he began teaching them many things" (Mark 6:34). His compassion led them to learning and growing in their faith.

A clear understanding of the compassion of both the Father and the Son of God was exhibited in the story of the prodigal son. Here was a young son who took his inheritance and squandered it in rich and lustful living, but when he found himself a pauper feeding pigs, he determined to go back to his father. "While he was still a long way off, his father saw him coming. Filled with love and compassion, he ran to his son, embraced him, and kissed him" (Luke 15:20). He restored him to sonship, clothed his boy once again with a fine robe, and celebrated his return with a party.

The word for compassion is only used of Jesus in the four Gospels; never of the people or of their leaders, whether Roman or Jewish. The exception to this usage is in these three parables: the master who had compassion (Matthew 18:33); the father of the prodigal son (Luke 15:20); and the good Samaritan (Luke 10:33).

What can we learn from all the incidences of the compassion of the Father and the Son of God in the Old and New Testaments?

- Compassion is linked to forgiveness and love. In fact, the compassion exhibited is as a result of forgiveness and love. We see this in God's forgiveness of Israel and the story of the prodigal.

- Compassion is a part of the DNA of a believer because it was a part of the life of our Savior, Jesus Christ. We are to be image bearers of him and compassion would be a part of that. We are called to exhibit it, for it will draw people to us to hear the story of the gospel.

- Compassion often led to further blessings and even the deliverance of God's people.

- We can, as Jesus was, be filled to the top with compassion; to the place where it is overflowing from us to those we come in contact with.

- There is a limit to compassion. Wait! You mean compassion can be ended? Yes. God can abandon people to their enemies as a discipline (Neh. 9:28). He can withhold his compassion to those who trivialize it (Ps. 77:9; Isa. 63:14). For this is a people without understanding; their Maker has no compassion on them (Isa. 27:11). And to those in Israel who became idolatrous, wicked, stubborn and prideful, God said through Jeremiah, "I will smash them against each other, even parents against children, says the Lord. I will not let my pity, or mercy, or compassion keep me from destroying them" (Jer. 13:14).

These are lessons to learn about compassion and its implementation, first in our hearts and then out to others through our hands. To be conformed to the image of the Son is to become compassionate. We cannot muster up compassion. When compassion springs from us to the states of people that cross our path, it is evidence of a heart changed by Christ. In that moment, the tender heart is "filled with compassion" and responds to whatever the need is.

Don't ask yourself "How can I have compassion?" instead "How can I have a heart changed by Christ?"

Key Takeaway: God the Father and Jesus Christ, the Son of God, both have an unlimited amount of compassion. However, the tap to compassion can be shut off by wicked and rebellious actions. We found five strong lessons to understanding more about compassion and when it is available to us and to others through us. When we link it up to forgiveness and love, compassion can be a key ingredient in softening hearts to be responsive to God.

Applications:

Reviewing the information above, how can you become a more compassionate person?

How can your family exhibit compassion to each other and to the neighborhood?

What would it take to enlarge the outreach of your church through compassion?

Confession Principle

My second son was only seven years old when he learned about confession and much more. He was in second grade and Pokémon was the rage. He and his friends had the cards and there was some serious competition among them. One day we noticed some new Pokémon cards he was playing with and asked, "Where did you get those?" His answer was a quick, "John gave them to me." That seemed odd because they were so valuable but we didn't follow up with another question.

The day turned into night and he got ready for bed. We were tired and prepared as well. Our bedrooms were just across the hall from each other. Lights went off and silence was all we heard for a while until he cried out almost weeping, "Mom and Dad, I was not given those cards. I took money to school and bought them." Ah, sweet confession.

Guilt was bearing down on him and so he confessed. The next day as I was shaving, he came to the door of the bath and we were discussing the night before. I said, "You better not do that again or you will get a guilty conscience." His reply was, "What's that?" I said, "That was what you had last night before you confessed to us." His young mind was instantly awash with a new understanding.

Let's understand that confession is a freeing experience. You have been holding down an act inside your soul. It's a secret and that requires lots of energy to keep it hidden. It happened a long time ago and you don't want to release it or it happened yesterday and you feel the same way. It's a hindrance, a burden, a pain in your heart.

The unconfessed action is your perpetual focus because if you are not holding onto it tightly in your mind, you might drift back to it and be disturbed by it once again. It produces the product of a guilty conscience.

What then does it mean to confess? I'm sure you want to get this right from the beginning. Is it an apology? Can saying you're sorry complete the task? These questions are important. We could think both are ways to confess but they don't fill out the definition for confession. It goes much deeper than cliché words.

One of the greatest verses written for believers was written by John the Apostle when he wrote, "If we confess our sins to him [God], he is faithful and just to forgive us our sins and to cleanse us from all wickedness" (1 John 1:9).

First, we have to confess, which is to say the same thing about your sins that God says about them. They are wrong, sinful, and important to confess. They may be just confessed to God, if it was just within the thoughts of our mind. But it may need to be confessed to another party whom you hurt with words.

The important thing is being truly repentant of those sins. Make an about-face by recognizing them as sin and agreeing with God's definition of them. They were not little white lies, fibs, or some other word except sin. Second, when others are involved, don't say, "I'm sorry" or "I apologize" because that does not give the person you are confessing to the opportunity to respond to what you have told them. It is best to use the words, "I have sinned against you, will you forgive me?" That gives them the chance to respond. It doesn't matter how they respond, "yes," "no" or "let me think about it." That's their issue, yours was to confess and you did that.

There are also several spheres of confession: to God only because no human was involved; to another person that was directly affected by your sin; or to a body of people, possibly the church, because the sin was known by all and confession has to be within that sphere.

Here's the second thing the verse says. He, that would be God, is faithful and just to forgive us. That's very important. We are not saddled with a sin that can never be forgiven or a God who is going to hold it over our head just for the fun of it. He is faithful to forgive and just to forgive on the basis of His Son's paid price on the cross for our sins.

But wait a minute. There is one more thing. If you confess, God will forgive that sin but because He can see into your heart, He knows if you are sincere or not. If sincere, the verse goes on to say that He cleanses you from all wickedness. That means other actions you have taken that hurt others will be exposed to you in order for you to seek forgiveness. And if you don't really know about a sin that was inadvertently done, God also forgives you of that.

It is also important to understand that God is not asking you to request forgiveness. You don't need to say," Father forgive me." Why? Because the verse already says He will if you will be humble and sincere in your confession. There is a release that confession provides; a relief and exhilaration to know that we are back in fellowship with God and with other believers affected by our sin.

Key Takeaway: Confession is good for your soul. It rids you of sin that can hold you back from growing as a believer. It is your responsibility to confess and God's responsibility to forgive, which He has no problem doing. He also covers you from other unrighteousness you were not aware of.

Applications:
When was the last time you confessed your sins?

How can your family apply confession to their lives at home?

What should be the church's attitude toward confession and repentance?

Courage Principle

In the Wizard of Oz, there were three characters that accompanied Dorothy to Oz; the scarecrow, the tin man, and the lion. Each of them desired something special from the wizard; the scarecrow a brain, the tin man a heart, and the cowardly lion courage.

What would you do if you needed courage? Where would you look for it?

Courage is essential when you are in the midst of change. There are two times in Scripture when change was huge and that is when there was a specific challenge to courage.

The first was during the transition of leadership from Moses to Joshua. Joshua had remained in the background during the forty years in the wilderness, but at the end of Deuteronomy, Moses spoke to the people and then to Joshua about courage.

He said to the people he had led for forty years, "Be strong and courageous! Do not be afraid and do not panic before them [the people of the promise land]. For the Lord your God will personally go ahead of you. He will neither fail you nor abandon you" (Deut. 31:6). And to Joshua, while all the people watched, he said, "Be strong and courageous! For you will lead these people into the land that the Lord swore to their ancestors he would give them" (31:7).

After the death of Moses, the Lord spoke directly to Joshua saying, "The time has come for you to lead these people, the Israelites, across the Jordan River into the land I am giving them" (Joshua 1:2). In this first chapter of Joshua, he is told to "be strong and courageous" four times (Josh. 1:6, 7, 9, 18). God knew that, for the people of Israel to be courageous, their leader needed these two attributes as an example to them.

It was the beginning of three major war campaigns, and fear could sneak in and derail them at any time, so strength and courage would be the two assets available to them from God. He spoke to Joshua, "This is my command—be strong and courageous! Do not be afraid or discouraged. For the Lord your God is with you wherever you go" (Josh. 1:9). Later on, we learn through the testimony of Rahab, that God had brought a spirit of fear and terror on the people of the land to allow the challenge to courage to be of consequence for Joshua and the Israelites.

The second huge change period was during the beginning of the church. It was movement away from the present Temple system and the Sanhedrin, made up of Scribes, Pharisees, Sadducees, and other leaders of Israel. Peter and John were some of the first to be confronted by them. They were first arrested and jailed for the night and then demanded to tell them, "By what power, or in whose name, have your done this?" (Acts 4:7).

Peter was filled with the Holy Spirit and told them the crippled man was "healed by the powerful name of Jesus Christ of Nazareth, the man you crucified but who God raised from the dead." (4:10) The Sanhedrin members were amazed at their courage to speak out because they saw them only as "ordinary men with no special training in the Scriptures" (4:13). Later in Acts 9-28, Paul would also face great suffering by religious leaders. But he continue forward with courage, knowing God was always in charge of his situation.

All of us are ordinary people who face ordinary days until something inserts itself into our lives and makes courage necessary. It has been described as the ability to do something that frightens you or to have strength in the face of fear or grief. It is a quality of heart that enables a person to face difficulty, danger, or pain with bravery. Courage suppresses fear and causes a person to dare to be bold.

In a 2012 article, Melanie Greenberg, Ph.D. suggested six attributes of courage:

- It is choosing to act while feeling fear
- Freeing your passion to do something great
- Persevering while in adverse conditions
- Standing up for right even when it isn't popular
- Letting go of the familiar and accepting change to go beyond your comfort zone
- And, facing suffering with dignity and faith[5]

Courage is a unique action that exerts itself in fear-filled, dangerous, and risk-laden situations. It can push fear out of the way and boldly move forward when the end is not yet evident.

Key Takeaway: Courage is rooted in a willful action that gathers information from the mind and emotion, and then dismisses some and believes the rest, despite the current circumstances.

Applications:

How would courage help you today to rise up and do something gutsy?

How could you example and teach courage to your family?

How could your church promote the action of courage?

Endurance Principle

Ernest Shackleton experienced the greatest survival story of all time and he didn't do it alone. You may not be familiar with his name, but in the early years of the twentieth century he was well known in England. A consummate explorer, he desired to cross the Antarctic from one coast to the other, passing by the South Pole. His crew of twenty-eight men, sixty-nine Huskie dogs, and three lifeboats, departed England on a sailing ship in August of 1914. It would be over two years before they would return.

Seeking the warmer weather of the southern hemisphere, and particularly the Antarctic, he navigated the ship closer and closer to the south pole. On January 19, 1915, his ship became surrounded by pack-ice. Slowly but surely, over the course of the next months, the ice pressed against the wooden sailing ship frame, until on November 21, 1915, his ship was crushed and sunk.

Left with meager supplies and only three lifeboats, the crew camped on moving ice floes for five months (156 days) and sailed on the open seas for seven days. They finally arrived at Elephant Island on April 14, 1916. They were beyond exhausted, hungry, delirious with thirst, frozen to the core, unable to sleep, and with constant diarrhea. They set up camp on this furthest north island as a launching point to go north. Their food supplies came from the sea as they ate seal, penguin, and fish, and cooked with blubber.

Gone now for 20 months, on April 24, 1916 the decision was made for Shackelton and Captain Worsley, with four other sailors, to set out in one completely covered lifeboat, to find help and eventually return for the rest of his crew. They sailed for South Georgia Island, 850 miles away, through the worst seas on earth. They were only able to take four navigational observations during the voyage. They were incarcerated in an iced-over lifeboat for seventeen hellish days, enduring the bitter cold, wet to the core, with the boat pitching, rolling, and jerking constantly as massive waves broke over her at all hours of the day and night.

They reached the South Georgia Island on May 10, 1916, only to realize they had landed on the wrong side of the island. So they hiked for thirty-six hours over snow-covered mountains to reach the whaling station, where they remained until they could acquire a rescue ship. On August 29, 1916, the fourth rescue attempt, they were able to return to the twenty-two sailors left on Elephant Island, surviving there for four and a half months. Not one man was lost in the whole endeavor. The story was chronicled by F. A. Worsley, the captain of the HMS Endurance, a fitting title for the ship of this story.

Endurance comes from a Greek word which means "patient enduring." It is found in verses that also include the words persecution and affliction, which indicates it is the positive movement of the soul and spirit in these situations. Note some of those here:

> "We patiently endure troubles and hardships and calamites of every kind" (2 Cor 6:4).
> "We also pray that you will be strengthened with all His glorious power so you will have all the endurance and patience you need" (Col. 1:11). "May God, who gives this patience and encouragement help you live in complete harmony with each other" (Rom. 15:5).
> "We proudly tell God's other churches about your endurance and faithfulness in all the persecutions and hardships you are suffering" (2 Thess. 1:4).

Endurance is an essential principle in the life of a believer, no matter what century they live in, because Jesus said to the disciples the night before his capture and crucifixion, "Here on earth you will have many trials and sorrows. But take heart, because I have overcome the world" (John 16:33). The world is full of tough times, and endurance is the way we make it through them. It is listed in a remarkable passage in a process that Paul wrote about,

> "We can rejoice, too, when we run into problems and trials, for we know that they help us develop endurance. And endurance develops strength of character, and character strengthens our confident hope of salvation. And this hope will not lead to disappointment. For we know how dearly God loves us, because He has given us the Holy Spirit to fill our hearts with His love" (Rom. 5:3-5).

Endurance is the resource that not only helps us in overcoming problems and trials, but also in that process strengthens our character. It is a vertebra in the backbone of our character which gives us a confident hope in God and eternal salvation.

An example of endurance can be recognized in the swaying of a tree. As it sways back and forth in the breeze, it is developing more vertical strength in its fibrous trunk to help it withstand strong winds. And, as the fibers increase in strength together, they are able to minimize the impact of external forces upon the life of the tree. That is what endurance is all about.

I wrote this note to a friend recently who was being persecuted and in need of endurance. "Problems can accomplish what God wants to develop in you, and three of the byproducts of endurance are a strengthened character and a stronger confidence and hope in God. He is allowing this to play out so you can gain endurance and its byproducts. If, in your pain, you can flip your thought process to an awareness of what endurance will produce, then you can defeat the negative suggestions of the enemy and come out with deeper character, confidence and hope."

Key Takeaway: Endurance is given to us by God in order to bolster our resolve to make it through persecutions, hardships, and calamities. In the process of facing all this, it helps to develop our character and align it with Christ's image, which the Holy Spirit is working out in us.

Applications:
Where in your life are you in need of endurance? Ask God for it.

How can you build endurance into the character of your children?

What could your church do to help its attendees deal better with trials?

Fasting Principle (Personal)

Fasting is a discipline that has almost been lost in this generation. The idea of denying your body anything in this age of overindulgence is hard to fathom. The lack of depth in spiritual experience today has also limited the suggestion to fast. So, to discipline our lives through the elimination of food or anything else for a spiritual purpose, strikes some as extreme.

However, Jesus, the believer's greatest human example, integrated fasting into his life. He fasted forty days at the beginning of his ministry" (Luke 6:16) and assumed that people did fast by starting his instructions concerning fasting with "When you fast..." (Matt. 6:16).

Fasting is a sound principle with Scriptural mention over thirty times in the New Testament; a practice of the early church, and originally a portion of the Levitical Law (Lev. 16:29-31), related to the Day of Atonement. It had the following guidelines:

- Keep it a secret (Matt. 6:16-18)
- Act normal, not revealing that you are fasting
- Abstain from food
- Focus your time and actions on the Lord

Fasting takes the emphasis off the physical you and places it on the spiritual you. It heightens sensitivity to God's Spirit and to His Word. It is a humbling of the soul (Ps. 35:13), and releases the bands of temptation on your life for the purpose of greater effectiveness in discerning and achieving the purposes of God (Isa. 58:6).

But there is a danger in fasting that you might be experiencing; to please yourself. Isaiah wrote out the discussion between Israel and God concerning their use of fasting. They asked, "We have fasted before you! Why aren't you impressed?" God answered, "It's because you are fasting to please yourselves. Even while you fast, you keep oppressing your workers. What good is fasting when you keep on fighting and quarreling? This kind of fasting will never get you anywhere with Me" (58:3-4).

God goes on to express the kind of fasting He desires, saying, "Free those who are wrongly imprisoned; lighten the burden of those who work for you. Let the oppressed go free, and remove the chains that bind people. Share your food with the hungry, and give shelter to the homeless. Give clothes to those who need them, and do not hide from relatives who need our help" (58:6-7).

The right kind of fasting is done in humility, not in pride. Here are some practical helps to this principle of conduct:

There are different kinds of fasts:

- Absolute fast – no drink and no food
- Partial fast – restricting your diet in some way
- Normal fast – no solids and drinking only water
- One-day or multiple-day fasts: 3-day, 7-day, up to 40-day

It is important to note that you may have medical reasons that prevent you from fasting; a medical condition that would respond negatively to your withdrawal from food and possibly water.

Here are some focuses you could have in fasting:

- Fasting to seek direction from God. The Israelites fasted to determine direction in battle (Judges 20:26), and Paul and

Barnabas fasted as a part of the process in the choosing of elders in several cities (Acts 14:21-23).

- Fasting when in deep sorrow as an expression of grief. This was done after the death of Saul and Jonathan by the mighty warriors of Jabesh-gilead (1Samuel 31:13; 2Samuel 1:12), and David at the death of Bathsheba's first child (2 Samuel 12:16).
- Fasting to express repentance for sin (yours, a church's, a city, state, or nation). Illustrated by all Israel at Mizpah (1 Samuel 7:6; Nehemiah 9:1-3); by Daniel repenting for himself and the people (Daniel 9:3-10:3); and the city of Nineveh repenting (Jonah 3:5).
- Fasting because of concerns for the work of God; the walls and gates of Jerusalem were broken down and destroyed by fire (Nehemiah 1:4).
- Fasting for deliverance or protection. Jehoshaphat and Judah fasted for deliverance in battle (2Chronicles 20:3); Ezra and the people fasted for deliverance from harm in their journey back to Jerusalem from captivity (Ezra 8:21-23); and the Jews fasted before and after Haman's plot was foiled (Esther 4:13, 16; 9:31).
- Fasting as a means of humbling one's self before God (Psalm 69:10-13). Anna used this as a way to worship God, along with prayer (Luke 2:37), and as a means of overcoming temptation (Isaiah 58:6).

The results are not always the same. God sometimes answers our prayers; maybe not in our timing, but eventually in His. We can gain spiritual discernment to help us make decisions that are pleasing to God, and our body is purged of the poisons present in what we eat.

Here is an example of a day of fasting that normally would also include prayer. It was used by a Christian who had an important decision to make or whenever he was asked to bring an important message. He would set aside a twenty-four-hour period prior to the meeting or the time for the decision to be made. The twenty-four-hours went from evening to evening.

- The first evening he would read many large sections of Scripture for general content and key ideas related to the subject of his need. When a particular section seemed significant, he would mark it for further study the following morning.
- Second, sleep through the night
- Second day, in the morning, his first act was to enjoy a time of personal edification from the Psalms and Proverbs to put his heart in tune with the Lord.
- Then he studied the significant sections identified the previous day by outlining each one, making special word studies, and looking up cross-references.
- He would use those scriptures in a personal prayer by sharing with God the insights gained in his study. As he did this, he would analyze his life and evaluate it on the basis of these insights laid bare before God.
- In the afternoon, selecting key verses, he would commit them to memory.
- Later, he would make melody in his heart by reading or singing Christian songs.
- Finally, he would seek to discover key Scriptural principles in his study through meditation by mentally reviewing all that he had studied so that it could be used to solve his present problem.

This was a labor of love and during this time he sometimes became weary. He would put himself to sleep by meditating on Scripture. He often discovered that during his nap, much would fall into place in his mind, making his meditation that much more significant later.

There is much to gain from fasting. We have reviewed several ways it can be implemented and also how it can become a regular part of the spiritual disciplines of your life. We have seen how we should not "show off" our fasting to others, but do it secretly. Fasting can expand your understanding of God and the Bible, too.

Key Takeaway: God is never far from us but we can be far from Him. Fasting and the accompanying study and meditation can realign us with His purposes and open our ears to His Spirit.

Applications:

What would it take to regularly incorporate fasting into your life?

How could your family participate in regular fasting?

How could fasting be incorporated into your church's regular calendar?

Generosity Principle

Generosity is a part of who God is. He was willing to give His only Son to the world which was the most generous act. Since we were created in His image, we also should be generous. Isaiah beckoned to the people, "Let the wicked change their ways and banish the very thought of doing wrong. Let them turn to the Lord that He may have mercy on them. Yes, turn to our God, for He will forgive generously" (Isa. 55:7).

God's generosity extends even further, "If you need wisdom, ask our generous God, and He will give it to you. He will not rebuke you for asking" (James 1:5). God is generous and willing to give His wisdom away. He did it with Solomon and He can do it with you. He does not ridicule or rebuke a person for asking to receive wisdom.

Selfishness, which is sin, convinces us to keep what we have, that would be greedy; give less than we can, that would be stingy; or say we are giving more, but are lying about it, that would be dishonest. We know in the last case, as seen in Acts 5, Ananias and Sapphira performed this very act and God struck them both with death.

We have another principle of life called Sowing and Reaping in the area of Conduct in which we talk about the seed sown and harvest reaped. This farming picture is also used in a statement of Paul about generous giving, saying, "Remember this—a farmer who plants only a few seeds will get a small crop. But the one who plants generously will get a generous crop" (2 Cor. 9:6) and "God is the one who provides seed for the farmer and then bread to eat. In the same way, he will provide and increase your resources and then produce a great harvest of generosity in you. Yes, you will be enriched in every way so that you can always be generous" (2 Cor. 9:10-11).

The influence of generosity in giving is touched on here. This type of giving enriches you, not in one way, but in every way. You are freed from the boundaries of selfishness and recognize an out of world principle, that you receive blessing when you bless others. Solomon links up with this by saying, "The generous prosper; those who refresh others will themselves be refreshed. People curse those who hoard their grain, but they bless the one who sells in time of need" (Proverbs 11:25-26). People know what you are doing and what you have, so any improper actions you do, will be disturbing to them.

Moses gave a series of statements related to the poor, soon to be in the Promise Land; most significantly was this one, "Give generously to the poor, not grudgingly, for the Lord your God will bless you in everything you do" (Deut. 15:10). And Solomon supported that by saying, "Blessed are those who are generous, because they feed the poor" (Prov. 22:9).

David's last message to the people of Israel in 971 B.C., before he gave the reins of power over to Solomon, had an interesting take on money. He is at the fund raiser for the building of the Temple, for which he had been gathering materials for a long time, and he reminded the people of Israel in his prayer to God, "Everything we have has come from You, and we give You only what you first gave us" (1 Chron. 29:14). A good statement to keep in mind when you consider giving.

Hezekiah, king of Judah, is experiencing a time of national revival in approximately 720 B.C., 251 years after David's prayer, and following the Celebration of Passover at the Temple. He required the people to bring a portion of their goods to the priests and Levites, so they could devote themselves fully to the Law of the Lord. He wanted to get the Temple back up and running with sacrifices.

When the people heard this request, they responded generously, and continually piled up great heaps of gifts from late spring until early autumn. "When Hezekiah and his officials came and saw these huge piles, they thanked the Lord and his people Israel" (2 Chron. 31:8). When right with God, generosity flowed from the people of God because, "The godly are generous givers" (Ps. 37:21).

Paul spoke of this, when he told the Corinthian church the attitude of another church, related to giving. "Now I want you to know, what God in His kindness has done through the churches of Macedonia. They are being tested by many troubles, and they are very poor. But they are also filled with abundant joy, which has overflowed in rich generosity" (2 Cor. 8:1a-2). "They gave not only what they could afford, but far more. They did it of their own free will. They begged us again and again for the privilege of sharing in the gift for the believers of Jerusalem. They even did more than we had hoped, for their first action was to give themselves to the Lord and to us, just as God wanted them to do" (2 Cor. 8:3-5). Here was a godly group of believers that didn't have much, but they kept on giving. They were not satisfied with a little; they wanted to give big for the Kingdom of God.

Here are important words that need to be said to leaders concerning rich people. Timothy was being mentored by Paul, and Paul considered him his son in the faith. As he taught about the people and activities of the church, he said this to Timothy concerning rich people. "Teach those who are rich in this world not to be proud and not to trust in their money, which is so unreliable. Their trust should be in God, who richly gives us all we need for our enjoyment. Tell them to use their money to do good. They should be rich in good works and generous to those in need, always being ready to share with others. By doing this, they will be storing up their treasure as a good foundation for the future so that they may experience true life" (1 Tim. 6:17-19). Here he is saying, that the rich should not trust in their money to save them or to always be there; he wanted them to also be generous doing good works. The rich needed to stay connected to the church body and not float high and away from interaction with people.

Paul identified giving as a spiritual gift, one of over twenty mentioned in Scripture. He said, "If your gift is giving, give generously" (Rom. 12:8). You receive the spiritual gift of giving from the Holy Spirit that lives in you, and the person aware of that gift recognizes God has given them the ability to have wealth, and want to give it away. In that case, Paul said he wanted them to give with no ulterior motive, but abundantly, and without any pomp and circumstance.

Here is a key to generosity, "Generous people plan to do what is generous, and they stand firm in their generosity" (Isa. 32:8). Whether a rich person, or a widow who just gives two small coins, or a church that keeps on asking to give more, generosity is a powerful blessing to those receiving, and also to those who are giving. It is a spiritual gift, but everyone can be generous, if not with money, then hundreds of other ways.

Key Takeaway: God is generous and He put generosity inside us when He created us. Generosity is needed because there will always be people in need. Those who give generously receive generously from God. It is important for believers to be generous in many different ways because it can have a huge impact on the hearts of unbelievers. Be generous every day with your praise, encouragement, thankfulness, teaching, leading, and giving.

Applications:

How can you increase your generosity this year?

What ways can you teach your children to be generous?

How can the church get this word out about generosity?

Honor (Giving it) Principle

How do you express honor to others? It seems like a different kind of question, but it goes to the heart of pointing others out instead of pointing yourself out. Many times we are self-focused and desirous of being honored to boost our ego, but what we find is that those who honor others receive their due honor at some future point.

Here's the kind of attitude we need to have; "take delight in honoring each other" (Romans 12:10). Paul knew it was the right action to take. This phrase is among over fifteen short sentences that represent action items for every believer in Romans 12:9-21.

To honor is to give a person high respect; to show the worth and value of someone. It is done in public, showing them great esteem. It is giving the glory to another for a job well done; an accomplishment well-completed. It is giving one credit where credit is due. It is the privilege of being associated with and bestowing distinction upon them. All of these definitions of honor could apply for God, but in God's particular case, it is worship of Him that shows courteous regard for Him.

Solomon said, "Honor the Lord with your wealth and with the best part of everything you produce" (Prov. 3:9). Honoring God involves releasing your hand from the first-fruits of your work and giving it to Him, realizing it is valuable to participate with God in His greater purposes. Understanding this directive to honor God by the giving of your wealth, time, and talent to Him will also help you understand honor in your daily walk with others.

There is a difference between giving honor and receiving it. Honor is due God at all times for He has done great things for us. Honor is due those around you for the suffering they endure, the successes they accomplish, and the services they provide.

Honor for ourselves must be given by others and not by us. Caution is always involved as you could be seen as tooting your own horn. Solomon said it well, "humility precedes honor" (Proverbs 18:12). That is to say that honor given to a person who is not humble will go directly to their head. So the best order is to find a humble person and then honor them.

And another challenge from Solomon was, "whoever pursues righteousness and unfailing love will find life, righteousness, and honor" (21:21). Living a good and righteous life will be cause for honor because it is not the norm, but a special life worthy of it.

Key Takeaway: Honor is necessary with God and others, and one should be careful to be humble when honor is given.

Applications:

How can you become better at honoring others and especially God?

On a regular basis, what are ways that your family could honor God?

What could your church do to honor its members who are doing special work for God?

Living Rightly Principle

A religious leader asked Jesus the question: "Good Teacher, what should I do to inherit eternal life? (Luke 18:18). Jesus was ready for a good discussion, so he answered the question with a question, "Why do you call me good?" (18:19). Jesus didn't wait for the leader to speak up; he proceeded to answer his original question, "You know the commandments: #7 You must not commit adultery. #6 You must not murder. #8 You must not steal. #9 You must not testify falsely. #5 Honor your father and mother.'" (18:20). (I have put the number of each commandment in front of each response for observation purposes.)

What commandments were left out? #10 coveting anything that belongs to your neighbor. And, #1-4 which dealt with having an exclusive relationship with God, not debasing yourself with idolatry, misusing the name of the Lord your God, and observing the Sabbath as holy.

The response of the religious leader was quick, "I've obeyed all these commandments since I was young" (18:21). Wow, was he proud and blind at the same time? Jesus could have said, "Aha! I caught you! Remember when you ......" but that would have only provoked an argument and that was not why he continued the conversation.

Jesus responded with, "There is still one thing you haven't done. Sell all your possessions and give the money to the poor, and you will have treasure in heaven. Then come, follow me" (18:22).

Did that statement catch the leader off guard? The question that passed quickly through his brain might have been, "Why do I have to sell, give away, and follow Christ? I am already doing what I need to do." This turned his heart to great sadness, seen from the last words Luke recorded, "for he was very rich" (18:23). He thought he was living rightly, and transitioning to be a follower of this Rabbi was too much of a change for him. He would keep doing what he determined would get him to eternal life.

Living rightly means putting God first, with no other gods at all in your life. His money was too important to him. Possibly he was looking to be affirmed in his strict adherence to the law, but Jesus didn't give him any satisfaction. In fact, he didn't allow him to think that he could even "inherit eternal life." He said he wanted to do something to get "eternal life" but wasn't willing to do it when it was suggested by Christ, which means he was insincere in his question.

Who sets the standard for living rightly? It's God; not any person. Paul saw spiritual development as a part of God's plan for each member of the churches he initiated. He gave to one of the most dysfunctional churches, Corinth, four parting challenges and a promise that would help them, and help us too, in living rightly.

He was inspired to say, "Be joyful. Grow to maturity. Encourage each other. Live in harmony and peace" (2 Corinthians 13:11).

"Be joyful." In other words, stop with the negative and cynical behavior, i.e., questioning the sincerity and goodness of people's motives and actions. Put in its place, joy, doesn't come out of good circumstances, but out of a pure heart, no matter what the circumstances. This would identify a heart dedicated to God.

"Grow to maturity." A chronologically older person shouldn't be acting like an infant. Growth happens as a natural process of living. When we stunt our growth or stop it, we die. Maturity of mind, emotion, and will should be the goal for every believer, because a mature person tends to exhibit better actions in their life, like patience, endurance, and wisdom.

There is a difference between being mature, which takes time and patience, and being spiritual. Spiritual is being right with God; no unconfessed sin or blind spots hiding sin, but maturity is being spiritual for a long consecutive time.

"Encourage each other." Wow, what would the world look like if those inside and outside the church encouraged each other? We have a tendency to pick on others; stand on the backs of others; hold others down so that we can rise. Paul wanted these believers to encourage everyone, all the time. Encouraging words are seldom spoken, but always appreciated. They can help a person over a hump in their progress.

"Live in harmony and peace." He was not saying that you all had to agree in every way and with every action. Harmony is different than melody in music. It augments the melody with different notes in the same key, and when all are sung together, they produce a great musical concert with each instrumental and vocal part in vertical alignment. Harmony is always beautiful. It generates peace, not discord, and that allows for even more growth.

The second part of "harmony and peace" is the presence of peace. Peace allows for all above and keeps the process recycling so that others begin to see the uniqueness to a body of believers.

There is a promise at the end of the 2 Corinthian passage. It reads, "Then the God of love and peace will be with you" (13:11). At the giving of the great commission, Jesus said, "And be sure of this, I am with you always, even to the end of the age" (Matt. 28:20). God never gives up on people, and delights in being present in their daily lives. He is here to help, comfort, and guide us into living rightly.

Key Takeaway: Joy is an internal delightful contentment. Growth is the path to maturity. Encouragement is a producer of hope. Harmony widens the concert of people. And peace allows you to rest in the assurance that you are living rightly. They all have the Holy Spirit as a promoter and prompter to keep us moving forward. Living Rightly empowers people and churches to fulfill their commission to disciple. These are the answer to the religious leader's question about inheriting eternal life.

Applications:

Which of the four challenges to living rightly do you already have in action, and which do you need to add to your present life?

How could you creatively work through these living rightly items with your children?

How could your church enhance the spread of these living rightly items?

Obedience Principle

You were once a child, required to obey your parents. Then you grew up, took the reins of your life, and became independent. You thought you no longer needed to obey and it made you feel free. Then you joined the Army, and your sergeant required your obedience. You got out of the Army and found a job, but your boss wanted you to obey. Your paycheck withheld money for paying your taxes, and you found out they would punish you if you didn't obey the law.

As life moved on, you hired a physical trainer, but they would only work with you if you did what they said. Then you got sick and obeyed your doctor. Police ticketed you for running a red light. I could go on and on, but you get the picture. Obedience is not a thing you once did as a child and now no longer need to do. It is an action that continues to follow you wherever you go throughout your life.

Consider Old Testament examples of obedience that made a difference in their lives. Noah obeyed God and built an ark which saved his family in the worldwide flood. Abraham obeyed God in taking Isaac to be sacrificed on Mt. Moriah. He then stopped him and inserted a ram sacrifice for Isaac. Eli, at one time a High Priest in Israel, told young Samuel to respond to the voice calling his name by saying, "Speak your servant is listening," indicating obedience to the voice (1 Samuel 3:10).

On the contrary side, consider the fates of those who did not obey. Adam and Eve disobeyed, choosing to eat the fruit of the forbidden tree, and look at the result to the human race. Saul disobeyed Samuel's orders and lost the kingdom of Israel to David. Jonah disobeyed and caused fear and dismay on a boat, and eventually ended up inside a large fish.

What about the New Testament? The Apostle Paul wrote about many situations in which people were to obey. They included a child to her parents (Exodus 20:12; Ephesians 6:1), slaves to masters, which could be expanded today to employees with bosses (6:5a), children of God to Christ the Lord of the Church (6:5b), citizens to their government (Romans 13:1), and church attenders to church leaders (Hebrews 13:17).

Obedience is not an option; it is an integral part of life where you learn self-control, where you are trained, where you live in freedom within boundaries. It is a test of who is in charge of your life. So when the test of faithfulness is upon you, will you respond with obedience or will you put up a fight?

Obedience is simply defined as doing exactly what you are told to do, immediately, and with the right heart attitude. When you do that, you are being completely obedient. Some might do what they are told, but do it in their own time and also murmur about it. This is not obedience. This is being stubborn and willful. This is not pleasing to people or to God, and is not helpful to your life. Here is a way that helps you remember what it means to obey:

Obligate yourself to another for learning, mentoring, and disciplining in order to grow

Bear up under their leadership because you know that they are not trying to break you, but to make you into a better person

Entrust yourself to them, their knowledge, their experience, and their wisdom in order to have direction, protection, and success

Yield your will to their will, believing they will help you get to where you want to be

Maybe we've stressed the strong side of obedience too much over the benefits side of obedience. How can we make it more about you than the person over you? Obedience has the following benefits:

- Protection from physical, spiritual, and emotional harm
- Long life promise given if you obey your parents (Exodus 20:12; Ephesians 6:1-3)
- Humility developer: Jesus "humbled himself in obedience to God" (Philippians 2:8)
- "Obedience is better than sacrifice" (1 Samuel 15:22)
- Faster and better results over trial and error learning
- Establishes boundaries in which you can live joyfully, patiently, and expectantly
- Opens the path for a higher and clearer picture of what God wants from you and for you
- Leads you to maturity

One last story to tell. David had been anointed King of Israel when he was sixteen years old. But Saul sought to kill him and give the kingdom to Jonathan, his son. So David lived off the grid with 600 men and became responsible for all their wives and children; to feed them, clothe them, house them, and govern them.

Tired of being chased by Saul, he moved into Philistine territory and made friends with King Achish. In fact, the king liked David and gave him the whole town of Ziklag to house his family, his men, and their families.

King Achish deserved to be obeyed because of this and because he cared about and respected David. However, the Philistines prepared to go to war against King Saul and his Israelite army. David and his men volunteered to fight on the Philistine side. As the army of King Achish gathered, several of his generals said they didn't trust David. He could destroy their plan and attack them from the rear and become a hero in Israel. They pressured King Achish to send David home. So when Achish said "leave," after some discussion, David and his men left.

When they arrived back at Ziklag, they found it in ruin and all their goods and families gone. David and his men hastily followed the trail of the raiders until they caught up with them, whereupon they killed them and recaptured their possessions and families. If David had not obeyed Achish, they might not have ever recovered their goods and families. They would have been too far gone.

As the battle between the Philistines and Israelites raged, Achish got the upper hand and killed King Saul and three of his sons. Had David been there, he would have blood on his hands, and the nation of Israel would have had a harder time making him king.

Obedience to a foreign king allowed David to have a clear conscience as he became the second King of Israel, and his men did not desert him because they had their families and their possessions. Obedience is always the better way.

Key Takeaway: Obedience is doing exactly what you are told to do, immediately, and with the right heart attitude. It is not hard to understand, but sometimes hard to execute. The story of David reveals that its benefits far outweigh the hardships it might seem to cause. Leadership does not rise to the top because they are disobedient and rebellious. One of the markers of a rising leader is the ability to obey those who are presently in charge.

Applications:

Based on the definition we have put forth, where are you on the obedience scale?

What is your level of willingness to obligate, bear up under, entrust, and yield yourself to those in charge of you?

It's hard to be a parent now, but understanding what we've said about obedience, how successful are you at teaching your children to be obedient?

How could your church teach proper obedience to the head of the church, Jesus Christ?

Patience Principle

You can speak of the patience of Job, but consider the patience of Joseph.

Here was a young man, who at seventeen was sold into slavery by his brothers. He was taken to Egypt as a slave; was later accused of wrong by his master, Potiphar; and thrown in prison to see years pass without hope of rescue. But God was at work behind the scenes, orchestrating Joseph's life.

When the time was right, he was brought to Pharaoh to be his dream interpreter. He had done this before, so he was prepared. Pharaoh rehearsed his dreams with Joseph, and he had instant clarity on their interpretations. Pharaoh was impressed. The interpretation of dreams built trust between the two men, and the organizational preparations, suggested by Joseph to address the dream issues, impressed Pharaoh again. Joseph was appointed to be second in command in Egypt.

Joseph never thought he would hear Pharaoh say, "I am Pharaoh, but no one will lift a hand or foot in the entire land of Egypt without your approval" (Gen. 41:44). Pharaoh raised this thirty-year-old man to the highest position in the land to address the coming famine. He dressed him in robes of fine linen, put his signet ring on Joseph's finger, and gave him an Egyptian name and wife. Joseph rode around in a special chariot of Pharaoh's, and all the people bowed to him. I'm sure Joseph pinched himself many times, for what had become reality, was truly like a dream.

The seven years of plentiful food for the nation passed, and along with the entire world, the seven years of famine began. But Joseph's wisdom and patience, given by God, had prepared him and Egypt to survive. He amassed great wealth for Egypt during the famine, as the world came to them for food supplies. He was still patient, as his greatest dream was not yet fulfilled until his brothers and father came to also buy grain, bowed down before him, and finally joined him in Egypt. Twenty-two years after he arrived in Egypt as a slave, Joseph was sitting on a throne before his brothers.

Joseph was a patient person. We can now see that the plan of God was to place Joseph in an influential position next to the Egyptian Pharaoh. The plentiful years brought him a stellar reputation, and how he handled the lean years only increased it. He made Egypt wealthier than it had ever been.

Joseph had patience in the pit, while his brothers decided what to do with him. He had patience on the trip, as he traveled to Egypt in slavery. He had patience in the home of Potiphar, in administrating his household and avoiding Potiphar's wife.

All his progress was seemingly destroyed as he patiently faced false accusations, lost his job, and was imprisoned. There, he had the patience to rise again, as the favorite of the warden, become the leader of the prisoners, and the dream interpreter of the two palace officials, also placed there. God was at work.

But patience became necessary again, as the cup-bearer, recently restored to his position in the palace, forgot about him. There was a two-year wait before the cup-bearer's memory reminded him of Joseph's ability with the interpretation of dreams. He was brought to Pharaoh, whose present magicians and wise men could not discern the dreams of Pharaoh.

It is important to note the humility of Joseph at this point; for before he began the conversation concerning the dreams, he said, "It is beyond my power to do this, but God can tell you what it means and set you at ease" (Genesis 41:16). God did work through Joseph to interpret what others could not.

Now in his new position, his patience enabled him to do the right things to protect his adopted nation. He set a great example that others, like Mordecai and Daniel, would later follow. Although he was busy in his work, he still had not received the fulfillment of his own second dream, but patiently waited until his brothers were bowing before him. His patience paid off.

The patience of Job was extreme, with his physical ailment, the grief over the loss of his children, and the thefts of his possessions. Its impact pressed hard against his heart, but he never gave in to it.

Joseph's thirteen-year rise to leadership was even more instructive, with its intermittent advances and steps backward, eventually rewarding him with extreme success. The restoration of his extended family, and their eventual move to Egypt, was an added bonus.

Solomon's proverb, "A man's wisdom gives him patience; it is to his glory to overlook an offense" (Prov. 19:11), aptly describes Joseph's life. He was the intelligent and wise person that he suggested for Pharaoh to find.

The principle of patience is not to get ahead of God, to be cautious of quick successes, and to wait on God for open doors. There is no need to hurry; God is going to use every high and low of life, if you will let Him. Being a patient person will keep you on track with God's plan for your life.

Key Takeaway: Joseph's story involves us in so many different aspects of his life; his dreams, his family, the jealousy of his siblings, God's timing and provision, and trust of God in the dark times, and joy with Him in the bright times. We can learn much more about Joseph by considering the twists and turns in his life and the patience he accessed throughout.

Applications:

How can you increase the level of patience in your life?

How can you, as parents, teach patience to your children?

What could your church do to encourage patience in all its attendees?

Repentance Principle

Overused, but certainly illustrative of what repentance means, the story of the prodigal son has received continual focus for centuries. Let's review it in story form as Jesus told it:

"A man had two sons. The younger son told his father, 'I want my share of your estate now before you die.' So his father agreed to divide his wealth between his sons.

A few days later this younger son packed all his belongings and moved to a distant land, and there he wasted all his money in wild living. About the time his money ran out, a great famine swept over the land, and he began to starve.

He persuaded a local farmer to hire him, and the man sent him into his fields to feed the pigs. The young man became so hungry that even the pods he was feeding the pigs looked good to him. But no one gave him anything.

When he finally came to his senses, he said to himself, 'At home even the hired servants have food enough to spare, and here I am dying of hunger! I will go home to my father and say, Father, I have sinned against both heaven and you, and I am no longer worthy of being called your son. Please take me on as a hired servant.'

So he returned home to his father. And while he was still a long way off, his father saw him coming. Filled with love and compassion, he ran to his son, embraced him, and kissed him.

His son said to him, 'Father, I have sinned against both heaven and you, and I am no longer worthy of being called your son.'

But his father said to the servants, 'Quick! Bring the finest robe in the house and put it on him. Get a ring for his finger and sandals for his feet. And kill the calf we have been fattening. We must celebrate with a feast, for this son of mine was dead and has now returned to life. He was lost, but now he is found.' So the party began" (Luke 15:11-24).

This parable is an illustration of the repentance process in an individual heart. Let's track the key phases for better understanding.

The younger son had been thinking about this for some time, since he left so quickly, and we know that he would not receive as much money as his older brother. Usually the split was one-third for second son and two-thirds for the first son, partly because the first son would be keeping up the land, animals, and crops.

But to ask for his portion before his father died, was to wish he was dead. This was an insult to his father and spoke to the son's rebellious nature. His purpose, we find out next, followed the nature of his actions. He was going to use his estate funds for wild living. He wasn't starting a business; or becoming a big money donor for some positive mission. And soon, the money was gone, so were his new friends, and a famine had begun. The lesson here was that wild living does not consider what tomorrow might bring.

But the boy was still trying to keep his independence, so he got a low paying, no eating job feeding pigs, animals Jews were not supposed to be around. As he watched them slop around in the mud, I'm sure he thought, "that's what I was doing with my friends!"

But he did have a brain, and "he finally came to his senses." This was a moment of clarity for him. He reasoned that his father's hired servants were now living better than he was, and that didn't sit well. So he decided to return to his father. Which brings us to our definition of repentance, which is a "coming to your senses."

Now he had to have a plan, and it involved four phases: initially, there had to be recognition that his life could be better; that he didn't need to live like he was. Next, he needed to confess that his actions were a sin against his father, but more than that, "against heaven."

This was important. On two levels he had been rebellious; to his father, but also to the Lord. There was a pass-through in his rebellion, from the physical act of sin expressed in wild living, to his spiritual act of rebellion against God.

A picture of a cross helps us here. The horizontal bar, where the hands of Jesus were nailed, represents the lateral world, those people around us that will be the hearers of our confession. They were hurt, and need to be asked forgiveness for that. The vertical bar, from the ground to its top, and upward into heaven, is recognizing we must also confess to the Lord our sin. He was harmed, just as much as those on the earth.

We have found, in both the Old and New Testaments, examples of this process with other Bible characters; such as, Israel's complaint of no meat in the wilderness directed against the Lord of Heaven (Ex. 16:8), Korah's rebellion against God by challenging the authority of Moses and Aaron (Num. 12:11), David's cry of "against you, and you only, have I sinned," when he came to his senses about his adultery with Bathsheba, and the murder of Uriah, her husband (Ps. 51:4; 2 Sam. 12:13), and Achan, who identified his theft in Jericho as a sin against the Lord (Josh. 7:20). As they all found out, saying, "I'm sorry" doesn't cut it, when in heaven your heart and motives are seen all the time by God. The writer of Psalm 119 declared his process to not need repentance, when he said, "I have hidden your word in my heart, that I might not sin against you" (119:11).

Repentance is recognizing you are sinning by acting independent of God. It is knowing that your wild living does not consider tomorrow's consequences and neither will it take you the right way. An understanding that repentance is where you admit that your life could be better, concede that your sin is against God as much as it is against a person, but then still express the need to punish yourself further, like the prodigal did in wanting to be a servant rather than a son, is still the wrong idea of repentance.

The right idea of "coming to your senses" is seen other places in Scripture. Saul came to his senses on the road to Damascus when he saw the risen Lord in person. The people on the Day of Pentecost, who heard Peter's message and asked, "What should we do?" received Peter's reply, "Each of you must repent of your sins and turn to God" (Acts 2:37-38). Jonah came to his senses inside the large fish (Jonah 2:7). And King Nebuchadnezzar came to his senses, after approximately seven years out in a pasture, acting like a cow (Daniel 4:33-34).

The last thing the prodigal did was determine to return to his father. Which he did, and then tried to use the punishment line of son to servant on him. The father interrupted him before he could say, "Please take me as a hired servant." He didn't expect the response his father gave him. It involved reinstatement as a son, with the robe, ring, sandals, and a celebration.

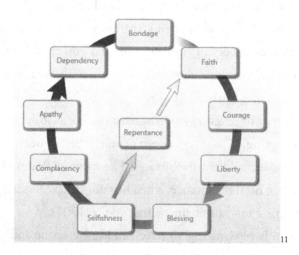

¹¹

Key Takeaway: Repentance is coming to your senses about sin and its cost to you. It is realizing that sin happens vertically against God, as well as horizontally against people, and both need to be addressed. It dismisses your need to punish yourself, in addition to seeking forgiveness, and it involves returning to the one who loves you unconditionally for eternity.

Applications:

Have you had the repentance experience, of coming to your senses, concerning Christ's substitution for your sins?

How could you make your children aware of the fact that sin is against God and someone else, and that both need to be addressed for forgiveness?

What ways could your church incorporate an understanding of repentance?

Respect for People Principle

How do you gain respect? Respect is something that has to be earned. It is being shown consideration, even admiration, for what you have done. Lots of people want respect, but don't do anything to deserve it. But there is a way for you to gain the respect of those around you.

Paul, in writing to the people of Thessalonica, shared a way to gain respect. Even though people may not have liked these believers or believed what they testified to, he felt they could still be respected. He said this to the church, "Make it your goal to live a quiet life, minding your own business and working with your hands, just as I instructed you before. Then people who are not Christians will respect the way you live, and you will not need to depend on others" (1 Thessalonians 4:11-12).

They were told to "make it your goal," or move forward, leading a quiet life, not a riotous one, or one immersed in controversy. They were not to be the life of the party. They were told to keep their eye on their own business, and not on the business of others. This was the nosy neighbor example; eyes and ears that watched and listened for problems which they could exploit. They were instructed to work with their hands; in other words, make a living for yourself, and provide for your family. This calls for respect.

Now, we can see these as today challenges for every one of us. Seeing people who are driven to quiet and private lives is a curious sight, and seeing people who mind their own business is even more rare, plus making a living with your own hands. These were essential, but why are these three things important in earning respect?

A quiet and focused life, and providing for your family, together create a strong testimony before the world. Paul said these ways would win the respect of those around them and they would not be dependent on others, a sense that God is providing for them and He is not ignoring them in their present state.

Knowing how to earn respect is of prime importance, but how do you show respect to others? We show honor and esteem for others by considering their positions in life, their age, and esteeming their accomplishments. That involves kindness and politeness to them, affirming them for who they are, and above all listening attentively to them without interrupting.

Peter wrote to believers that were experiencing persecution, and he had encouraging words to say about how to behave and act toward others. Here are his major thoughts:

- Primarily, you are representing Christ, who is our example of properly respecting all (1 Peter 2:21-25)
- Respect everyone, leaving no one out (2:17a)
- Respect the king, or in our time the president (2:17c)
- Slaves were to "accept the authority of your masters with all respect" (2:18-20). In our day, this is showing respect for your boss or manager.
- Wives were to respect their husbands, then their "godly lives will speak to them without any words. They will be won over by observing your pure and reverent lives" (3:1-2).
- Husbands, in the same way "give honor to your wives" (3:7)

We could add three more that are suggested in other places:

- Respect for the elderly (Lev. 19:32)

- Respect for those who minister among you in the church (1 Thess. 5:12)
- And, children are to respect their parents (Eph. 6:1-3; 1Tim. 5:4)

Respect needs to be earned and given to others. Peter is speaking about respect, not as an encouragement to do this simply out of duty or dread of consequences, but to do it out of love and devotion to God. A proper respect of others provides a foundation on which to build a relationship of trust, that leads to your testimony of faith.

Key Takeaway: Respect is much more essential than most of us think. It is a precursor to the hearts of others being open toward you. It is not just for one class or age of people; it is for all. How different life in our cities and towns would be if this principle was taught and put into practice.

Applications:
Of the actions that Paul mentioned above, which are you doing now?

How can you, as parents, make it easy for your children to see respect exampled in your actions to others?

How could the church instruct and example respect to its congregation?

Reverence for God Principle

What is the most freeing action you could do that would bring you peace, satisfaction, and contentment? It is not a fear of man or of circumstances, but a fear of the Lord. The wisest man on earth, Solomon, wrote, "The fear of the Lord is a life-giving fountain; it offers escape from the snares of death" (Prov. 14:27).

We can explain it two different ways: it is a true fearfulness of God; who He is, and the power He holds. It is a respect and reverence for God, recognizing He is the eternal king of the universe, and that we are but a speck of dust.

This fear is enhanced by reading His Word, saturating yourself with the wisdom of its truths. He rules, no matter what is happening, and "everything serves His plans" (Psalm 119:91).

Moses gained this fear of God in the desert of Sinai. He came there after he had fled Egypt and found a family, which he married into. Reuel was the father and Zipporah was one of his daughters that Moses married. He was there for forty years, when he met God at the burning bush near Mount Sinai (Exodus 3:1).

God warned him, "Take off your sandals, for you are standing on holy ground. I am the God of your father—the God of Abraham, the God of Isaac, and the God of Jacob" (Exodus 3:5). When Moses heard this, he covered his face, because he was afraid to look at God. God spoke of the people of Israel, and his awareness of their suffering, and He commissioned Moses to go and release His people from slavery.

At the end of his life, after forty years with the people of the exodus, Moses recited a song he created. In it he said, "I will proclaim the name of the Lord; how glorious is our God! He is the Rock, his deeds are perfect. Everything he does is just and fair. He is a faithful God who does no wrong; how just and upright he is!" (Deut. 32:3-4). Moses had learned to reverence God.

Joseph revealed his respect for God in his comments to his brothers, after the death of their father, Jacob. He said, "Don't be afraid of me. Am I God that I can punish you? You intended to harm me, but God intended it all for good. He brought me to this position so I could save the lives of many people. No, don't be afraid" (Genesis 50:19-21).

Through all the ups and downs of his life, since he was sold into slavery at the age of seventeen, Joseph learned to respect God. It was about twenty-two years after his slavery began, and after his ascension to leadership in Egypt, when he said this to his brothers. He was not God, but God intended good to come out of the years since that significant action of his brothers.

Peter and John, when warned to stop speaking about Jesus, said, "Do you think God wants us to obey you rather than Him? We cannot stop telling about everything we have seen and heard" (Acts 4:19-20). Their respect for God and his Son, Jesus Christ, caused them to abandon their safety, and deny the demand of the council of all the rulers and elders and teachers of religious law of their nation, to not speak again of Jesus. Instead, they declared their loyalty to God.

Paul, in his later years as a believer, evidenced his allegiance to God when he spoke to the sailors aboard the ship, bound for Rome. He said, "Take courage! None of you will lose your lives, even though the ship will go down. For last night an angel of the God to whom I belong and whom I serve stood beside me, and he said, 'Don't be afraid, Paul, for you will surely stand trial before Caesar! What's more, God in His goodness has granted safety to everyone sailing with you.' So take courage! For I believe

God. It will be just as He said" (Acts 27:22-25). Paul belonged to God, he was his servant, and he believed God.

Reverence of the Lord is a fountain of blessing to our souls. A fountain of water is essential to human life, but we understand this fountain as essential to spiritual life. This respect for God gives us eternal life. And further than that, "it offers escape" from the snares and temptations of this world.

When you are focused on a fear and respect for God, you are not focused on what you need to please yourself. You remain in the world, but you are not of the world (John 17:14).

Living inside the boundaries God established for you gives you freedom, which brings peace, joy, rest, assurance, and all the feelings and thoughts you need to keep going and to keep praising Him.

"The Lord is a great God, a great King above all gods" (Psalm 95:3). "Great is the Lord! He is worthy of praise! He is to be feared above all gods" (1 Chron. 16:25). "Fear of the Lord leads to life, bringing security and protection from harm" (Prov. 19:23). Do you fear God? Growing in your ability to fear Him has lasting and life-giving results.

Key Takeaway: The fear and reverence of God is not bad; it is a good thing, with benefits that last eternally. It can release you from a fear of men, and give you the ability to tell the story of salvation to everyone around you.

Applications:
What could you do to enlarge your reverence for God?

How could you help your children understand that reverence for God is the most important thing they could ever learn?

How could your church regularly bring this important truth to light?

Sacrifice Principle

How much do you know about sacrifice? Growing up in America, where most of us maintain a lifestyle that is high above the majority of the world's population, you may not understand what sacrifice really means. Let's take a deep dive and clear some things up.

When the people of Israel exited Egypt after four-hundred years of slavery, they were led to Mt. Sinai by Moses. There God defined how the people would worship Him and what that would require. He also established the Levites as His tribe of religious workers, dedicated to the Tabernacle which was soon to be built and furnished with all its accessories, and the ministry guidelines of the priests that would offer the sacrifices with the types of animals that could be offered.

Further than this, on Mt. Sinai, God met with Moses and He [God] wrote on two stone tablets the Ten Commandments. These clearly defined actions that were called sins. It was divided into three sections: the first four commandments directed at worship and love for God, the last five commandments directed at love for neighbor, and the fifth commandment, placed between the first four and the last five, dealing with honoring parents. This commandment acted like the pin in a door hinge. It was the parent's responsibility to teach their children how to love God [1-4] and how to love your neighbor [6-10]. These commandments would identify for the people sins that needed to be confessed and then sacrificial steps were given to complete the atonement action. There's a lot more to talk about related to the sacrificial system and a good book to help you understand it all is, *The Temple, Its Ministry and Services*, by Alfred Edersheim.

In the Old Testament sacrifice referred to an action like, "I sacrificed, through the ministry of the priests, an offering on the altar" which meant you offered a lamb, bull, goat or turtledoves on the altar with a perpetually burning fire below to atone for your sins. This indicated the act and the item of the act, both necessary for guilt to be removed.

For the people of Israel, the whole book of Leviticus emphasized the necessity and activity of sacrifice, and especially the need for a blood sacrifice concerning sins. The purpose was to cover the offeror's sins and put them back in right relationship with God. The Levites dedicated themselves to properly preparing and offering sacrifices on behalf of all Israel.

This meant that the Levites needed to be properly prepared internally and externally to facilitate their work. Much is said about the state of their heart, the clothing they wore, and also the washing of their body. If they were not "clean" (we could say "holy"), then they dishonored the sacrifice and were in grave danger of punishment. The sacrificed animal also had requirements of purity. No one was to offer a lame animal, or one with other defects.

Sacrifice was important to God as He taught the people their necessity to atone for sin, but even in the Old Testament there were other passages that suggested other items to sacrifice.

- When Samuel came to Saul after his battle with the Amalekites, it was revealed that King Saul chose not to destroy them completely as commanded, but spared the life of King Agag and brought the "best of the sheep, goats, cattle, and plunder to sacrifice them to the Lord" (1 Samuel 15:21). Samuel responded to Saul, "What is more pleasing to the Lord: your burnt offerings and sacrifices or your obedience to His voice? Listen! Obedience is better than sacrifice, and submission is better than offering the fat of rams" (15:22).

- When the psalmist decided what he would do after he was rescued from his suffering and pain, he said, "I will praise God's name with singing, and I will honor Him with thanksgiving. For this will please the Lord more than sacrificing cattle, more than presenting a bull with its horns and hooves" (Psalm 69:30-31).

- Solomon in his wisdom said, "The Lord is more pleased when we do what is right and just than when we offer Him sacrifices" (Proverbs 21:3).

- The prophet Hosea, who married an unfaithful woman to illustrate the nation's unfaithfulness, spoke God's words to the people of Israel, "I want you to show love, not offer sacrifices. I want you to know me more than I want burnt offerings" (Hosea 6:6; Matthew 9:13; 12:7).

What we learn from these passages is that although sacrifices were necessary in the Old Testament for atonement, there were other actions, i.e. obedience, worship, love, and doing what was right, which were also important to God.

Why so? Because sacrifices had to continually happen, they were a work that could not fully resolve the offeror's sin issue. There was a covering over of sins for a while but not permanent removal. Jesus' sacrifice was the ultimate sacrifice. The Lamb was slain to remove all past, present, and future sins once and for all for mankind. His lasting sacrifice removed the need to repeat offered sacrifices for sin, but the other actions spoken about in the paragraph above were still to be upheld.

Today you don't need to kill an animal and sacrifice it on an altar for your sins. You depend on Christ's sacrifice and understand that you have much greater and glorious sacrifices to offer than the Old Testament required. The writer of Hebrews adds the words of the psalmist into his book when he quotes, "You did not want animal sacrifices or sin offerings…I have come to do your will, O God…" (Hebrews 10:5,7; Psalm 40:6-8). This is Christ saying, as he comes into the world as an infant, that he wants to do the will of the Father, which is to offer himself as the lasting sacrifice for all sin.

Further, what God wanted, as King David understood, was "the sacrifice.…of a broken spirit" for "you will not reject a broken and repentant heart, O God" (Psalm 51:16-17). Giving to God's work is also a sacrifice God accepts. Note Paul's response to the giving of the Philippians, "I am generously supplied with the gifts you sent me…They are a sweet-smelling sacrifice that is acceptable and pleasing to God (Philippians 4:18).

Here are some of the actions you can participate in today that are viewed by God as better than animal sacrifices:

- Obedience
- Worship
- Showing Love
- Right Living
- Doing His will
- Broken spirit
- Repentant heart
- Giving to God's work

Further, Paul said, "I plead with you to give your bodies to God because of all He has done for you. Let them be a living and holy sacrifice—the kind He will find acceptable" (Romans 12:1). This is truly the way to worship Him. All the above actions take place when your body is a living and holy sacrifice.

Key Takeaway: God no longer requires an animal sacrifice to cleanse us from sin due to the once for all sacrifice of His own Son. We can now perform many sacrificial actions to God, using our lives as the mechanism through which they are offered.

Application:

How could you increase your sacrificial actions toward God in the next six months?

How could your family, whether large or small, increase their sacrificial actions toward God?

What could your church body do as sacrificial actions for other believers?

Sowing and Reaping

This principle is clearly stated by the Apostle Paul as he writes to the Galatian believers, "So, don't be misled—you cannot mock the justice of God. You will always harvest what you plant" (Gal. 6:7). The process of sowing and reaping never changes; the seed of whatever you plant is what you harvest, never anything different.

Jesus told a parable about sowing and reaping. I have chosen to intersperse Jesus' teaching with the explanation he gave to the disciples to help you see the physical and spiritual ramifications of sowing and reaping. That's why there are verse numbers by each statement:

"Listen! A farmer went out to plant some seeds. [4] As he scattered them across his field, some seeds fell on a footpath, and the birds came and ate them. [19] The seed that fell on the footpath represents those who hear the message about the Kingdom and don't understand it. Then the evil one comes and snatches away the seed that was planted in their hearts.

[5] Other seeds fell on shallow soil with underlying rock. The seeds sprouted quickly because the soil was shallow. [6] But the plants soon wilted under the hot sun, and since they didn't have deep roots, they died. [20] The seed on the rocky soil represents those who hear the message and immediately receive it with joy. [21] But since they don't have deep roots, they don't last long. They fall away as soon as they have problems or are persecuted for believing God's word.

[7] Other seeds fell among thorns that grew up and choked out the tender plants. [22] The seed that fell among the thorns represents those who hear

God's word, but all too quickly the message is crowded out by the worries of this life and the lure of wealth, so no fruit is produced.

⁸ Still other seeds fell on fertile soil, and they produced a crop that was thirty, sixty, and even a hundred times as much as had been planted! ²³ The seed that fell on good soil represents those who truly hear and understand God's word and produce a harvest of thirty, sixty, or even a hundred times as much as had been planted" (Matt. 13:3-8, 19-23).

This parable showed the connection of sowing to reaping. It distinguished the results that happened depending on what type of ground the seed landed on. There are other stories about sowing mentioned in the Bible and they reveal the same connection of that which was sown to that which was reaped. This principle extends beyond the grain of the farmer to the lives of people of the Bible.

A well-known observation of Solomon on sowing and reaping stressed the results related to the seed: "Those who plant injustice will harvest disaster, and their reign of terror will come to an end" (22:8).

The voice of God through the prophet Hosea encouraged the people of Israel to, "Plant the good seeds of righteousness, and you will harvest a crop of love" (Hosea 10:12). However, that was not the seed they planted. Hosea tells us, "They have planted the wind and will harvest the whirlwind" (Hosea 8:7). He reviewed the actions of Israel as "rejecting what is good," "appointing kings without my [the Lord's) consent," and "making idols for themselves" (8:3-4). This caused them to reap their own destruction at the hands of their enemies.

The New Testament also compared the difference between sowing only to satisfy self and sowing to please the Spirit. Sowing to satisfy the flesh reaped decay and death; sowing to please the Spirit of God reaped everlasting life from the Spirit. Paul's admonition was to not get tired of sowing good. "At just the right time we will reap a harvest of blessing if we don't give up" (Gal. 6:8-9).

James explained the results of the work of a peacemaker saying,

140

"Those who are peacemakers will plant seeds of peace and reap a harvest of righteousness" (Jas. 3:18). He identified these seeds as peace loving, gentle at all times, willing to yield to others, full of mercy and good deeds, impartial, and always sincere. He said these "seeds of peace" would produce the result of an "harvest of righteousness."

We can conclude that the principle of sowing and reaping continues to operate throughout the centuries with no respect to the nation, city, or people. It is an unfailing principle; active and powerful. A basic message all should consider as they sow seeds.

Key Takeaway: Life is full of sowing and reaping actions. We cannot hide from the principle and we cannot hope that the harvest will not match the seed sown. It just won't happen. The ground it falls on and the seed type are most important in the process, and that is under your control. The Bible, which was written over a 1,400-year period, is full of stories that affirm this principle as correct.

Applications:
What seed have your sown that you are waiting to harvest? Will it be a good or bad harvest?

How could you teach this simple principle to your children? What words and what actions would help?

How is your church communicating this age-old principle to the congregation?

Suffering Principle

Beautiful pictures were created of Jesus with thousands gathered around him as he spoke to them and fed them. His compassion was overwhelming, and his love for friend and enemy was strong. He earnestly desired the salvation of all, even the scribes, Pharisees, and Sadducees, who plotted to kill him.

When Jesus informed his closest disciples that he would "suffer many terrible things at the hands of the elders, the leading priests, and the teachers of religious law" and "would be killed" (Matthew 16:21), his disciples, through the voice of Peter, told him it couldn't be so. "Peter took him aside and began to reprimand him for saying such things" (16:23). It surprised them. And Jesus' response was, "You are seeing things merely from a human point of view, not from God's" (16:23).

Sometime later, Jesus wept in the Garden of Gethsemane, was put under arrest, and bounced from the Sanhedrin to Pilate, to Herod, all night long. He was beaten and ridiculed by soldiers, his back was severely torn open by the cat of nine tails whip, was forced to carry his cross, and in his feeble state, fell under its weight. He struggled to walk to Golgotha where he faced the final insult of being hung on a cross. This is suffering, substantiated and serious, that he endured for all humanity.

Paul listed the many events in which he suffered: put in prison often, whipped times without number, three times beaten with rods, once stoned, three times ship-wrecked, once spent a whole night and a day adrift at sea, faced danger from rivers and robbers, Jews and Gentiles, in cities, in deserts

143

and on the seas, endured many sleepless nights, was hungry and thirsty, and shivered in severe cold (2 Corinthians 11:23-27).

In light of this, Paul instructed young Timothy in his closing remarks of the second letter to him, "Don't be afraid of suffering for the Lord" (2 Timothy 4:5). And Peter, in his first letter to believers scattered in the provinces of what is today the country of Turkey, said, "Dear friends, don't be surprised at the fiery trials you are going through, as if something strange were happening to you. Instead, be very glad—for these trials make you partners with Christ in his suffering, so that you will have the wonderful joy of seeing his glory when it is revealed to all in the world" (1 Peter 4:12-13).

Any suffering you are experiencing needs to be reviewed through these three statements: "You are seeing things merely from a human point of view." "Don't be afraid of suffering for the Lord." "Don't be surprised at the fiery trials you are going through." The wrong viewpoint, fear, and surprise are normal reactions to terrible situations that bring pain into your life. But Jesus, Paul, and Peter challenged us to ignore them.

If we are to ignore these viewpoints when suffering, what should we do? We should be prepared. This raises the question; how does one prepare for suffering? Here are ten suggestions given by Peter in chapters 3-4 of his first book:

1. "Worship Christ as Lord of your life" (3:15a).
2. "Always be ready to explain your Christian hope" (3:15b-16a).
3. "Keep your conscience clear" (3:16b).
4. "Remember, it is better to suffer for doing good if that is what God wants, than to suffer for doing wrong!" (3:17).
5. "Arm yourselves with the same attitude he had, and be ready to suffer, too" (4:1).
6. Stop participating in "the evil things that godless people enjoy" (4:3).
7. "Be earnest and disciplined in your prayers" (4:7).

8. "Continue to show deep love for each other" Peter identified this as "Most important of all" (4:8).

9. "Cheerfully share your home with those who need a meal or a place to stay" (4:9).

10. "Use them [your spiritual gifts] well to serve one another" (4:10).

Paul would totally agree with Peter's suggestions and add one more. He chose to put his suffering in perspective. He said, "We were crushed and overwhelmed beyond our ability to endure, and we thought we would never live through it. In fact, we expected to die. But as a result, we stopped relying on ourselves and learned to rely only on God, who raises the dead" (2 Corinthians 1:8-9).

This was trouble that was severe and mortal, but Paul focused on God's purpose for the suffering, not the trouble it caused him. This perspective carried him through the trial and the lesson learned was not to, in any way, rely upon himself, but on God.

Preparation for suffering involves deepening your relationship with Christ and with other believers; for it is this communion and community that will help in times of suffering. This means there are two questions you need to ask yourself: How am I deepening my relationship to Christ? And, how am I deepening my relationship with other believers?

It is not getting easier to live on planet Earth as a believer. The devil is ramping up his forces to destroy us and darkened hearts are ready to join into the persecution. My wife and I recently watched the movie *The Insanity of God*. We listened to the words of persecuted believers around the world and a statement that was common to all was that they considered persecution to be a normal part of their daily Christian lives. That is having the right perspective, preparing for suffering.

Although it is not something to court or complain about, if we are a Christ follower, we are able to count ourselves worthy to suffer personal dishonor for the name of Christ, who suffered so much for us.

Key Takeaway: Suffering is to be expected since we are part of the family of God through faith in the work of Jesus Christ. He suffered, leaders of the initial church suffered, and believers throughout the centuries have suffered. We are not to view it from our human viewpoint, neither be afraid of it, or surprised by it. Our focus should not be on the suffering, but on the benefit of learning how to better rely on God daily.

Applications:

How will this essay change your thinking and actions concerning suffering?

What could you do to explain the possibility of suffering for Jesus to your family?

How could your church help attendees to expect suffering and not be fearful or surprised by it?

Temptation Principle

The picture of a shiny apple handed to you temptingly is the picture of temptation's allurement. We all face it, we all fall to it, we all dream of winning over it. There is no limit to temptation's treats; they are innumerable and always match up well with our weaknesses. What can we do about it? Do we continue to fail and be resigned to defeat? This may be true for some, but not for those who are in Christ, and trust God.

Initially, we must understand that temptation is not sin, but rather a precursor to sin. The Apostle James identified the pathway of temptation to sin as "temptation comes from our own desires, which entice us and drag us away. These desires give birth to sinful actions. And when sin is allowed to grow, it gives birth to death" (James 1:14-15). What desires is he talking about?

The categories are noted for us by the Apostle John: "A craving for physical pleasure, a craving for everything we see, and pride in our achievements and possessions" (1 John 2:16). Other translations use the strong desires of the flesh, the strong desires of the eyes, and the pride of life. These three areas draw us away from that which is right. We become proud and selfish and that begets sinful actions which, when unhindered, bring forth eventual death. This is not a pretty picture and it is portrayed in almost every movie. The degradation, pain, sorrow, selfishness, rebellion, and many more words describe the results of temptation to the lead character and brings them to an eventual reckoning.

The enemies that present us with temptations are three-fold: our own flesh, burdened from birth with a nature prone to sinfulness; the world system, "under the control of the evil one" [Satan] (1 John 5:19); and the devil himself, along with his demon cohorts. James described the two allurements as "enticing" us, trying to convince us of the need to have, and then when we give in, "dragging us away." That description could scare the noblest person. Pulled down, dehumanized and degenerated from the glorious creation God initially made us to be.

But let us pause here for a moment and see three positive things in our James passage. One, God is not tempting us, so don't try to blame your temptations on Him. Second, God blesses those who patiently endure both testing and temptation. And third, in eternity the one who resists temptation will receive the crown of life, promised to those that love Him because love of God is the deterrent to temptations end, sin.

Paul wrote to a community that was plagued with sin, the church at Corinth. He spoke clearly about sin problems and provided solutions. When it came to temptation, he said the following, "No temptation has seized you except what is common to man. And God is faithful; He will not let you be tempted beyond what you can bear. But when you are tempted, he will also provide a way out so that you can stand up under it" (1 Corinthians 10:13).

He writes this just after he has addressed the four biggest sins faced by Israel in the wilderness wanderings: idolatry, sexual immorality, testing God, and grumbling. These were incredibly harmful to the Israelites.

Paul says, in essence, that there is nothing new under the sun; it is all common to man, not particular to some, and never seen by others. We all face generic temptation in all its variants.

Paul also reveals the two actions of our trustworthy God to enable us to stop temptation. The first is to understand that we are never tempted above what we are able to bear. In other words, God does not delight in our failure, but permits only temptation which we truly can succeed over.

This means He knows our inner being and does not seek to discourage or cause us fear, but does hold back the tempter from destroying us.

This is specifically seen in the first two chapters of the book of Job where God actually revealed His conversations with Satan in reference to Job's life, and Jesus said to Peter at the Last Supper, "Simon, Simon, Satan has asked to sift each of you like wheat. But I have pleaded in prayer for you, Simon, that your faith should not fail" (Luke 22:31-32). And it did not fail. Peter was used mightily by God, as seen in the book of Acts.

The second action of God in regards to us is to provide a way of escape. God has specific ways out of temptation. He wants us to deal with the temptation before we have to deal with the sin it led to. He wants us to lift our eyes to His escape plan. Take this into consideration as you meet temptation today.

Temptation's purpose is to make us recognize our own insufficiency and God's all-sufficiency; thus God said to Paul when he asked for release from his thorn in the flesh, "my grace is sufficient for you" (2 Cor. 12:9).

Temptation is allowed to help us develop spiritual resistance to our fleshly desires and strengthen the spiritual muscles of our soul and spirit. We then operate more out of our spirit and less out of our fleshly five senses.

God wants obedience and willingness on a full or empty stomach. Paul said it best, "I have learned how to be content with whatever I have...I have learned the secret of living in every situation, whether it is with a full stomach or empty, with plenty or little. For I can do everything through Christ, who gives me strength" (Philippians 4:11-13).

Key Takeaway: Temptation is common; no one is immune to it. But God is faithful, trustworthy, interested in our success, and willing to help. We have to join with Him in the process, with the confidence that we are never tempted above our ability to overcome it. Then we have to look for the way of escape provided by God; not just find it, but actually use it.

Applications:

How can you become more aware of temptation in your life and your ability to see God's way of escape?

As a parent, when will it be a good time to explain temptation to your children?

In your church, what could be done to encourage more discussion about temptation and how to deal with it?

Testing Principle

When was the last time you participated in a test that you really enjoyed? Your answer is coming through loud and clear. We don't like tests because they reveal our lack of mastery of material or maybe we never do well on any of them because we feel rushed or blocked.

Whatever, the result is a grade supposedly representing our effort or lack thereof. How would you feel about receiving a grade from God every time He put you through a test?

Why can't we just live a nice, quiet, normal life going about our own business and enjoying our days? Part of the answer to that is, a quiet, normal, life lulls us by its routine into a state of non-growth.

The Apostle Peter in his first letter to believers under persecution said,

> "There is wonderful joy ahead, even though you have to endure many trials for a little while. These trials will show that your faith is genuine. It is being tested as fire tests and purifies gold—though your faith is far more precious than mere gold. So, when your faith remains strong through many trials, it will bring you much praise and glory and honor on the day when Jesus Christ is revealed to the whole world" (1 Peter 1:6-7).

Tests of God "for a little while" will end in joy, reveal the genuineness of your faith, glorify God, and bring you a reward. There really is light at the end of the tunnel.

The fact that God tests believers cannot be denied. Job stated, "But He knows where I am going. And when He tests me, I will come out as pure as gold" (Job 23:10). Job experienced this confidence, not because he liked being tested, but because of the actions he took before he found himself in a test.

Just after saying this, he explains, "For I have stayed on God's paths; I have followed His ways and not turned aside. I have not departed from His commands, but have treasured His words more than daily food" (23:11-12). Direction, righteous living, obedience, and God in the prime position, all helped Job remain strong in his faith under God's refining hand.

The test of God was there for Job to consider God; to keep centered on Him. When Job did that, his righteousness was validated. Job came out as gold from the fire of the test. He had the dross burned off his soul and became a refined believer.

Solomon saw the tests of God in a similar way. He said, "Fire tests the purity of silver and gold, but the Lord tests the heart" (Proverbs 17:3). Fire is a powerful tool that melts down silver and gold, and the higher and longer the heat, the more impurities are burned off or float to the surface for removal. As fire tests precious metals, so God tests precious souls, with a good end in mind.

The idea of refining gold in a fire is used to help us see the positive outgrowth of trials. In the east, a goldsmith would keep the metal in the furnace until he could see his reflection in it. That was an indication of its purity. The eternal purpose for our trials is for God, the refiner, to see Christ reflected back from us.

We understand from his statement that God's tests are not designed to destroy, but to purify; not to break us, but to make us more aware of our inclinations while still living in the flesh. Some He tests with riches, power, or physical strength; others He tests with poverty, slavery, or weakness. Solomon was tested with riches and power; Samson was tested with physical strength; the widow of Zarephath was tested with poverty; Joseph was tested with slavery; and Gideon was tested with weakness.

Job experienced testing in three different areas. There was the loss of personal property. A messenger told him that Sabeans arrived suddenly and drove off his oxen and donkeys, and killed all the farmhands that protected them (Job 1:15).

Then a second messenger arrived with the news of fire falling from heaven and burning up all his sheep and their shepherds. Not too long after that, he received word that three bands of Chaldean raiders had stolen his camels and killed his servants (1:16-17).

While he was still sorting out these losses, the last messenger arrived with the gut-wrenching news of the loss of his family. All his sons and daughters were feasting together in the oldest son's home, when a powerful wind swept in from the wilderness, hit the house on all sides, and it collapsed, killing all his children. It could have been an EF-5 tornado.

Job is trying to process the sudden loss of his wealth and heritage. He tore his rob in grief, shaved his head, and fell down to worship. Wait a minute, he did what at the end? Worship would not be the final action for most of us. We would be halted by the massive loss, start asking "why," and never get to worship. But here's what Job said in that moment:

> "I came naked from my mother's womb,
> and I will be naked when I leave.
> The Lord gave me what I had,
> and the Lord has taken it away.
> Praise the name of the Lord!" (1:21).

Job is not advocating surrender; he is recognizing the true nature of his temporal status that he came into the world with nothing and his ownership of things and connections to people is short lived, if not an illusion. He is accepting God's plan, for under inspiration it is recorded, "In all of this, Job did not sin by blaming God" (1:22).

But the testing was not over yet, for he was soon to experience the loss of his health. Job was struck with terrible boils from head to foot. He scraped his skin with a piece of broken pottery as he sat among ashes. And further, his wife, who had experienced all of this too, told Job to "curse God and die" (2:9). She was overwhelmed with the loss of her children, the family's security, and wealth, too.

Before all this started, we are privy in Job 1 and 2 to conversations between God and Satan in the throne room of heaven. What we see is that God allows Satan to do all that we have just written about because He is confident in the integrity of His servant Job. These were mere tests.

God did not ask Job if this would be okay; He acted sovereignly. But the friends who came to console him heaped insults on Job, trying to convince him that he had sinned. It didn't work, and at the end of Job's book, his life after testing is analyzed:

- God spoke directly to his friends and demanded a burnt sacrifice of seven bulls and seven rams for their misstatements and false accusations against Job.
- Job was instructed by God to pray for his friends who had berated him.
- When he did this, the Lord restored his fortune, in fact, He double it.
- Job's brothers, sisters, and former friends (enemies), feasted with him in his home.
- They consoled and comforted Job because of his trials.
- He was given, by each of them, money and a gold ring.
- He was blessed more in the second half of his life, living 140 more years.

- He was given seven more sons and three more beautiful daughters, to the joy of his wife.
- And, he put the girls in his will, which normally only sons were in.

Not one of us would desire the testing that Job went through, but all of us would be elated to have the blessings after his testing ended. The true nature of testing is in the hands of God. We don't know what conversations are held in heaven concerning us. We must trust that God is a good God and worthy of our praise.

Key Takeaway: You cannot float downstream and become a better believer. You will face tests that are meant to refine you into Christ's image. Recognizing life's circumstances as such, and continuing to hold fast to God, helps you begin and end well.

Applications:

What attitude adjustments will help you to weather the storms of life today and tomorrow?

How would you explain the difference between a test and a temptation to your children?

What could your church do to make the congregation more aware of testing by God?

Thankfulness Principle

Today is not Thanksgiving Day, but today should be a day of thankfulness which can have a powerful effect on your life.

Leupold in his book on Psalms wrote, "True thanksgiving is a truly spiritual matter. It is worship on a higher level."[6] A thankful heart is a heart that will praise, worship, and glorify God. It remembers God as sovereign and honors Him by recognizing His part in all that has happened, is happening, and will yet happen in your life. It reveals a clean heart and brings you to a state of peace with regard to your circumstances. It opens your mind and eyes to positive alternatives for your situations.

In the fiftieth psalm, Asaph, the writer, explained that God does "not need the bulls from your barns or the goats from your pens" for sacrifices (Psalm 50:9-13). After all He owns the animals of the forest, the cattle on a thousand hills, the world and everything in it.

The psalmist is comparing all the items you think God needs you to sacrifice with the item He thinks is the greatest sacrifice and that is thankfulness. Asaph continued his words with, "Make thankfulness your sacrifice to God, and keep the vows you made to the Most High" (50:14). God spoke through him saying, "giving thanks is a sacrifice that truly honors me" (50:23). Thankfulness is called a "sacrifice" and it is a form of worship. God seeks worshipers, and being thankful is truly a way to worship Him.

Thankfulness recognizes what God has given you and how to be grateful for it. His Son is the greatest of His gifts, along with His sending of the Holy Spirit to abide within us, but it also does include smaller things like a fruitful earth that provides all your food, shelter and clothing. When you are thankful your perspective changes; you see yourself as needy, which you are, and you see Him as the solver of every need.

And, thankfulness will be rewarded. It prepares the way before you and leads you into a new reality with God as central in your life. It opens the way to more right actions, such as obedience to God's ways.

When your eyes open in the morning, thank God for a new day of life. When good happens or even when bad happens to you, it is important to have the thankfulness perspective, for God is always at work for you.

Key Takeaway: It seems like such a small thing, even a natural thing to be thankful. The power of wholesome thankfulness is beyond measure and blesses us with clarity, connection and courage to move forward in life. Experiencing thankfulness to God daily expands and renews your life.

Applications:
How can you create a life of thankfulness to God, and to others?

What would be ways to teach your children to be thankful?

What could your church start doing that would emphasize their thankfulness to God, neighbors, and their community?

Walking with God Principle

It takes 750-1,000 short steps and many falls for an infant's brain to get her balance right to walk. It comes natural for us after the initial two years of life; so much so that we take for granted how much time it took to create that ability. Now we can do much more than walk; we can run and jump.

There's so much in the physical life that is an illustration of the spiritual life. Learning to walk with God takes time to master and there are always moments when we falter; but overall, we can get to the place where it is natural to walk with God. We can enjoy a good and right walk with God. John relayed this truth when he said, "Whoever claims to live in Him must walk as Jesus did" (1 John 2:6). And Peter said, "He [Christ] is your example, and you must follow in his steps" (1 Peter 2:21).

As a child learns to walk physically, we are challenged to walk spiritually. In the midst of a crooked and perverse generation, Noah "walked with God" (Genesis 6:9b). Noah found a way to design his life with God at the center. He communicated with Him even though he lived in a time when there was limited revelation about God and from God. There was no Bible yet either.

This impactful action, that Noah "walked with God" is hard to explain, but we know it involved discussions with God because that's where the plans for the Ark came from and they are still available today in the book of Genesis. In fact, many "arks" have been built through the centuries from these instructions, trying to replicate the original.

Noah had a really great memory at 500 years old, but surely he wanted to write down the dimensions rather than keep coming back to God to verify. That was better than assuming he heard this length or height correctly and ended up with beams that didn't come together or protruded out of the frame. This may be similar to some of our attempts at putting together children's toys the night before Christmas without the directions. You know what I mean. The last time you did that, how many parts did you have left over?

I don't think that was Noah's way and it certainly would have produced a large wood pile of mistakes. Of course, the positive person would see the benefit of those mistakes as a lot of extra fire wood.

We know that Enoch, "walked with God" from the time he was sixty-five and for three-hundred more years. He could have been an example to Noah, but departed sixty-nine years before Noah was born. Enoch's son, Methuselah, lived a total of nine-hundred and sixty-nine years, all the way through the birth of his son Lamech and his grandson Noah. He died the year of the flood. Lamech, Noah's father, died five years before the flood. Perhaps Noah was mentored in walking with God through the stories about Enoch as they were relayed through Methuselah and Lamech.

Adam and Eve walked in the Garden of Eden with the pre-incarnate Christ. Jacob walked with the pre-incarnate Christ; even did a little wrestling with him. Abraham's walk and discussion about Lot's family living in Sodom is another illustration of walking with God. God called to young Samuel as he served in the Temple. Gideon's discussion with the angel of the Lord, while he threshed wheat in a winepress under an oak in Ophrah, was quite a discussion. David's journeys through danger, depression, exhilaration, and battle with the Lord as his shepherd, is very familiar to us. Peter walked with the risen Lord on the shore of the Sea of Galilee, and the walk of the disciples with the risen Christ on the way to Emmaus reveal it is possible to walk with God.

In Joseph's twenty-two (from 13 years as slave plus 9 years as ruler = 22) year sojourn in Egypt there are no words recorded of God saying anything to him, and none recorded of Joseph crying out to God. No "why's" were spoken, no questions raised to heaven, and no seeming anger about his ups and downs. No response to the injustices he endured until we hear these words as he stood in front of his brothers in Egypt, "I am Joseph, your brother, whom you sold into slavery in Egypt. But don't be upset, and don't be angry with yourselves for selling me to this place. It was God who sent me here ahead of you to preserve your lives....God has sent me ahead of you to keep you and your families alive and to preserve many survivors. So it was God who sent me here, not you! And he is the one who made me an adviser to Pharaoh—the manager of his entire palace and the governor of all Egypt" (Genesis 45:4-8). Notice the repetition of "it was God who sent me..." Joseph walked with God and agreed with what He was doing. Here Joseph makes God the chess master.

What can we learn from these experiences? Here are some helpful statements to remember about what it means to "walk with God." Walking with God...

Requires agreement to His standards. You must identify the standards of His holiness and the requirements He has given in His Word for your life and meet them wholeheartedly (Amos 3:3).

Requires discipline to do what is necessary over and over until it becomes a positive routine which is easy to fall into every day. It takes about thirty repetitions or days to form a new habit.

Requires two-way communication. Reading His Word and talking with Him has input and output in it. This daily time of reading and praying can also include a quiet time when you are listening to God, to make it two-way.

Requires same direction. Purpose speaks to what we are doing every day and there are plenty of admonitions and teachings in the New Testament letters to help us there. The purpose of God must be our purpose, and His direction for us in the Scriptures and through our quiet time must be carried out.

Requires trust and faithfulness. Trust in what He is wanting to happen in your life. Be faithful even when it is dark, rugged and cold (circumstances); and when sadness, fear, and other negative emotions threaten to overwhelm you (feelings/emotions).

Requires respect. It is a reverence for who He is and what He is capable of doing in and for you, or even in spite of you. Respect grows through time and events cannot be rushed or purchased. You must understand He is always operating for your good; He is never caught off guard; He is a compassionate Father who will discipline you when you do wrong.

Requires gratefulness. You must have a thankful heart, and learn to be thankful in ALL things. You must allow this thankfulness to expand your vision of what God is doing in and through you.

Walking with God leads to obeying God and, when you obey Him, He blesses you and that leads you to worship Him, which leads you to walk more with Him. This cycle created in walking with God draws you closer to Him and deepens your life with Him, and that is what He desires.

Key Takeaway: Walking with God takes time, obedience, patience, a listening ear, and a righteous heart. Those who have walked with God are evidence that it is the only way to live a life on earth.

Applications:
How does your life need to change to incorporate "walking with God" into it?

How can your family learn to walk with God?

What can and can't the church do to help members walk with God?

Living A Principled Life
Confidence Area

Confidence is a certainty in one's abilities, assurances, and boldness. The Apostle Paul said, "we have placed our confidence in Him" (2 Corinthians 1:10b)

Belief Principle

Where does your belief lie? What are the things you believe about God? We live in a world focused on the five physical senses. We have to see, taste, touch, smell, or hear it to believe it, much like the disciple Thomas who was not convinced unless he saw the nail prints in Jesus' hands and the scar in his side. And Jesus afforded him the opportunity to even place his hand on those places.

When we live out of our five physical senses, we miss the blessings of a robust belief that encourages and sustains us in the good and bad times. Belief is a trust and confidence that what is not seen will come true. It takes us out of the limited physical world, into the larger spiritual world, to realize that our earthly existence is just the start of our eternal life.

A friend has been a realtor for over fifteen years and he has lived well on his hundred percent commission job. There are no bi-weekly checks to depend on. All his work is done before he receives a commission check. That is not to say he doesn't advertise, meet people, and work his sphere. But beyond doing the work to find clients and homes for sale, he trusts God for supply. His belief is stretched every day by working in this field. How would your belief fare in a commission-based job?

Joshua, in writing the book by his name, chronicles the conquering of the Promise Land by the tribes of Israel. There were many victories, one defeat, a lot of new lessons learned, and at the end of three campaigns the tribes were all allotted land. These people believed God and He brought their belief into what He had promised, the reality of a land they then possessed. Their belief became sight as they could taste, touch, see, hear, and smell it right in front of them. They found rest after they battled for over six years with those who sought to keep their land. These peoples were removed because of their gross immorality and disbelief in the God of the Jews.

Very close to the end of his book, Joshua wrote the following testimony: "And the Lord gave them rest on every side, just as He had solemnly promised their ancestors. None of their enemies could stand against them, for the Lord helped them conquer all their enemies. Not a single one of all the good promises the Lord had given to the family of Israel was left unfulfilled; everything He had spoken came true" (Joshua 21:44-45). Conquest brought rest and His solemn and good promises were kept; every one, none were left unfulfilled.

But that was not the end of their story because there were many pockets of resistance still to conquer, so their rest was short-lived. It would take much longer to expel those pockets controlled by these Canaanite tribes than their initial years of war.

The writer of Hebrews discussed this to emphasize the rest that is now ours to obtain. He said, "God's promise of entering His rest still stands, so we ought to tremble with fear that some of you might fail to experience it. For the good news—that God has prepared this rest—has been announced to us just as it was to them...For only we who believe can enter His rest" (Hebrews 4:1-3).

As persons of belief who accept the Bible as trustworthy, we are also aided by God to conquer what is within and around us. Rest comes because we obey completely and our future happens based on the belief that we have accepted Jesus Christ as our substitute and have rested in his work to save us from past, present, and future sin.

Where does your belief in God need to be strengthened? Is it with living a victorious life, in praying with belief, or whatever else comes to mind for you? Belief eventually brings about the sought-after future if it is accompanied with obedience.

Key Takeaway: Belief is not based on our works, but on the finished work of Jesus Christ on the cross and in his resurrection from the dead. We cannot base our life merely on the physical senses which are limited, but must move our belief beyond all that.

Applications:

What is your level of belief?

As a parent, what are you teaching your children to believe in?

How could your church expand the understanding of belief of your attendees?

Boundaries Principle

Do you live with boundaries or without them? You might say you have no need of them. If so, it is possible that you have too narrow a definition of boundaries. Consider boundaries that surround you: stop lights, white stripes on a roadway, money in your bank account, walls in your apartment or home, a survey of your property, time to be at work, bills that have a due date, and you are probably thinking of some others right now. These are just a few of the multitude of boundaries that each of us encounter every day.

There are many boundaries in the Bible. The beginning of Genesis is full of so much about God, man, and the eco system He placed us in. Its emphasis was that boundaries are important and actually freeing, unless you stepped over them.

Boundary one was the earth. Creation was not the same outside the earth as it was on the earth. Look at Mercury, Venus, and Mars as examples. All are planets in our solar system but none created like the earth. Man was meant for earth and God gave us everything we need to exist here.

Boundary two was the light. It enabled us to see what we were doing. Day and night became boundaries. They illumined or darkened the planet, making a difference for humanity, plants, and animals.

Boundary three was the land and waters. There were oceans and land created with the sands on the sea shore being the boundary. God made man to live on the land. He could travel the seas, but found it hard to sustain his life there. Sea creatures thrive in their boundaried environment of oceans, seas, and rivers.

Boundary four was the Garden. Man was not sent out by God to find his own place to live on the land. He was placed inside the God-made Garden of Eden. It was full of food and water and became the place of his responsibility. He later had to exit it because he broke a boundary.

Boundary five was what you eat. A vegetarian diet was initially given to man and the animals. That would change later, but in the beginning, Adam was into fruits and vegetables rather than a thick juicy steak.

Boundary six was your kin. Animals, sea creatures, and birds of the air were not to be our family. Eve was given to Adam as his helpmate and together they produced children, starting with Cain and Abel, and later many more. These would make up the family of man, one race with eventually many ethnicities.

Boundary seven was purity. Adam and Eve were naked and unashamed. It would take disobedience to make them shame-filled enough to cover themselves before they met with God. He saw right through their disguise and spoke with them about crossing a boundary.

Boundary eight was how they worshiped. Abel brought a lamb to sacrifice in worship to God. Cain brought the work of his hands to worship God, but that was not acceptable because the boundary in sacrifice was that it must be a blood sacrifice. Their mother and father had learned that lesson already since they were clothed with the skins of animals before leaving the Garden.

Boundary nine was life's sacredness. Cain killed Abel and paid a high price for it. He was banished from God and his parents and lived as a homeless wanderer after that. Murder was stepping over the boundary of life.

And then we go to Exodus 20 where God gives the children of Israel the Ten Commandments. If not kept, these boundaries revealed sin. There were four initial Commandments that set up some boundaries in reverencing God, the fifth Commandment was the boundary of honoring your mother and father. You could figure out what it looked like to honor and not honor. And, the final five commandments provided boundaries for life, people, possessions, and neighbor's property.

After the nation of Israel entered the Promised Land and warred for six years with the possessing nations, the tribes of Israel were all given land with boundaries. They still had work to do in removing the groups still left, but they knew what land they all owned.

God established boundaries for priests of the tribe of Levi who would work for Him. He put strict boundaries on everything used and performed in the Tabernacle and the later Temple. If they were not kept, people died. He also established food boundaries for the nation of what was able to be eaten and what was not.

Today, all sports, travel, manufacture of food products, and all else have boundaries. Boundaries are an important part of our life, and God, who has unfailing love for us, has created boundaries that keep us safe, protect us and hold back sin within us.

The purpose of boundaries is to help us know what our responsibilities are. Adam was given things to do in the Garden. We are given responsibilities as a believer. It is up to us to find them and obey them in order to grow, mature and be of use to God.

Boundaries separate good and evil by defining them both and setting a line where one ends and the other begins. We cannot turn around without dealing with boundaries for our physical body, our mental and emotional health, and our spiritual connection to God. Words and behaviors also have boundaries; when broken they hurt others and when recognized they bring life.

An excellent resource to expand on this principle is the set of books known as *Boundaries*, by Henry Cloud and John Townsend. They focus on kids, adults, dating, your soul, marriage, and finding peace. They speak to whatever we need to know about boundaries in life.

Key Takeaway: Boundaries exist all around us and we do well to recognize and obey them. They keep us out of trouble and alleviate pain that we would cause ourselves and others by stepping over them. An understanding of the boundaries in your life is necessary for your health.

Applications:

What boundaries have you crossed and what penalty did you receive?

What could parents do to help their children understand the place boundaries play in their lives?

How could your church emphasize this principle to all those who attend?

Clarity Principle

How many times have you had a discussion with a friend, spouse, child, someone at a business, or someone in the government and thought you were on the "same page," only to realize later that there were differences in the way you or they understood your conversation? It happens to all of us and the end result is a mess because one or both were not clear.

The Roman army used trumpets as a means of communicating to troops on the battlefield or in camp. There were many different types of sounds that could be played, some were telling the soldiers to tear down their tents, to assemble, to come for food, to retreat, or to charge ahead. They developed a school for training trumpeters so that the sound of each man for each of the messages was identical. There was no room for an unclear trumpet. The troops needed to clearly hear the message from their commanders so they could respond quickly and correctly. It could mean the success or failure of a military offensive or the proper placement of troops to ensure strength and deny surprises attacks from the enemy.

Clarity is clearness of mind. It breaks up the clouds that exist and clears the path for correct understanding. Lack of clarity brings confusion, anxiety, assumptions, fear, tentativeness and paralysis. Being clear, without misunderstandings or assumptions, brings assurance, confidence, enthusiasm, awareness, and peace. It is central, not peripheral, to success and provides the perspective needed to then evaluate the options available, chose one, and begin to focus on that.

In writing a letter to Timothy, Paul said, "You should keep a clear mind in every situation" (2 Timothy 4:5a). He was referring to his earlier warning that people were going to stop listening to Timothy's sound and wholesome teaching, follow their own desires, look for those who would affirm their decisions, reject the truth, and follow after myths.

Paul went on to write, "Don't be afraid of suffering for the Lord. Work at telling others the Good News, and fully carry out the ministry God has given you" (4:5b). Here Paul was refocusing Timothy on clarity of his purpose.

Initially he wrote, "Don't be afraid of suffering for the Lord." Keep a clear mind. Sometimes suffering brings out the worst in people. It's easy to blame God, others, or yourself for your suffering. That is shortsighted and misses the point. Our suffering should bring glory to God because we are, through that suffering, being conformed into Christ's image. If we permit the Lord to transform us, we are also strengthened by suffering, if we don't step in the way and short-circuit the process. We can be a comfort to others who are going through suffering, too, because as we are comforted by the Spirit in our suffering, so we will be able to comfort them (2 Corinthians 1:4).

Further, he wrote, "Work at telling others the Good News." Keep a clear mind. The idea of working to make your presentation of the Good News effective to others is hardly thought of today. We shy away from sharing our faith, and when we do share, we need to ask, "What is my objective in sharing?" Am I here to argue and berate? No, you are there to tell your personal story and extend the love of God to them as you have received it. Let the Spirit do His job of convicting of "sin, righteousness and judgment" (John 16:8). Your objective is to take advantage of every opportunity as you are challenged to do so in Ephesians 5:16 and Colossians 4:5.

Finally, he wrote, "Fully carry out the ministry God has given you." Keep a clear mind. Paul talked to Timothy as his son in the faith. His ministry was as a preaching elder and Paul's challenge was not to complain, criticize, or rebuke everyone in the church. They were all supposed to be serving in the church; that's what spiritual gifts are for. Timothy and others should apply this desire for clarity in order to fully carry out ministry in a positive way.

All these were to be done by Timothy with a clear mind, not with a cluttered, angry, or distracted mind. He was to pray well, speak well, discuss well, and sing well. Everyone in the church was to minister as they were gifted, and not to do it out of dread or duty, but out of devotion to God.

In the Corinthian letters, Paul wrote about many negative issues inside the church and at one point he illustrated his point by saying, "Even lifeless instruments like the flute or the harp must play the notes clearly or no one will recognize the melody" (1 Corinthians 14:7). This church's negativity did not produce clarity in message within and outside the church walls. If they were all clear about their roles and responsibilities, then clarity would lead to proper action.

Key Takeaway: Clarity is the doorway way to understanding, which then helps us to find possible solutions, and move to action on one of them. When you have clarity, you will be confident, knowledgeable, wise, ready to risk, and at peace.

Applications:
- If you understand that clarity is essential to growth, then you must ask yourself these questions:
  o "What is unclear to me right now?" Make a list.
  o "How could I get clarity so that I can grow?" Find ways to clear the clouds away.
- Where is there not clarity with your children?
- What would be necessary for the principle of clarity to be operating in your church?

Contentment Principle

Living in this world makes it easy to go with the flow. We have used our five senses so long to obtain what we wanted that it's easy to feel like you can continue to satisfy self all the time. It doesn't help to have all kinds of ads continually promoting a variety of products that would better our lives. It's easy to be enticed by a pitch here and there.

If we're not careful, the pile of stuff that we acquired to satisfy us will get larger and our bank account will get smaller. There are no guarantees in life about health, longevity, or comfort and the draw of immediate pleasure keeps us away from thinking about these more crucial areas.

At some point, it should be a no brainer to think about what it would mean to experience contentment, fulfillment, or satisfaction. Each of these words used the other two to define them in the dictionary, so in most cases they are defining the same thing.

Contentment is a place where you do not desire something more temporally. You have been furnished enough to meet your physical, mental, emotional, and social needs and you want to focus on growing your spiritual desires to a greater level to impact the eternities of others.

How do we find contentment?

Many believers find it in their possessions, family, and the money they have amassed, just like an unbeliever does. They don't think toward eternity or life after death, they only deal with the present. Does that help us to find contentment? I'm not sure it does.

The writer of Hebrews said, "Don't love money; be satisfied with what you have. For God has said, 'I will never fail you. I will never abandon you'" (Hebrews 13:5). Keeping this perspective lodged in the front windshield of your life is of primary importance.

We are not saying that everyone needs to be content at the poverty line, or that there is only one level of contentment. What we are saying is, that at some point in your life, there needs to be contentment that extends past the temporal into the eternal. The ads are muted in your ears, the draw of new just to always have new doesn't reason out, and the need to have what the Jones' have is squelched.

If you are having trouble living by faith and finding contentment with what you have, here are some possible ideas as to why that is so:

- You are not thankful for God's provision for you now.
- You are disappointed in your "lot" in life.
- You are "enticed and drawn away" to have more things.
- You may be jealous, envious of other's belongings.
- You have not learned to rest in God.
- Your head does not have an eternal focus but is captured by the temporal.

Does your security lie in the physical world, where health and finances can change quickly and leave you with less than you think you need, or in the eternal world, where God promises not to fail you and abandon you? We are His children and no good father walks away from his children.

Further, there is a good thing that could be called spiritual discontentment.

- It is induced by the Holy Spirit
- It comes out of your spirit, which is where you connected with the Holy Spirit, and He speaks into your soul (mind, emotion, and will) to make a change.

- It is a continual burden on your heart, not based on circumstances of the day, or anything specific.
- It could relate to your spiritual gifting because you are not able to use it to the best of your ability any longer at your present church.
- It might show up as a sadness, dissatisfaction, or a restlessness.
- And when the decision is made to change, you will go through a form of the grieving process related to the loss you are experiencing because of that change.

Some would say this is a bad thing, considering that the Bible, specifically Paul, encouraged people to be content in whatever state they were in. But we are speaking of something much deeper than what could be suggested as a circumstantial problem you face that you don't like and complain about to God. That's the negative side of spiritual discontentment.

The usage of the word "spiritual" says much about the nature of this discontentment. How we would define it is helped by this illustration. A friend had gotten increasingly aware that he didn't feel at home in his present church anymore. He took time to discuss this with his pastor and prayed, even fasted, about it. He felt led to start to attend another church and noticed that his heart was at rest there.

All this started when he experienced some spiritual discontentment. He didn't know just what it was then, but he could tell that it had to do with the church he was attending. For change to take place, it would be necessary to think about or actually separate from that church, group of friends, or whatever the Spirit was telling him to do because we don't normally give up what we have until we initially decide to make a change, which is the initial step in transition.

The following are the major points of spiritual discontentment:

- Awareness of something happening in your spirit and soul
- You must validate what it is, and where it is directing you

- Start working through it
- Ask God, "Where do I go from here?"

Key Takeaway: Contentment is crucial to resting in God and keeping your eye on eternity. Finding a way to hold yourself accountable for what you do with the resources God gave you should be a matter of prayer and planning. Spiritual discontentment is a positive action that can move you forward in your Christian life. It's also crucial to your growth as a believer.

Applications:

Where are you stuck in the temporal and can't capture an eternal view?

When is a good time for your family to find a balance with "toys" for the kids, or for the parents?

What could your church do to enlarge the idea of contentment in the lives of its attendees?

Counting the Cost Principle

Solomon, in his God given wisdom, warned how dangerous it would be for someone to make a vow to God and then later count the cost of that vow when he said, "Don't trap yourself by making a rash promise to God and only later counting the cost" (Proverbs 20:25).

During the period of the Judges, which took place after the nation of Israel had secured the land, Jephthah became the eighth judge in the nation. He was the son of a prostitute and his father was Gilead. Jephthah was chased off the land of Gilead by his half-brothers in a tiff related to inheritance. Settling in the land of Tob, he grew into a mighty warrior and gathered to him a band of worthless rebels.

At one point in his eighteen-year judgeship, the Ammonites began to war against Israel, so the elders of Gilead said to Jephthah, "Come and be our commander! Help us fight the Ammonites! (Judges 11:5). He questioned the sincerity of their request so they up the ante by promising, "we will make you ruler over all the people of Gilead" (11:8). He returned with his men and became the commander of the army.

He also made a vow to the Lord, "If you give me victory over the Ammonites, I will give to the Lord whatever comes out of my house to meet me when I return in triumph. I will sacrifice it as a burnt offering" (11:30). He crushed the Ammonites and devastated twenty towns and when he returned home to Mizpah his one and only daughter was the first one who came out of his house to meet him. This greatly saddened Jephthah. He granted her request to spend two months with her friends in the hills and "when she returned home, her father kept the vow he had made, and she died a virgin" (11:39). This story is a sad example of how much pain and sorrow you could experience if you do not count the cost of your vow before you make it.

At the peak of his ministry, Jesus spoke to the people about becoming his disciples by giving this warning, "don't begin until you count the cost" (Luke 14:28-30). He talked about calculating the cost of constructing a building before you started, lest you get into it and realize you don't have the money to finish. The response of your neighbors would be to laugh at you and consider you foolish.

He also talked about a king who wanted to go to war against another kingdom, discussing this with his counselors to see if his army could really defeat their foe. If he did count the cost of war, then he might just send a delegation to their foe to discuss terms of peace (14:31-32).

Whether becoming a disciple of Christ, building a structure, warring with another country, vowing to God or starting any endeavor requires you count the cost before you begin. Counting the cost means contemplating, calculating, conferring with counselors and more, before you start, so that it pays off in a finished product.

Solomon said, "Do your planning and prepare your fields before building your house" (Prov. 24:27). Otherwise, you will come up short on your ability to continue. Then it will be identified as a "rash" decision and others will mock you.

Here are some steps in counting the cost:

- Plan from beginning to completion.
- Lay a foundation deep in thought, planning, and finances.
- Pray over your plans and lay them before the Lord.
- Kick haste and immature judgment out of your process.
- Gather experienced counselors and listen intently to what they say.

Key Takeaway: "Plans succeed through good counsel; don't go to war without wise advice" (Proverbs 20:18). Terrible endings are bound to happen when you don't count the cost before you begin any endeavor. Take the time to make sure the finished product can be achieved.

Applications:

Where do you need to count the cost before you begin?

How can a family train its' children to count the cost?

What would it look like for your church to establish this principle in the hearts and actions of its congregation?

Discipline Principle

Andrew seemed to be a curious one-year-old and one day while Debi was preparing dinner, he wandered into the kitchen and over to the trash can. As his little hand reached to open it, his mother said, "ANDREW, NO!"

That made him move away for a moment but something, whether smell or color, drew him back. This time he was a second ahead of his mother and going for the junk. She saw him and slapped his hand. It brought a surprise to his face and a little murmur to his lips and a new lesson to his mind. I know all this because I have the video preserved for future use.

Debi was not slapping Andrew's hand in anger but rather to imprint on his little mind that the trash can was off limits. She did this out of love for Andrew. There were sharp lids, gooey rotted food and other stinky stuff in there.

The positive word for discipline is correction not abuse. The end product of any discipline is to see positive adjustment in the way you live that will benefit you for the rest of your life.

Solomon suggested, "don't reject the Lord's discipline, and don't be upset when he corrects you. For the Lord corrects those he loves, just as a father corrects a child in whom he delights" (Proverbs 3:11-12). Have a right attitude about correction, don't reject it, and don't be upset about it. Why? Because it is given out of love for us and delight in us. "You are more valuable to God than a whole flock of sparrows" Jesus said (Matthew 10:31). So respect God for his disciplining love.

The writer of Hebrews discussed this when he said, "don't make light of the Lord's discipline, and don't give up when He corrects you. For the Lord disciplines those He loves, and He punishes each one He accepts as His child" (Hebrews 12:5b-6). How about that? Do you think it's not important? It is, so don't give up under correction, benefit follows.

The proper attitude is to submit to the discipline or correction, meaning to bear up under it, and recognize that "God's discipline is always good for us, so that we might share in His holiness. No discipline is enjoyable while it is happening—it's painful! But afterward there will be a peaceful harvest of right living for those who are trained in this way" (Hebrews 12:10b-11).

King David talked much about his life with God in the psalms. There seemed to be ups and downs and sometimes the discipline of God was evident in his life. In this line of thought he wrote, "When you discipline us for our sins, you consume like a moth what is precious to us. Each of us is but a breath" (Psalm 39:11).

Leupold commenting on the last part of this verse said, "When the Lord makes His correction felt to draw a man away from his sin, then a new realization of the vanity of the things formerly regarded as precious becomes overwhelmingly clear; they are as though they had already been consumed by moths, worthless like a moth-eaten garment."[7]

Leupold further expressed how much vanity we have before the correction and how we finally understand, through the discipline, that we are mortal and live only for a breath of time. It is discipline that brings us back to a place of humility; to a new recognition of how short life is. This is discipline's end.

God is not angrily striking out in rage and frustration because we crossed the sin line. He is well aware of our propensities. He disciplines in love to redirect us to better actions.

Key Takeaway: Discipline never comes without pain, but always leads to a better life. We see that David, Solomon, and the writer of Hebrews agreed that discipline happens and that, if you don't rebel in the midst of it, you can learn lessons that will help you through life.

Applications:

What difference has discipline made in your life?

How do you feel when you have to discipline your children? God feels that way, too.

How does your church deal with the discipline of believers?

Discretion Principle

"Discretion is the better part of valor."[8] This proverb was spoken in Act V, Scene 4 of Shakespear's play, *Henry IV*, Part One, by Falstaff, a corrupt knight, who faked his own death on the battlefield to survive and then falsely claim victory over the rebel leader Hotspur so that he could receive fame and glory from Henry IV.

To understand this proverb we need to understand the words discretion and valor. Discretion is the quality of being discrete and wise and valor is personal bravery or acting rash to do something brave. So, Falstaff was saying it was better to be wise and live than be brave but seriously wounded or dead.

A story which we will see in three acts, reveals discretion clearly:

Act 1 – David was anointed King of Israel by Samuel but it was fourteen years before he sat on the throne. King Saul saw his glory fading and the people were impressed with David, so he searched to kill him. David spent years hiding from Saul by wandering in sparse areas of Judea and at this time was in the wilderness of Maon about eight miles south of Hebron.

His six-hundred men were low on supplies and acquainted with a land owner, Nabal from Maon. They had protected his property and never harmed the shepherds, sheep, or goats belonging to him. So David sent ten men to Nabal requesting provisions for his troops. Nabal was a selfish and self-centered man who responded with the questions, "Who is this fellow David? Who does this son of Jesse think he is? There are lots of servants these days who run away from their masters. Should I take my bread and my water and my meat that I have slaughtered for my shearers and give it to a band of outlaws who come from who knows where" (1 Samuel 25:10-11)?

So, David's men returned and told David what Nabal said. His response was "Get your swords!" and he readied four-hundred men to march to Nabal's property.

Act 2 – Back at Nabal's ranch, servants went to his wife Abigail, who was a sensible and beautiful woman, and told her of the incident. They said Nabal screamed insults at the ten men and did not understand how beneficial David's army was in protecting their herdsmen and flocks. They expressed their fear of soon retribution on all Nabal's possessions and family.

Abigail wasted no time in gathering stores of food, packing them on donkeys, and leaving to intercept David's army before they got to the ranch. David had just been saying, "A lot of good it did to help this fellow. We protected his flocks in the wilderness, and nothing he owned was lost or stolen. But he has repaid me evil for good. May God strike me and kill me if even one man of his household is still alive tomorrow morning" (25:21-22)!

Abigail and David met in a mountain ravine. There was no way around her. She quickly dismounted, bowed low, and fell at David's feet. She blamed herself for not fulfilling the men's request, agreed that Nabal was wicked and ill-tempered, and stated she had never seen the men while at her house. Abigail suggested her presence was there to keep him from murder and vengeance, and revealed the many food-ladened donkeys. She asked forgiveness if she had offended David in any way and encouraged him not to blemish his record with violent acts against Nabal's ranch and people. She assured him he would one day be king.

Act – 3 David praised the Lord for their meeting, thanked God for her good sense, and blessed her for keeping him from vengeance. He then accepted her gifts and said, "Return home in peace. I have heard what you said. We will not kill your husband" (25:35).

Abigail arrived home, found Nabal drunk in the midst of a big party, celebrating like a king. Using discretion, she held her news of the meeting with David until the next morning when he was sober. Then she told him of the impending doom on him, had it not been for her quick action. He had a heart attack, was paralyzed, and died in his bed ten days later.

When David heard the news, he praised God for avenging his insult, and sent messengers to Abigail to ask her to become his wife. She bowed low and affirmed her desire to marry him, and quickly went to join David.

Abigail was a woman of discretion and full of wisdom. She anticipated David's action to come attack Nabal, and quickly acted to prepare supplies for his men and intercept them before they got to the ranch. She took the blame, excusing herself because she didn't know the men had come, and sought forgiveness if she had offended David by her actions. She affirmed David's right to the throne and convinced him not to put a stain on his reputation by the slaughter of all the family. And then she accepted his marriage proposal and immediately joined David.

What can we learn from this story of discretion? Solomon said, "Discretion is a life-giving fountain to those who possess it" (Proverbs 16:22). "Pleasant words are persuasive" and "a gentle answer deflects anger" (Proverbs 16:21; 15:1). So Abigail was the perfect picture of a person of discretion by listening more, talking less, and letting her actions speak for her. Abigail was careful and cautious, and this is the best way to describe what it means to have discretion.

Key Takeaway: Discretion is the ability to use your freedom and power to make cautious choices and be filled with wisdom in challenging circumstances. It is a gift made possible with humility as its sidekick. To use discretion can provide an alternative way of dealing with a problem to the benefit of all involved. It is knowing what to do or say and what not to do or say.

Applications:

Where have you needed discretion in the past five years?

How could you teach discretion to your children?

How could discretion enhance the reputation of your church?

Hope Principle

In the *Lord of the Rings, Return of the King,* on the Pelennor Fields in front of the city of Minas Tirith gathered a great multitude of orcs, trolls and other evil forces. In the midst of the battle, six-thousand riders from Rohan appear on the hill, a powerful number of men on horseback. They cry out and begin their descent onto the fields and crash head long into Sauron's forces, using the brute strength of their horse's body to crush their adversaries.

The fortress of the Hornburg at Helm's Deep also saw Gandalf the White coming at a crucial moment with Erkenbrand and a thousand cavalry. They, too, pressed through the orcs and Uruk-hai, trampling and dispersing them.

These two scenes, as powerful and victorious as they were, do not fulfill God's desire for men. The psalmist remarked about all war, "His pleasure is not in the strength of the horse, nor His delight in the legs of a man; the Lord delights in those who fear Him, who put their hope in His unfailing love" (Psalm 147:10-11).

What differentiates us, from those around us, should be hope. Not a mystical hope or a pipe dream hope, but a hope based on solid facts. Facts about what God has done through the people of Israel, making them His nation. Facts about the death and resurrection of Christ and its' benefits. Facts about the presence of the Holy Spirit in the lives of those who believed. And promises He has made about the future for believers.

God knows the beginning, middle and end of all things. He is confident in His abilities, victorious in His actions, and certain about the future. So why wouldn't our hope rest in Him?

David understood this when he said, "my hope is in you [God my Savior] all day long" (Psalm 25:5). Paul said to the Roman believers, "May the God of hope fill you with all joy and peace as you trust in Him, so that you may overflow with hope by the power of the Holy Spirit" (Romans 15:13). To overflow is to exceed a fixed number or measure and to exist in abundance. This kind of hope is possible for every believer.

Earlier in the same chapter, Paul said, "For everything that was written in the past was written to teach us, so that through endurance and the encouragement of the Scriptures we might have hope" (15:4). Hope is built on the truth of the Word of God. It is found to be dependable. Everything that has happened to people like us before in the Scriptures teaches us to hope and to know that God has been there for them and will be there for us.

Though hope is not one of the nine fruits of the Spirit, it is foundational to them all and woven into their definitions. It is not the greatest of the triad of faith, hope, and love, but it is an equal part of it. Being a person that is overflowing with hope is being a person who is getting to know God better every day through His Word, his own experiences, and the "power of the Holy Spirit" in his life. Abound with hope. Bubble over with hope. Spill it on everyone you meet.

Hope must be put in someone or something. Here are some reasons to put our hope in God:

- "I have put my hope in His word" (Ps. 130:5).
- "Why am I discouraged? Why is my heart so sad? I will put my hope in God! I will praise Him again—my Savior and my God!" (Ps. 42:5, 11; 43:5). Repeated three times.
- "May integrity and honesty protect me, for I put my hope in you" (Ps. 25:21).

- Paul asked the question, "Am I on trial because my hope is in the resurrection of the dead" (Acts 23:6).
- "We rejoice, too, when we run into problems and trials, for we know that they help us develop endurance. And endurance develops strength of character, and character strengthens our hope of salvation. And this hope will not lead to disappointment" (Romans 5:3-5).
- "We, too, wait with eager hope for the day when God will give us our full rights as His adopted children, including the new bodies He has promised us" (Romans 8:23).

Hope is looking forward to something we don't yet have. It is a positive view of the future. It is a solid trust in God's ability to fulfill His promises.

Key Takeaway: My hope is built on nothing less than Jesus' blood and righteousness; I dare not trust the sweetest frame, but holy lean on Jesus' name. On Christ the solid rock, I stand; All other ground is sinking sand, all other ground is sinking sand. (Hymn The Solid Rock, Edward Mote and William B. Bradbury).

Applications:

How could the hope of Jesus be built into your everyday experience?

What could you do to make sure your family is hoping in the things provided by God?

How could your church expand people's hope in God?

Intentionality Principle

Intentionality does not just mean you began, but intentionality also means you finished; that has to happen to expect more progress toward your goal. The dictionary defines the word intentionality as "done purposefully." The word "intended" means planned and purposed. It is an act of moving forward with a plan with the intention to see it to completion.

It can be addressed in any area of your life or your whole life in general. There is no vacation from it, no holidays when you rest from it, and no Saturday and Sunday days off. Intentionality is intense. For some personalities, being intentional might be harder than for others, but they can still do it, their implementation might just be quietly working in the background.

On September 14, 2001 President George Bush stood at ground zero on the rubble of the Twin Towers in New York City with a fireman beside him and bullhorn in his right hand. He was saddened and angry by what he saw surrounding him and considered it an act of aggression by Islamic extremist. To the people standing there and to those who perpetrated this destruction he said, "I can hear you, the rest of the world hears you and the people who knocked these buildings down will hear all of us soon!" He was intentional in this statement. For a long time, the whole military apparatus and all the civil intelligence agencies intentionality began to seek and destroy those associated with the militants who created this calamity. We are twenty years beyond that day and the Afghanistan war has just concluded. What will their next intentional focus be on?

Intentionality has a lot to do with your process which can include the following five actions. First, if you're intentional, you have to be S-specific, to hone in on a particular area. Second, you must M-measure so you know how much to do and when you need to do it. Third, A-achievable assumes you can finish, if it is not achievable why are you wasting your time on doing it? Fourth, R-realistic gets to the heart of the matter. Intentionality presumes it is realistic, not just an unattainable dream. And fifth, T-time-oriented means dates have to be set, to start, to be halfway done, and be completed.

After Joseph revealed himself to his brothers in Genesis 45 and all the surprise and joy that accompanied that reunion had passed, he invited them to move to Egypt. The brothers returned to their father and suggested they go. When they had settled and after years there, Jacob died. At this point the brothers thought that because their father was dead, Joseph would feel free to pour out his wrath on them.

He understood this and gave them comfort and a promise, "Don't be afraid of me. Am I God that I can punish you? You intended to harm me, but God intended it all for good. He brought me to this position so I could save the lives of many people. No, don't be afraid. I will continue to take care of you and your children" (Genesis 50:19-21).

We can gather from this interaction with the brothers that intentionality if used in wrong actions on the one side, can be used by God on the other side to intentionally bring about His purpose. Joseph, as God's chosen man, was the savior of Israel. Without him the brothers would never have prospered as they did in Egypt.

Intentionality is important for everyone of us and for every part of our lives. To have it in some areas and not in others can bring confusion. Certainly, intentionality means change and periods of transition to accommodate that change, but that's okay, that is what life's all about.

Key Takeaway: Intentionality is powerful and drives us forward to achievement. It will influence every area of your life as you set a direction.

It is important to not ignore the change that will happen because of it and to keep pursuing what you want in life.

Applications:

What area of your life is lacking in intentionality?

What would it look like for you to become an intentional parent?

How can your church become more intentional?

Joy-filled Principle

Everyone needs some joy. Can you imagine a life without a deep inner joy? When we speak of joy, we are not referring to what some call happiness. These two, joy and happiness, cannot be equated, for they are different in the simplest of ways. Happiness is an emotion in your soul based on circumstances, while joy is an attitude of your spirit, unconnected to circumstances. You might think you are exhibiting joy when you just have circumstance-related happiness.

The first time your new car gets a dent in it, there goes that feeling of happiness in your soul. You are now sad and mad. Happiness cannot abide when sadness comes. On the other hand, joy is the inner attitude that can abide with sorrow, for it sits far above temporal experiences.

Think about this statement of the Apostle James, "when troubles come your way, consider it an opportunity for great joy. For you know that when your faith is tested, your endurance has a chance to grow. So let it grow, for when your endurance is fully developed, you will be perfect and complete, needing nothing" (James 1:2-4).

Troubles and great joy meet together in the same moment. Joy's perspective is to acknowledge your faith is being tested and that you will endure and grow because that will eventually make you complete in Christ. You see much more out of troubles than sadness, badness and pain. Joy comes because you look at today's circumstances and see tomorrow's gains. Joy views the eternal; happiness views the temporal.

Paul said it very clearly, "We are ignored, even though we are well known. We live close to death, but we have not been killed. Our hearts ache, but we always have joy. We are poor, but we give spiritual riches to others. We own nothing, and yet we have everything" (2 Cor. 6:9-10). There's more in this passage, but these two verses are sufficient to understand that joy is not based on circumstances, and sorrow and joy can happen at the same time.

Joy can be maintained through trials, sorrows and even through persecution. The apostles at Jerusalem were flogged and told never again to speak in the name of Jesus and they "left the high council rejoicing that God had counted them worthy to suffer disgrace for the name of Jesus" (Acts 5:41).

A true definition of joy would be an attitude that is the result of rightness with God through Jesus Christ. This is the initiation of genuine joy in your spirit; however, it is not the joy of being trouble free, but the joy of being free in trouble. It has no hold on your soul.

After Christ's ascension, the disciples began to travel to different cities and speak to Jews and Gentiles. Luke states that they were "filled with joy and with the Holy Spirit" (Acts 13:52). Paul recognized the growth of the believers in Thessalonica when he said, "You became imitators of us and of the Lord; in spite of severe suffering, you welcomed the message with the joy given by the Holy Spirit" (1 Thess. 1:6).

Conforming to Christ's image means you will be filled with joy by the Holy Spirit. It cannot be worked up or passed on to another. It will be in every heart that has connected with God, believed in His Son, and now is conforming to his image. It abides in your heart as evidence that you are a believer. As you submit daily to Christ, your joy will be full.

Therefore, we can see joy as necessary to share your faith effectively. A complete joy which penetrates your whole being from the inner spirit to the outer smile affects your witness in action and word. You are sharing a joy that is unconsciously yearned for in every life, yet so missing.

Let joy be evident in your words and actions. Let it remove you from living under circumstances; after all, who wants to live under those? Move to living in the joy of your spirit, filled with the Holy Spirit.

Key Takeaway: Joy is not circumstantially produced and comes out of the spirit of a person, rather than their soul. It can share the same heart with sorrow, suffering or burdens. It is a fruit of the Spirit and necessary if you are going to witness.

Applications:

When was the last time you were filled with joy? (Remembering the difference between happiness and joy).

When does your family experience joy?

How could your church help believers live more of their time joyfully?

Liberty Principle

Liberty is a principle that proclaims we are no longer in bondage and are given by God all-inclusive liberty to do anything we like and no one can forbid it. This is a serious misunderstanding of liberty and causes the liberty taker to become a stumbling stone in the body of Christ, the Church.

Paul spent time explaining this to the Corinthian church that was abusing liberty. He said, "You say, 'I am allowed to do anything'—but not everything is good for you. You say, 'I am allowed to do anything'—but not everything is beneficial. Don't be concerned for your own good but for the good of others" (1 Corinthians 10:23-24). Liberty does have boundaries.

Paul is saying that the principle of liberty has limitations within the boundaries of holiness, and is best applied when combined with the principle of love. Liberty seeks her own interest, but is never done in a vacuum. If your liberty hurts, harms, damages, or destroys others or even yourself, that act of liberty should not be chosen. So he says it is improperly applied when it cares nothing for the interest of another person.

The Romans needed to understand this truth as they applied it only selfishly. In the book of Romans, chapters 14-15, Paul wrote to them about this sibling rivalry related to the weaker and stronger brother or sister in the faith. He was not talking about authority positions; everyone was viewed as equal in the passage. He was not talking about issues within the faith that were clearly stated as right or wrong with evidence to back them up in the Scriptures. He was talking about people equally dedicated but who varied in their spiritual maturity (14:6). He was also talking about personal preferences in disputable matters including food and holy days as illustrations.

There are six emphases in these chapters that help us understand the case Paul made for those who were weaker and stronger believers in the faith. Let's look at them briefly:

- Accept one another (14:1-4). The weaker was not to pass judgment on disputable matters and not to condemn the person doing it. The stronger should not to look down on the weaker. They were to realize that God was seeking to mature both of his children at the same time so to maintain their fellowship together.

- Be convinced in your own mind (14:5-8). Regarding something special, do it as to the Lord. Eating meat, do it as to the Lord. Abstaining from meat, do it as to the Lord. He encouraged them to understand their motivation.

- Each will give an account of themself to God (14:9-12). Christ is the Lord of both and both shall stand before the Judgment Seat of Christ for their rewards. They were to bow before the Lord and confess their faults to Him considering He is the judge of all.

- Make up your mind to build up your fellow believer (14:13-21). Watch your actions and don't be a stumbling stone, or any obstacle, to other believers. Perception is everything, so weigh the differences and work for peace and growth. Perspective is everything, remember you are both part of God's Kingdom. Progress is everything; so don't destroy others, rather, release your right to liberty. Look, think and act lovingly.

- Keep unclear beliefs inside you (14:22-23). Don't overstep your conscience; stay cool inside and out.
- Unify rather than divide (15:1-7) Seek after unity by bearing with the failings of the weak and please your neighbor for his good. The result will be hope and God will be glorified and praised.

Interestingly, both believers could be the weaker and the stronger person, it all depended on the circumstances. The weaker could be more fully educated in Scriptural truth, but still hung up in an area of legalism. Both could be filled with pride and look down on or outright condemn the other for what they believed to be right in their own eyes. The stronger person could be insensitive and impatient, ridiculing the weaker person for their stand. And the weaker person could be judgmental about the stronger person's overt actions.

The following understanding shared by Paul was precisely what both individuals needed to hear. "The Kingdom of God is not a matter of what we eat or drink, but of living a life of goodness and peace and joy in the Holy Spirit. If you serve Christ with this attitude, you will please God, and others will approve of you, too. So then, let us aim for harmony in the church and try to build each other up" (Romans 14:17-19).

Christian liberty mixed with love measures its effect on others and chooses not to enact that liberty if it is only in selfish interest and causes hurt to others. Your sinful flesh does not regard others and that gets you into problems in the body of Christ when you say you are a Christian, yet you act out your liberty at the expense of others. The principle of liberty must always be tempered by the principle of love.

Paul wrote about this love extensively in 1 Corinthians 13. He shared several statements which help bring clarity to the boundaries of liberty.

- "Love is patient and kind,
- Love is not jealous or boastful or proud or rude.
- It does not demand its own way.

- It is not irritable, and it keeps no record of being wronged.
- It does not rejoice about injustice but rejoices whenever the truth wins out.
- Love never gives up, never loses faith, is always hopeful, and endures though every circumstance" (1 Corinthians 13:4-7)

Do you use your liberty no matter who is around you? Then you are being selfish rather than selfless and have forsaken the purpose of the church to build others up. This can even harm your testimony to unbelievers.

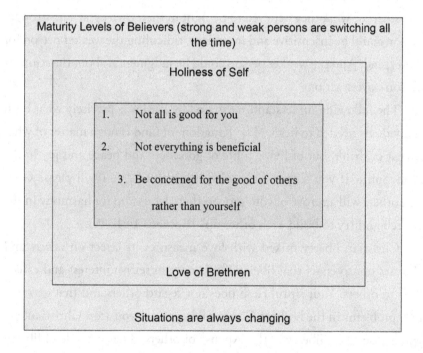

Key Takeaway: Love has to be linked to liberty. You must think about yourself less and others more. Liberty is only freeing if it is not putting another person in bondage. The strong must be considerate of the weaker person and both should live their lives to honor the Lord and build up the church.

Questions to ponder:

What actions of yours hurt others who might be weak? What should you do about it?

As a parent, how are you helping your children understand the difference between clearly stated rules to follow in the Bible, and gray area actions that are a matter of preference for other believers?

How can your church do more to build up the spiritual strength of attendees and stop condemnation and judgment?

Living Wisely Principle

Could you say you live wisely? Would you say all your relationships are wisely chosen? How about your money, is it all wisely spent? What about your activities, yes, those daily activities, are they all wisely done?

It seems like such an easy thing to live wisely, but is more difficult than you might think when you consider the depths, widths and lengths to which you have to go to accomplish living that way.

Paul wanted Titus to be an example to those in his church body and also "promote the kind of living that reflects wholesome teaching" (Titus 2:1). He was to challenge all the different sectors of the church; older men and women, younger men and women, the rich, the poor, the slaves along with business persons and contractors, to live wisely. No believer was excluded from the challenge of living life wisely.

He meant living life to the fullest but with the warning that it was all to be done wisely. Every thought, every act, and every word were to be encased in wisdom. That would make it even harder to live, but it would allow each person to be more effective in godly living.

Paul said this about living differently than before you became a believer, "Don't copy the behavior and customs of this world, but let God transform you into a new person by changing the way you think" (Romans 12:2a). The mind and heart were the places where change started.

He also suggested to the Corinthian believers a way to directly attack what were important centers of focus in their old lives. He said, "Those with wives should not focus only on their marriage. Those who weep or who rejoice or who buy things should not be absorbed by their weeping or their joy or their possessions. Those who used the things of the world should not become attached to them. For this world as we know it will soon pass away" (1 Corinthians 7:29b-31).

What he didn't say is to forsake your family or detach from your marriage. He said, don't make that your only focus. Consider a focus that is wider and runs parallel to your marriage. Keep the directives concerning marriage, yet make your life about more than just that.

Secondly, he admonished them not to be absorbed by sorrow, joy, or possessions. Sorrow can capture you and put you in an endless loop of depression and that doesn't lead to positive thoughts or accomplishing anything. Further, being always joyful and not considering any sorrow or serious moment is not living in reality. Neither is letting your possessions make you unsatisfied with what you presently have, or to think that just getting more will bring you satisfaction. All possessions wear out or become outdated, useless at some point in the future.

Finally, Paul said that you still have to be in the world and use the things of the world, but you must not become attached to them or they will abuse you. Yes, the word was abuse. When we attach to them, they start requiring more from us; more than we can give, and that causes us trouble.

There is another world coming for you. It is heaven, and if you focus completely on your earthly life, you miss the truth that you were made for heaven. Physical life is not the end, only the beginning. Physical emotions and things are not the end either, but can capture you so that you forget that you are just passing through.

Their eternal life was not to get lost in their temporal actions. Paul was communicating the breadth of opportunity that was before them, that they must be wise about every decision. This was not a time to follow fleshly desires; it was a time to excel in their love for God and for others and make sure they were taking good care of their hearts.

Key Takeaway: Living wisely means knowing yourself and God deeper, for all life and wisdom comes from Him. To live wisely means you are deliberate in all you do, filled with the Holy Spirit who guides you, and submissive to the Lord of your life.

Applications:

How would your life have to change to become more effective and productive in living wisely?

As a family, how could you adjust your lives to live wisely?

How could your church teach you to live life wisely?

Maturity Principle

It has been said, if you stop growing, you start dying. That is something to ponder and ask yourself the question, "What are the activities I am engaged in that cause me to grow?"

Even at an early age, while Jesus was still under the direction of his earthly parents, Luke chronicled his developmental areas. He wrote, "Jesus grew in wisdom and in stature and in favor with God and all the people" (Luke 2:52).

The four areas of development he identified were intellectual, physical, spiritual and social. Although Jesus was God, his human body and soul still had to develop. A normal person is physically at their final stature by their early twenties.

Beyond that was his intellectual development, the experiential part of life which brings the ability to obtain wisdom. Jesus was growing in that as well, although he was not trained in the synagogue.

Then, his favor with God. At Jesus' baptism and transfiguration God the Father spoke from heaven and said, "This is my dearly loved Son, who brings me great joy" (Matt. 3:17), a commendation of epic proportion. Jesus was in continual communion with God the Father.

Finally, he gained favor with all the people. He was viewed as sociable, loving, friendly, responsible, caring and respected. This often gave him the opportunity to speak into their lives or be of service to them.

This is a blueprint for our own development. Not much more can be said about our physical development, however, growing in wisdom, favor with God and with all people are important. But let's focus on our spiritual development which is a key area for maturity that influences wisdom and connection to God.

There is an upward call that starts the day of our salvation and continues throughout our life. This is a call to maturity in Christ, to holiness of life, to live in Him and by Him. It is possible because we are free; no longer in slavery to the flesh. We live the "new life" by living through the new nature provided by the Holy Spirit at the moment we are saved.

At this point there are two words we need to differentiate. Sometimes a person uses the words spiritual and spiritually mature to mean the same thing but there is a distinct difference. Spirituality is the place you are at where you are living righteously, sins confessed, having a repentant heart, and do not grieve or douse the Holy Spirit living within. Your actions and attitudes are spiritual.

But a person identified as spiritually mature has been in the process of being spiritual for many years. She has learned a lot about God, speaks with understanding about the Bible, has a dedicated prayer life, and concern for unbelievers. So, spiritual applies to us all, whether young or older believers. But spiritually mature persons are not everyone, much fewer, and takes more time to develop.

The writer of Hebrews used the terms milk and solid food to illustrate growth levels. He said to believers, "You have been believers so long now that you ought to be teaching others. Instead, you need someone to teach you again the basic things about God's word. You are like babies who need milk and cannot eat solid food. For someone who lives on milk is still an infant and doesn't know how to do what is right. Solid food is for those who are mature, who through training have the skill to recognize the difference between right and wrong" (Heb. 5:12-14). He also called the babies spiritually dull and not able to listen very well. The word infant is not speaking of a family birth relationship in the context, rather, it is a different word which means "immature" which could be an infant for sure, but also an older believer relating specifically to their spiritual development.

We grow toward normal maturity in several areas. Physically we have already talked about. To be mentally mature for most happens at a later date when they have experienced and educated themselves deeper. It is much harder to become emotionally mature as that means they have worked through the earlier years of life and have fit them into their personal psychological picture. For the most part, most believers are at the milk drinking phase.

The writer emphasizes that solid food, not talking about physical food here, helps us spiritually mature. That food would be the Bible, prayer, Christian life experiences, and the Holy Spirit's work in our lives. Those who are spiritually mature are eating solid food so they can distinguish between righteous and sinfulness. Milk doesn't make this happen; you are still dependent on others to identify that for you.

This is the reason God has created the Bible. It is a textbook on righteousness and unrighteousness; a revealer of the processes necessary to become mature. It applies to all ages and generations and continues to be relevant throughout every millennium. Eating spiritual meat will develop your spiritual strength.

It is suggested that most people quit learning at age forty and live the rest of their life on the basis of what they learned in their first forty years. That means that there is not much change taking place in their lives. We are not to follow that example. We are to continue to spiritually mature and be involved in helping others mature, too.

Key Takeaway: Spiritual maturity comes in a similar way that gaining wisdom and being emotionally mature come. It is hard work requiring righteousness and trust in God to lead. Dedicating your life to God and asking Him to help you be mature starts you on the journey of a lifetime that you will never regret.

Applications:

Divide a piece of paper into four quadrants and write one of the areas for maturity at the top of each section. Now consider what you are presently doing to develop yourself in each area and also brainstorm one or two actions you might begin to increase your development in each one.

How could you help your family develop their spirituality and train them to recognize righteousness and sinfulness?

What path could your church map out for believers so they can follow it and grow?

Peace Principle

The very nature of the word peace creates visions of trickling streams and crystalline lakes nestled between white capped mountains or of people smiling and clasping hands and walking together.

Chaos in the world reflects the loss of peace in individual hearts and requires the settlement of grievances by hostile parties and opposing factions. This is a tough job, but it is something to desire personally, something to dedicate your life to, and something to encourage in your neighborhood, city, state and nation.

The Bible reveals peace as being three dimensional, like a cube. There is height to it, for it reaches into the third heaven where God eliminated the barrier of sin which had separated us from Him. This peace was achieved for us by God's Son dying on the cross, but is conditional on our personal acceptance of Jesus as Lord and Savior.

There is a depth to it, for it reaches into a person's heart, into their inner being and calms the soul once at war with God. And, there is width to it, as it spreads to your relationships with others and extends the possibility of God's peace to all in the world.

It is worth noting that inner peace is necessary to any advancement in spiritual growth. If you are perpetually in doubt of your salvation, then it will be hard for you to grow as a Christian because that doubt nags at you when you desire to grow. Your inner voice says, "Why, you don't even know if you are a believer, so why try to be a better one?" The peace with

God must be assured before the peace of God can mature. Your spiritual growth depends on your assurance of salvation.

The height and depth previously referred to constitute peace WITH God, bestowed on each person at the instant salvation takes place. Paul said, "since we have been made right in God's sight by faith, we have peace with God because of what Jesus Christ our Lord has done for us" (Romans 5:1). Peace isn't found in the absence of conflict, but in the presence of both the recipients and the dispensers of forgiveness. "This is the message of Good News for the people of Israel—that there is peace with God through Jesus Christ, who is Lord of all" (Acts 10:36).

The second is the peace OF God which is an inner tranquility achieved by conformity to His will and progressive yieldedness to the Holy Spirit living within. Paul wrote concerning this to the Philippian Christians, saying, "Don't worry about anything; instead pray...Then you will experience God's peace, which exceeds anything we can understand. His peace will guard your hearts and minds as you live in Christ Jesus" (Philippians 4:6-7). The psalmist declared concerning peace, "In peace I will lie down and sleep, for you alone, O Lord, will keep me safe" (Psalm 4:8). And Isaiah in a song of praise wrote, "You will keep in perfect peace all who trust in you, all whose thoughts are fixed on you" (Isaiah 26:3).

Key Takeaway: Peace is not an ethereal thing; it is an experienced calm that expands from the depths of the soul to the outward expressions of your face. There is nothing you can do to own it; it is given by God so that you can have peace with Him and have the peace of Him. This is only found in becoming a believer, all other peace is circumstantial and subject to change at any moment.

Applications:

How sure are you that you have experienced peace with God?

What is the level of peace in your home, dependent on circumstances or on God?

What could your church do to help attendees experience the peace with God and the peace of God?

Providential Principle

In the time of King Xerxes, who reigned over 127 Provinces stretching from India to Ethiopia during the years of 483 B.C. to 473 B.C., there were two men living in Susa, Haman an Agagite, an archenemy of the Jews, and Mordecai a Jewish man exiled from Jerusalem. Haman was after control, wealth and prestige. Mordecai was seeking to be faithful to his God, and be a good citizen as a captive in a conquering nation's capital.

Mordecai was hated by Haman because when he was elevated above all other nobles, making him the empire's most powerful official, Mordecai refused to stand and bow to him in respect. So, Haman created a plan to not only kill the Jew but also all Jews living in the kingdom. It was put into action by a decree signed by the king and then the ripples started. The city of Susa, the home of the palace, fell into confusion related to the decree.

During the same time, Queen Vashti and King Xerxes hosted huge separate banquets for the women and the men in responsible empire positions. After the men were fully saturated with wine, the King sent for Vashti to parade her before the men. She declined to come, which started the King's advisors thinking about the ramifications of her decision. Their solution was to depose her, take her royal crown and banish her from the king.

The advisors initiated a search for a new queen with candidates coming to Susa. Hadassah, a young Jewess, also called Esther, lived there with her cousin Mordecai. She had lost her parents, was adopted by Mordecai who became her guardian, and told not to divulge her nationality. Life was good for them before the king began the search for a new queen. Esther was taken as a candidate, and providentially chosen to the position as queen.

Later, after she was crowned queen, Mordecai informed her of the plot to kill all the Jews and urged her to go to the king and seek his mercy. They both fasted and prayed for three days before she appeared at the throne room entrance. The king happily invited her in.

She requested his and Haman's presence at a banquet that night. They both came and the king inquired as to her request. She asked him and Haman to come to another banquet the next night and she would share her request.

That night, after the first dinner, the king couldn't sleep, so he sent for the national records and asked them to be read to him. Since it was government business it was sure to put him to sleep. Instead, as the reader began, he read of the story concerning the King's attempted assignation by two of his eunuchs who guarded the door to the king's private quarters.

Mordecai had learned of the plot and shared it with Esther who presented it to the king who foiled it. But no reward was yet given to Mordecai. So, the king planned to honor him and received a suggestion from Haman, who thought the honor was for him. He suggested a special ride on the king's horse for the honoree around the city led by a person declaring that this was a reward from the king for services rendered. But Haman ended up being the spokesman and Mordecai the one sitting on the horse. The whole story is shared in Esther 4-8.

During the second banquet at the king's inquiry, Esther told the king of her nationality and how Haman's decree would allow her to be killed along with all other Jews. The king was incensed and Haman was impaled on a seventy-five-foot pole which he planned to use on Mordecai. Mordecai was given his position and was able to counteract the first decree by a second decree, giving the Jews permission to fight back during any attacks. It all turned out for the best and God saved His people in the process.

This story is shared to emphasize that no coincidences ever happen.

God is walking through life with all people and weaving His will and plan through the good and bad which is initiated every day. He is mightily involved and the following considerations help to support that statement.

a. Esther's loss of her parents put her under the care of Mordecai, later to be an important part of a successful story of protection for God's people.

b. Mordecai's personal interest in adopting her and treating her like a daughter developed trust, loyalty, and an obedient heart in her which would also be important later.

c. Vashti's refusal to come before King Xerxes, led to the queen's demise.

d. A search for a new queen swept up Hadassah/Esther, as well as many other young women into the king's harem.

e. Esther gained favor with Hegai, the eunuch in charge of the harem, who helped her properly prepare for her time with the king.

f. She was now in an influential position to the king of the empire.

g. She had acquired the position, but God had connected her to Mordecai, given her beauty, and put her there.

h. Her nationality being hidden, which was done at the request of Mordecai, was revealed at the right time when she confronted Haman in front of King Xerxes.

i. Haman's great pride kept him blind to any downside. He was just happy to say, "I'm going to dinner with the King and Queen!" It seemed his life was great.

j. Haman's evil plot came straight from Satan, because the devil works to destroy God's people all the time. Revelation 12 shows us more of this hatred.

k. When Esther was told of the plot and realized the gravity of the situation she did not shrink back from her role in the plan of God.

l.   Acknowledgment that it might cost Esther her life, she stated to Mordecai, "If I must die, I must die" (Esther 4:16). She realized the stakes were much higher than just her welfare.

m.   These two stories, the rise of Haman and the decree, and the life of Mordecai and Esther, ran along parallel paths until they clashed together at the second banquet.

n.   The solution to the larger problem was not fully realized by Esther's help, but her actions were an important step toward the final protecting of God's people.

o.   King Xerxes had to lose favor with Haman. He had to be discredited and removed from his office of power, which he was at the second banquet.

p.   Mordecai's previous warning of an impending plot of the king's assassination had to be discovered so that the king would favor Mordecai. The king's sleeplessness caused him to request the reading of government records. That was when Mordecai's warning of the assassination was read to the king.

q.   Haman's leading of Mordecai around the city, declaring this was a reward from the king, was his first humiliation, and the city's look at the emerging Mordecai.

r.   Haman was sentenced to death at the second banquet and Mordecai was appointed to his position, so that he gained the authority to write and send out a new decree for the Jews to have permission to fight back at their accusers.

s.   The Jews had to take advantage of the second decree, not accept their fate, but fight.

t.   Mordecai never lost faith in God. He prayed for deliverance of the Jews, even though Babylon had destroyed Israel and Jerusalem and he lived in Susa as a result of his captivity.

u.   Satan was not able to warn Haman of impending doom because Satan does not know the future, but his wife, Zeresh, did say to him, "Since Mordecai—this man who has humiliated you—is of Jewish birth, you will never succeed in your plans against him. It will be fatal to continue opposing him" (Esther 6:13). She was right.

We share this story of God's prevention of the killing of all the Jews in King Xerxes empire to capture an understanding of all the moving parts God brought together to accomplish His goal. From the death of Esther's parents, her adoption by Mordecai and their move to Susa as captives, the crowning of Esther as queen because of Queen Vashti's rash action, the prevention of the King's death by Mordecai, the rise of Haman and the first decree, to Mordecai's eventual empowerment to provide a second decree so the Jews could fight back, were not coincidences, they were in God's plan.

This gives us pause to reflect on our past and present actions. Are they just coincidences or are they linked to the larger plan that God? We cannot call them coincidences, but must instead call them certainties of God's continual work with us, around us, and in the greater world.

Robert J. Morgan in his book, *The Red Sea Rules*, reflects on this, saying, "Throughout most of the Bible, God helped His people in ordinary, providential ways rather than in overtly supernatural ones. The same is true today. That's why mature Christians pay special attention to the accidents, misfortunes, and coincidences that befall them. For in reality, there are no such things. Only the providential ordering of God who watches over His prayerful, trusting children, and whose unseen hand is guiding, guarding, arranging, and rearranging circumstances."[9]

Key Takeaway: God is present as we live each day and there are no coincidences in our lives. Rather, it is the unseen hand of God guiding us, protecting us and providing for us. To attempt to live a life thinking that luck or fate is on your side, is to miss the powerful actions of God that are unfolding around you.

Applications:

How have you shrugged off personal happenings as luck or fate rather than God's hidden hand at work?

What would be a way for your family to capture all life's incidents around you so you can look for God's hand in them?

How could you and your church become better at looking for the miraculous in the ordinary of life?

Purpose Principle

When someone asks you, "What is your purpose in living every day?" or "What brings meaning to your life?" How do you answer? Will your answer be concise, understandable, and reasonable to others? It can be only if you have taken the time to identify what is your purpose.

In being a coach of men and women over the last two decades, I have come to the conclusion that not much can be accomplished until a person has clearly identified their values built on their past, the purpose they are accomplishing in the present, and their vision for their future. Here is a story that confirms this.

Elijah is remembered for the great spiritual battle he fought on Mount Carmel against eight-hundred and fifty false prophets that had detoured the people of Israel from serving God. Two altars were built and two sacrifices prepared, but only one was accepted. God by fire from heaven fell on Elijah's and burned up the drenched sacrifice, the stone altar, and the water in the trench around it, in direct answer to the prayer of Elijah.

But most of us don't know about the struggle of Elijah after that event. King Ahab's wife, Jezebel, who was a treacherous and powerful woman, directly threatened his life (1 Kings 19:1-2). His response was to run. He traveled one-hundred miles from Mount Carmel to Beersheba, left his servant there, and then traveled another one-hundred-fifty-miles to Mount Sinai to hide in a cave.

Once there, God asked Elijah, "What are you doing here, Elijah?" to which Elijah responded with the facts as he knew them: "I have zealously served the Lord God Almighty. But the people of Israel have broken their covenant with you, torn down your altars, and killed every one of your prophets. I am the only one left, and now they are trying to kill me, too" (19:9-10).

His journey to Sinai took forty days and nights and you can just imagine him working out his feelings as he walked. Some say he was complaining but others, including myself, see this more about getting the facts out as he knew them to be. But his facts were skewed because he just had his impressions of how things were.

God suggested he stand outside the cave for a moment and in so doing, the Lord passed by. A mighty windstorm blasted the mountain, then an earthquake, and finally a tremendous fire followed, but after each of them it is written, "but the Lord was not in" the windstorm, the earthquake or the fire. However, the Lord was in the sound of a gentle whisper that then repeated His question, "What are you doing here, Elijah?" (19:13).

Elijah had lost his purpose. He was focused on the terrible state of things rather than the tremendous power that ruled over all things. So, what was God doing? He was helping Elijah get refocused on his purpose. He was commissioned to represent God, and if so, then it didn't matter what the facts were on the ground, and it didn't matter if it seemed like everything was going to hell in a handbasket, he was to be living out his purpose.

So once refocused, God then said, "Go back the same way you came... anoint Hazel to be king of Aram. Then anoint Jehu...to be king of Israel, and anoint Elisha...to replace you as my prophet" (19:15-16). Elijah still had more to do in the purpose given to him by God and these activities would transform the present conditions in Israel.

It's very important, like a ship, to have a compass, something that continually shows you which direction you are going and helps you to stay on course. Your purpose is like a "plumb bob" which is a weight on the end of a string used as a vertical reference line for vertical level. It is essentially the vertical equivalent of a bubble level. With your purpose in hand, you are able to evaluate your actions, responses to circumstances, relationships, and issues that surface in your daily life.

Your purpose should be written in a terse statement. It speaks about you in the present tense. It is what you are about every day. It describes the passions you have as a person. That sounds like a lot to be put into a terse statement but it can be done. Here are a few that I have found:

- My purpose is to encourage, teach and challenge others.
- The Jones Group exists to provide clients a joy-filled real estate experience.
- John exists to help people connect to beliefs, relationships, and causes that bring meaning and purpose to their lives.
- Judy exists to connect others to God through consultation and restoration, directing them toward worship.

The important point about these statements is that all are in the present tense. They are actively in process every day and therefore can help the person evaluate whether they are on target or not. If they are not, it can show them where to get back on track.

It is inspiring, exciting, engaging and clear. It is twenty-five words or less and in one sentence. It should be simple enough to be understood by a twelve-year-old and large enough to encompass a lifetime of activities. It will be specific to you and your talents, skills and giftings.

God gives us all purpose, a way to be of help to the world. However, we can get distracted by the circumstances around us if our purpose is not clear. He wants us to keep our purpose in focus and do it every day. Finally, let God deal with the greater problems and let us be a part of the solution by maintaining our purpose in His plan.

Key Takeaway: Living without a purpose is floating downstream without a paddle. Finding purpose enhances your ability to decide what you will and won't do. It is carried out daily and easily evaluated every night.

Applications:

How could you find or refocus your purpose today?

What would you do first to establish a purpose statement for your family?

What is your church's purpose? Is it clearly stated by the congregation regularly as a reminder?

Strength Principle

Hollywood is raking in the money for putting *The Avengers, X-Men, Superman, Wonder Woman, the Thor series, Spiderman,* and many more sci-fi thrillers on the big screen. They all portray human beings, and some assorted gods, that have special strengths and become saviors of earth against alien and earthly enemies.

It has made an impact on the younger generation's psyche who hate to be normal in comparison to these large characters and wish for something extra-special to make them stand out for hero like worship.

Society suggests much about what depicts a strong person including bravery, rawness, macho-ness, violent, self-centered, powerful and unmerciful. Movie after movie displays these suggesting that strength is physical prowess, mental acuity, and emotional coldness. However, these traits when isolated can actually be weaknesses that mask insecurities or inabilities and short-circuit what is real strength.

The Bible has many great examples of strength. Samson, during the period of the Judges in the Old Testament, killed thousands of Philistines, performed seemingly miraculous feats like carrying off the gates of a city, and eventually broke the Philistines bondage of Israel. He could probably be a stand in for the Hulk, however, he was controlled by his passion for women and that eventually led to his downfall.

The other, Goliath, is one of the most well-known stories in the Bible of how a little guy beat the big guy who supposedly had all the strength. He stood nine and a half feet tall and with a cynical voice taunted the Israelites for forty days. He seemed invincible, but David found his weakness and dropped him to the ground. David's connection to God and his belief, even passion for Him, made that victory possible.

The reality is that mental, physical and emotional prowess were present in some ways but these were not where the strength came from. It came from God. He provided strength to persons who were conscious of their weaknesses, and who looked to Him for support. A few verses, out of many on the subject, affirm this in both the Old and New Testament:

- In the midst of an enemy's theft of everything that David and his men owned, including family, "David found strength in the Lord his God" (1 Samuel 30:6) and he stated, "You encourage me by giving me strength" (Ps. 138:3).

- An exuberant psalmist wrote, "What joy for those whose strength comes from the Lord" (Ps. 84:5).

- The psalmist encouraged his readers to "Search for the Lord and for His strength; continually seek Him" (Ps. 105:4).

- Hanani the seer came to King Asa and reminded him, "At that time you relied on the Lord, and He handed them [Ethiopians and Libyans] over to you" but this time "you have put your trust in the king of Aram instead of in the Lord your God" (2 Chron. 16:7-8).

- Isaiah's message from God was, "Don't be afraid, for I am with you. Don't be discouraged, for I am your God. I will strengthen you and help you. I will hold you up with my victorious right hand" (Isaiah 41:10).

- Paul shared about his troubles, "We were crushed and overwhelmed beyond our ability to endure, and we thought we would never live through it. In fact, we expected to die. But as a result, we stopped relying on ourselves and learned to rely only on God, who raises the dead...We have placed our confidence in Him, and He will continue to rescue us" (2 Cor. 1:8-10). He went on to say,

"This makes it clear that our great power is from God, not from ourselves" (4:7).

- Paul prayed for the Ephesians, "I pray that from His glorious, unlimited resources He will empower you with inner strength through His Spirit" (Eph. 3:16).
- And he prayed for the Colossians, "We also pray that you will be strengthened with all His glorious power so you will have all the endurance and patience you need" (Col. 1:11).
- Paul testified to the Lord's work in his time of need, writing, "Everyone abandoned me. But the Lord stood with me and gave me strength so that I might preach the Good News in its entirety for all the Gentiles to hear. And He rescued me from certain death" (2 Tim. 4:16-17).

What can we understand by relating just these few places where strength was received? Key words or statements are used that help us understand that real strength comes from the Lord. Believers were encouraged and joy-filled by strength given to them from God. They were challenged to search for it in the midst of His presence. Reliance was on the Lord's strength alone, not their own. Fear and discouragement were pushed aside by the Lord's strength. Paul prayed that the same strength available to him would be available to believers in the churches that he visited.

The conviction must be that His strength is both available and applicable to every situation we could ever encounter. Connection to God would be required and calling on His name is the essential starting place. Second is abandonment of our own strength and trust in God's power and strength would be necessary to access that strength. Sometimes that might mean waiting on the Lord's perfect timing but certainly worth the wait.

Key Takeaway: There is a strength that trumps all human power. It comes from God and is available to believers who are in right relationship with

Him, are accepting their weaknesses, and are eager to call on God for the application of His strength to them.

Applications:

When have you relied totally on God's strength to bring you through trouble?

How could you family learn to rely on God for strength?

How could you church affirm and teach this principle to all its attenders?

Trusts Principle

"In God we Trust" was the motto adopted in 1957 as a replacement for the unofficial motto of "E Pluribus Unum," which means, "one out of many" which was on our paper currency since 1782. "In God We Trust" had sporadically appeared on coins from the year 1864 after Reverend Mark R Watkinson of Ridleyvilate, Pennsylvania, sent a letter November 13, 1861 petitioning the Treasury Department to, in some form, add a statement recognizing Almighty God on our coins "in order to relieve us from the ignominy of heathenism" and to declare that God was on the Union side of the Civil War.

The phrase was first placed on paper money in 1957, appearing on the one-dollar silver certificate, put there because of a Joint Resolution by the 84th Congress and approved by President Dwight Eisenhower on July 30, 1956, declaring "In God We Trust" must appear on American currency.

From that day until now there have been those who desired its removal on the basis of separation of church and state but it has survived this unfounded pressure. It is a statement of trust in someone greater than the government. It points quietly to what the Scripture urges, "Trust in the Lord with all your heart; do not depend on your own understanding" (Proverbs 3:5).

Trusting only in ourselves is the first mistake we make and the whole of humanism supports this independence from God. Isaiah challenged his readers to not "put your trust in mere humans. They are as frail as breath. What good are they" (Isaiah 2:22).

The second mistake is to trust in government, which is riddled with bureaucracy, greed, partisanship and not worthy of complete trust. It needs auditing on a regular basis.

Instead, King David declared, "The Lord is my strength and shield, I trust Him with all my heart. He helps me and my heart is filled with joy. I burst out in songs of thanksgiving" (Psalm 28:7). We spoke of the wholehearted principle as being a desired goal for each heart as they live before God. This means trusting God with our mind, emotion and will, all our heart every day, without reservation. Declaring that we can't fully depend on ourselves, any others, idols, the church, or the government to direct our life should be the reality that leads us to vow to trust God only.

A trusting heart is a heart freed from beliefs that would deceive and disappoint. It is a leap of faith that moves our soul and spirit to a new level of spirituality. No matter what comes, what circumstance crosses our path, who remains faithful or unfaithful to us, or any other temporal situation, wholehearted trust in God will suffice to bring us through it all. It is a deep dependence on the God who is the creator, sustainer, savior, guide and Lord.

David was identified by Samuel in the Old Testament and by Paul in the New Testament as a "man after God's own heart" (1 Samuel 13:14; Acts 13:22). His intimate relationship with God was deepened in the field as the shepherd of his father's sheep. He was alone with a flock of sheep and responsible for their well-being. They depended on David to lead them to water and green pastures. And, we know that he killed a bear and a lion to protect them, before he killed Goliath (1 Samuel 17:34-36).

It would be easy for David to see himself as a sheep of the Great Shepherd. God could act the same way that David acted with his sheep by providing for his needs, protecting him, and guiding him every new day. We see this clearly in the prayer of David in Psalm 86. It is an intimate prayer of dependence on the Lord:

"Answer me, for I need your help.

238

Protect me, for I am devoted to you.

Save me, for I serve you and trust you.

Give me happiness, O Lord, for I give myself to you.

Listen closely to my prayer, O Lord; hear my urgent cry" (Psalm 86:2-4, 6).

I left out verse five. It gives us an indication of how David saw God. He said this in the midst of his prayer, "O Lord, you are so good, so ready to forgive, so full of unfailing love for all who ask for your help" (86:5). God blesses, forgives, and loves us so much was what David conveyed and to not accept that love and live with a trusting heart would seem illogical.

Trust is a statement of confidence; it is a reliance on God solely and that is a statement any believer should be able to make. David said under inspiration of God that He was "so good," "so ready to forgive," and "so full of unfailing love." Seeing God this way and trusting Him through the good and bad of our life is the challenge to everyone who puts their faith in Jesus Christ as Savior.

Key Takeaway: Trusting God is the only complete answer for our lives. It is recognizing our insufficiency and His all sufficiency. His steadiness, power, unfailing love, and forgiveness have taught us that. Making the decision to pray the prayer of David regularly in earnest moves us deeper into a trust-based way of living.

Applications:

How can you develop your spiritual walk with God to the point you have this kind of trust?

How could you show your family that you are relying on God daily?

What could your church do to emphasized the idea that trust in God is the only alternative in life?

Vision Principle

People in every nation, ethnic group, gender, age, economic status and more have created their own personal vision. Some enjoyed quick success in obtaining it and others struggled longer but eventually reap its rewards. There is nothing as satisfying as viewing a vision accomplished in three dimensions. The struggle fades to the background when success is present. It might be like having a baby. There is a gestation period, then labor, then birth and wow, there is the child held in your arms.

Vision is powered by passion from deep in your heart. It seems most likely that your vision will align with your personal values and purpose than it would move in a different direction. So, its important to have all three defined, written out, and available for review at any time. Here are some helpful points about a vision:

- Vision is values and purpose based.
- Vision is passion fed.
- Vision is dream fed.
- Vision must be authentic to you.
- Vision is about you, but not all about you, it is also about how it affects others.

It is a clear picture of a possible future. It is a mental portrait, a realistic, credible, concrete, and visible future you desire. It is the expression of what you feel you are called to create in your time and place; hence it gives you a distinctiveness and an attractableness. People are drawn to it because it is unique and creates a new possibility for others.

To encourage a person to think visionary is to invite them to envision what their life will look like in five or more years. It is a photographic image that guides the journey to what it depicts.

A statement of destination. All visions, big or small, begin with the end in mind. They answer the question, "What if?"

We've spoken of purpose before, so what is the difference between a purpose and a vision?

- Purpose answers the question, "What do you love to do every day?"
- Vision answers the question, "Where are you going?" It speaks to your destination but is always written in present tense as if it is already completed.
- Vision is accomplished when several strategies unite to fulfill it. They define the elements of the vision and answer the question, "How are you going to get there?"

There are several essential elements that help you write your vision statement:

1. Reflection - You cannot create a vision statement without imagining your future. This is seeing the whole forest by getting above the trees. Answering these following questions can help you in building a statement.
   a. At what are you best? What do you do with excellence and imagination?
   b. What are you passionate about? Vision is intuitive and emotional.
   c. What do you aspire to become?
   d. How are your values and daily purpose linked to your vision?

2. Long-term thinking - Assesses the past and present with a view to shaping a different future. Usually, you don't want to be just like your parents. You desire something more and better. What are dreams you want to accomplish?

3. Focus - Vision is directional, brings clarity (doesn't deal in generalities) Where do you want to develop your life as a person, as a worker, as a leader?

4. Imagination - It is out of the box thinking and planning; accomplishing the impossible. It pushes you to your limits and beyond; being imaginative, bold, and visual. What would you like to see be true of you when you are an older adult?

5. Hope - It is about possibilities, believing that obstacles can be overcome. What are obstacles you think need to be overcome?

6. Counsel – Including others in the process of filling in your vision is important. Who do you know that knows you and would share what they have heard you say about where you want to go?

With all of this said, there is one other understanding that will help you in your vision quest. It is called, the death of a vision. Many decades ago, I was introduced to it and it has significant ramifications.

The death of a vision is exactly what it says, the vision given by God tries to be fulfilled out of your own strength, so it dies before your eyes. Some people at that point call it quits, but what they don't understand is that this is a normal part of any vision process.

Let me illustrate:

Born in Egypt under a Pharaoh ignorant of Joseph's leadership, Moses was adopted by a princess and afforded every opportunity of education and the military. Still able to converse with his parents, they spoke with him about his infant deliverance and supposed that God would use Moses in their deliverance from slavery.

Grasping at an opportunity to do just that, he did deliver one Israelite from a beating by an Egyptian guard and then murdered the assailant.

Word got back to Pharaoh and he was out for the blood of Moses. "Moses fled from Pharaoh and went to live in Midian, where he sat down by a well" (Exodus 2:15). He thought he was going to realize the vision of helping his people but instead he learned the principle of the death of a vision.

God does give visions to individuals but does not release them to carry it out in their own strength. There are three phases to realizing a vision: one, the birth of the vision where it is implanted in your head and heart; two, the death of the vision when you try and fail to bring it to fruition independent of God; and three, the rebirth of that vision when God steps in and works alongside you to see it accomplished.

It happened to Moses, to Abraham with the promise of a son, to Joseph and his teenage visions, to the disciples and the promise of a kingdom only to see Jesus, their King, die on a cross.

What we learn is that timing can be off for us and our vision, but God is never early, never late, and always right on time for your vision.

Key Takeaway: Vision is an essential part of moving forward in life. God wants to work with us to accomplish great things. His timing is often times not our own and we end up waiting patiently. The death of a vision is just the middle of the process, so hang in there for the next step.

Applications:

What dream has God given you that you are trying to fulfill on your own?

How could sharing with your children the death of a vision process, like in Moses or Joseph's life, help them in the future?

How could your church begin to help people find out what their values, purpose and vision are?

Living A Principled Life
Community Area

Community is a group of people who are living together with similar beliefs and interests and act as a natural or spiritual family.

Agreement Principle

It seems our country struggles in this area. Agreement has become an unheard-of thing. No one wants to "give in" or "link hands" with another unless it is in opposition to commonly held honorable things like our flag or laws. We seem to be very proud and full of bluster. Humility is hard to find.

Paul knew that agreement was important and essential for believers in the church. He suggested that there be agreement "wholeheartedly with each other" (Philippians 2:2). Only two of the original spies who went secretly into the promise land had this kind of agreement. The Lord noted that Caleb and Joshua had a "different spirit and followed wholeheartedly" (Numbers 14:24, 30), and further defined it by the words complete, consecrated, dedicated, and making full. To be in agreement is to be completely aligned with others in the same direction. There is no wavering, no grumbling, no fear, no doubt, but complete faith and belief. Hezekiah in his purge of false religion in Israel many centuries later was identified as one who "sought his God and worked wholeheartedly. As a result, he was very successful" (2 Chronicles 31:21). He had a pureness of heart, his motive was innocent, and his success was real.

Agreement has to start in the heart and flow out through words and actions that express a pureness of heart. Maybe at first you can't see it another's way, but is it time to argue or listen? Is it time to examine their viewpoint and understand what it actually is? If so, then how do you move forward in discussions to get to a point of agreement?

In order to change how you and they act toward each other you have to change how you and they feel. To do this, you need to find out whether the story each shares is accurate. This happens best when you set aside any preconceived ideas and ask questions that take you to the truth, rather than the story each is telling themselves. You are looking for the truth for both parties and identifying where any disagreement lies.

Here are some questions that might help.

- What is the story you each are telling yourself about this particular issue?
- What was your process in coming to your story?
- What do each of you want?
- Where then are you both?
- Where do you want to go from that place?
- What would have to change to bring you both into positive agreement?
- What would each of you do?
- How would you prove your sincerity in agreement?
- How are you feeling at the end of this process?

These questions and the responses that follow can nip in the bud disagreement by bringing clarity and honesty to an issue. Remember that it takes two to tango, so it's important for both to view their story honestly so that they can get to the truth.

Paul knew that wholehearted believers worked well together because their agreement keep them representing Christ correctly. It also provided a foundation for a good testimony to those outside as they looked into the church. This was Paul's desire for all the churches he had established, that each one would be the mechanism people could look at to see a new type of life available to all.

Key Takeaway: Agreement is one of the key ingredients to fellowship among believers. It requires wholeheartedness and clear communication. It takes persistence and humility to find, and requires a recognition by both parties that it has importance beyond their immediate spheres.

Applications:

In what areas do you have agreement with others, and where do disagreements still exist? What are you willing to do to work them out?

How could a parent train a child in the essence of agreement?

What could your church do to foster agreement among its attenders?

Association Principle

We are known by our associations. Community is about finding new connections and partnering with other believers in fellowship and purpose. It is aligning yourself with the people who want to know God more and are willing to do the right things to stay connected.

In his first letter to the Corinthian church, writing to raise awareness about deceivers who rejected the resurrection and ridiculed its idea, Paul wisely admonished that young church, "Don't be fooled by those who say such things, bad company corrupts good character" (1 Cor. 15:33).

Bad or worthless company, that company which does not build up and encourage your faith, is not the kind of people you want to associate with. It is true that because of our flesh, it is more natural for a good man to be pulled down to a vile man's level than a vile man be raised up to a good man's level. The influence of sin is easily spread from one to another like a disease.

Paul preferred that Corinthian believers who seek after lives of good character find their associations among others of like pursuit. It has always been true that the company you keep has a direct influence on your development or destruction. At fifteen, I allied myself with friends who were taking me in a direction opposite my faith. It was by God's grace that we moved soon after from Tucson to Denver where I found new associations among students at our church. It definitely made a difference in my trajectory.

There were many in Scripture that associated with wrong people, like

251

Absalom, Balaam, Samson, and others, but Solomon's son Rehoboam was a notable one. He ascended to the throne after his father's death and had groups of advisors. The first were older men who had advised his father. The second were young men who had grown up with him and now taken positions as his new advisors.

Jeroboam, a strong leader of Ephraim and a representative of the ten tribes of Israel, came to Rehoboam to request him to lighten the harsh labor demands and heavy taxes Solomon had imposed on the people. Rehoboam asked for three days to review his request and during that time spoke with both camps of advisors. The older men encouraged him to do as requested so that the people would always be his loyal subjects, but the younger group advised him to make the burden even heavier. Three days passed and he chose to respond to Jeroboam with the advice of the younger counselors which caused him to rebel, gathered the ten tribes to form the northern Kingdom of Israel, and become their king. Bad associations broke Israel in half, created more war and death, limited the impact of God's nation on the world, and led to the captivity of both nations.

Solomon cautioned about the path and results of bad associations. He wrote, "Don't befriend angry people, or associate with hot-tempered people, or you will learn to be like them and endanger your soul" (Proverbs 22:24-25). Not only will you be molded into one of them, but your heart will be destroyed in the process. Earlier in Proverbs he wrote, "Walk with the wise and become wise; associate with fools and get in trouble" (13:20). This is a key danger of bad associations. They are people that get you into trouble, they live for now with no regard to the future, and they alienate you from those who really care about you.

So what benefit do good associations bring? Let's start with the obvious, the twelve disciples. Living with Jesus for over three years produced a wonderful end. Once the betrayer, Judas Iscariot was replaced, these twelve became the apostles that proclaimed the gospel to the utter most parts of the world. Saul, converted and now going by the name Paul, had many associates like Luke, Barnabas, Silas, Aquila and Priscilla, Timothy and Titus, and quite a few more. Just look at the last verses of the books he wrote in the New Testament and you can see the great group of positively associated people that Paul influenced and worked along side. Their success in starting churches and seeing the transformation of people within them was incredible and attributed to their undying commitment to the Lord Jesus Christ and the power of the Holy Spirit.

All of this being said, it is not the suggestion of Paul to isolate from unbelievers so that you have no one to witness to. It is to develop your friendships carefully with unbelievers and recognize where close association could take you, if you let it. At the same time, build your closest associations with those who will encourage you positively, challenge you to righteousness, and expand your faith in God. Choosing your company well for the journey of life has a direct bearing on where you will eventually end up.

Associations are important. They set the tone for your future growth or destruction. It is important to find positive community so that you can align yourself with those who seek to conform to the image of Christ. You can never go wrong there.

Key Takeaway: Our associations, whether it be with individuals or corporately in the church, do put us on a glide path to a better landing. We always have to be vigilant about who we let into our lives as influencers and friends, and we do need to recognize the cost of alignment with them.

Applications:
How are the people you associate with helping you to be a better person?

How could you as a parent raise awareness in your children of the dangers and blessings of their associations?

What could the church do to enhance their attendees' understanding of how important their associations are?

Belonging Principle

Belonging is an essential in life. The story is told about a college student who returned to the campus after experiencing the funeral of her grandmother. It seemed that her grades began to drop immediately. Her counselor assumed she was affected with sadness of loss and that she would soon recover; however, her grades continued to drop.

One day she caught up with her and asked about this and the student assured her it was not the loss of her grandmother that was affecting her. It was the fact that while home she opened the front of grandma's Bible and discovered on the family record page that she was adopted. "I don't know who I belong to," she told her counselor. "I don't know where I came from!"

The desire for belonging is something that is present in every one of us. It is the way God made us, and reveals itself as a drive to become a part of a group, to be connected, to feel companionship. Adam felt this when Eve walked into his life after God created her. God had used Adam's naming of the animals to make Adam aware that he didn't belong, he was the only one like him.

As soon as Isaac was born, Ishmael started to feel he didn't belong. He was the son of Hagar, Sarah's servant girl, and Abraham, Sarah's husband. Sarah despised Hagar because she could have a child but eventually, in God's timing, Sarah birthed Isaac. Approximately sixteen years after Ismael was born, he and his mother, Hagar, were sent away to fend for themselves. This was the beginning of what we know as the Arab peoples.

Today, students of all ages seek friends to connect with and belong to. When you start a new job, you desire to belong with the people of the company, and if you don't connect, you might leave for greener pastures. Belonging is different for each person; some don't need a lot to belong and some need much to assure themselves that they belong. It is not an "all or not at all" scenario; the differences in each person make finding community a challenge. But you know it when you find it.

Joseph Myers in his book, *The Search to Belong*, identifies myths concerning belonging. Maybe these will help you know that you are not unique when belonging doesn't come to you through a formula.

Myers reveals that there are multiple avenues you may travel expecting to find belonging, but will be disappointed because they are unfulfilling. These myths "dilute and confuse the definitions we employ to describe our journey to connect"[10] and that leaves us longing but not belonging. Which ones have you bought into?

- More time = more belonging – Time should not be a part of the criteria of belonging. People process at different speeds and in different ways and more time will not necessarily make everybody end up singing, kum-ba-yah.
- More commitment = more belonging – People want to connect, but that doesn't mean they want to commit.
- More purpose = more belonging – A common purpose, vision or goal does not guarantee that people will feel like they belong.
- More personality = more belonging – This myth is accentuated by a misconception we have about introverts and extroverts. Just because a person is sociable doesn't magically reward them with belonging.
- More proximity = more belonging – Living geographically close doesn't guarantee belonging. Life in the twenty-first century is

highly electronic. There are multiple ways to connect, share, and experience without entering the door of a home or church.

- More small groups = more belonging – Although small groups do help people begin their journey, they do not fulfill all that's promised in belonging. The percentage of adults in the church that actually commit to small groups hovers around fifty percent. We don't assume that the other fifty-some percent all feel like they belong either.

Let's be clear. There is a lot that needs to take place for a person to feel belonging. All the above are good attempts at making that happen, but, however lofty that goal is, we understand that several people together or all in a group does not guarantee belonging will happen for everyone.

The human psyche is a wonderful thing and God has created us all unique. Belonging is not making a mold for everyone to fit into, because everyone has a different idea of what belonging is.

So can we ever belong? I believe we can and here is an illustration to help. Have you ever played three-dimensional chess? They use multiple boards representing different levels and allow the chess pieces to move in three physical dimensions. You need to make completely thought-out decisions before you move and remember what's above and below you as much as what is in front and back of you.

Using that as an illustration, we believe that belonging is also multidimensional. Multiple areas of your life, like your emotional, mental, spiritual, physical and social areas, are seeking belonging for you. Belonging is best achieved when several, but not necessarily all life areas, find it.

Another illustration might help. I have several Realtor friends and they experience a similar situation when a buyer finds the perfect home. Amazingly, it usually happens in the entry area of the house. The Realtor might show them many homes and none connect with them. Then, they walk into the one and say, "This is it. We like this one!" Whoa, what changed? They were just inside the door. How could they know for sure this is the right home when they hadn't seen the den, master bed and bath, the back porch, the three-car garage, and the kitchen? The answer is that their eyes are taking in massive amounts of data all at once as they stand in the entry and the mind is gathering that input and sending out a positive signal of satisfaction. There is no simple way to explain the feeling present; it all clicks together in milliseconds to make an offer on that house.

How can we translate that to belonging? Considering how great God made us and how many systems we have up and running all the time, we can know belonging is happening instantaneously because of the multidimensional aspect of our being. There is alignment, satisfaction, hope, and a sense of rest present inside us. Hard to understand but definitely possible. Go back to the drawing board on all the above myths and ask this question. How can we create multiple dimensional opportunities for family, church, neighborhood, school, or workplace that provide ways to link in? This would enhance the ability to provide belonging based on their uniqueness, not yours.

Key Takeaway: Belonging has multiple dimensions to it and to think that one specific opportunity can guarantee belonging for everyone is as likely as winning every time you go to Las Vegas. The odds are against it. But there is hope because people do connect and find belonging.

Applications:

Where do you want to belong and what would affirm in your heart that you did belong?

How could you, as a parent, create multiple opportunities to belong for each person in your family?

What multiple opportunities could your church create to make belonging by new attendees occur?

Caring Principle

Do you really care? I know you say you do, but do you?

Recently, a Real Estate Broker made an inciteful decision related to the ongoing follow-up of clients by her realtors after each closing. She decided follow-up needed a new name and heart, so she renamed the ongoing connection of realtors with closed clients to Client Care. This produced a new attitude in realtors about how to care for each client. It changed their perspective as to why they were making calls, sending monthly cards or even texting closed clients. It became real care.

Are there actions which are not real care? Let's review two false interpretations of what the word "care" means.

Say your friend came to you, saw you were troubled and said, "Hey, seems like you are hurting. Do you want to tell me what's up?" So you poured out your heart to them and their response was, "Boy, that's tough. I hope you get over it. I got to go." Seems a little bit curt, doesn't it? That friend was being sympathetic. She saw your suffering and was sorry you had to go through it, but did not want to hang around to see how you would fare. Her mind was thinking, "they need to take care of this, and I don't want to get involved."

How about this scenario? Your friend listened as you poured out your heart about your present financial problem. Your child was in the hospital and you didn't have the money to pay the bill. Then they whipped out their checkbook and wrote a check to cover the hospital services. Doesn't happen as much as the sympathy scenario, but there are some people that take on other's problems and relieve them of bad situations through gifts of money. That person would be called an over-identifying friend. It was never their problem but they took it on as such. It's very nice of them and beneficial for you on the financial side, but not beneficial for you on the spiritual growth side.

These two scenarios show you how caring can go astray and miss the mark. You see, if you are faced with a problem, God doesn't want you to experience a short-circuited solution. If that happens, you are not learning anything from facing the problem. And even if you don't see accepting the funds as a problem right now for a short-circuit solution, it could have unintended consequences later. You might depend on that friend to come through on other occasions and lead you down a path to dependency on them, and not God.

In the larger scheme of things, maybe the problem was meant to help you start using what money you do have in a better way or to trust the timing of God to help you solve your problems. The result then doesn't leave you crippled, but helps you walk by faith in God. Now we are not saying, don't be sympathetic and listen to problems people have. Or don't deny financial help from others when it is properly given and you know it came from God because you didn't advertise for it.

Let that initial sympathy or desire to solve another person's problem turn into empathy. The difference between it and our two initial scenarios is emotional, mental, and spiritual identification with the hurting person. It is to experience the problem with them, but not to take it on or just feel sorry for them. Empathy allows us to come alongside a person, to be present in their pain, and to encourage them.

CARING CHART

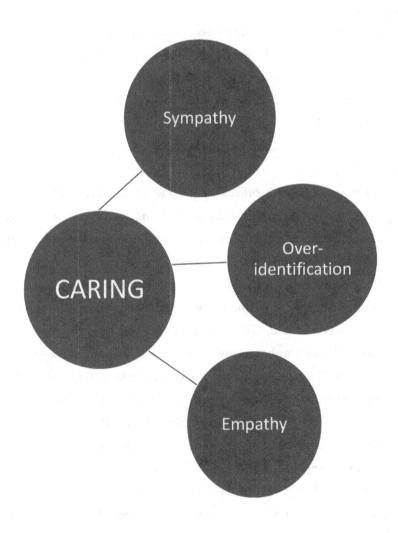

It may have some or all of the following traits:

Our attitude should be one that expects to care for others and will make the necessary changes so that the caring can be more than just praying for them, not that that is not an important component.

Our will decides to make care one of our values; a deep-seated conviction of our life.

Our emotions are linked with the hurting person and our heart goes out to them.

Our actions confirm we care over and over again by showing up, being present, and praying with them. It is clearly committed action.

Our words express we care. They are not telling others you care and then being only sympathetic, as we discussed above, because that can destroy the soul.

You want to be remembered as the one who left pieces of your life with the hurting person.

What would be some other ways that describe real caring? Awareness, respect, compassion, encouragement, listening, observing, asking good questions, and having clarity on what your responsibility is concerning "neighbors."

The Apostle Paul suggested that we all should "be kind to each other, tenderhearted" (Eph. 4:32) and the writer of Hebrews sought to encourage his readers when he said, God "will not forget how hard you have worked for Him and how you have shown your love to Him by caring for other believers" and "keep on loving others as long as life lasts" (Hebrews 6:10-11).

A recent study concluded that the only statistically significant factor differentiating the very best leaders from the mediocre ones is caring about people. Life often provides the possibility for compassionate action for the disenfranchised and if you are in doubt as to whether to care or not, care more. Engaging in simple acts of kindness and love is satisfying. Live so that when others are reminded of you, they think of compassion and caring.

Key Takeaway: Caring involves compassionate action and wholehearted involvement. It is not something you can do frivolously; it is a commitment to come alongside, talk with, cry with, or pray with the person who is facing an issue bigger than their abilities. Being kind, caring and loving is at its heart.

Applications:

How could you expand your ability to care for others?

How can you make sure your family feels cared for?

What can the church do to expand sincere caring among the body of believers?

Comforting Principle

What's it like to be comforted? My experience has been that it makes you feel that you are not alone, your experience is common to others, and when the person comforting you has been through a situation similar to yours very assuring. It might be divorce, could be the death of a family member, or the loss of a job, to name a few troubles. It's a comfort just knowing your experience is common to others. We all need comfort once in a while. So, how does God provide the ultimate comfort?

At the beginning of 2 Corinthians, Paul wanted to encourage the believers in Corinth concerning this. He said, "God is our merciful Father and the source of all comfort. He comforts us in all our troubles so that we can comfort others. When they are troubled, we will be able to give them the same comfort God has given us" (1:3-4).

God is the source of comfort. He is not an angry and petulant Father. He is full of mercy, which is not getting what we do deserve, and He extends grace, which is what we don't deserve. So, here we see the cyclical nature to comfort. One, "He comforts us in all our troubles." He does not remove us from our troubles; that would defeat His purpose. He is with us through our experience and provides comfort. This is occurring through the work of the Holy Spirit who indwells us. The Father sent Him to "teach you everything and remind you of everything I have told you. I am leaving you with a gift—peace of mind and heart" (John 14:26-27). "The Spirit will tell you everything He receives from me [Jesus Christ]" (16:15). So, all three persons of the Trinity are involved in us receiving comfort.

Second, we learn that in his experiences, Paul was crushed and overwhelmed beyond his ability to endure. He thought he would never live through it, and he expected to die. In this moment, he realized the secret to comfort. He "stopped relying on [himself] and learned to rely only on God, who raised the dead" (2 Corinthians 1:9). Did you get that? When Paul came to the end of his ability to deal with his trouble, he relied on God alone because He raised Jesus from the dead! This is faith at work, believing that if God's power is sufficient to go beyond death, then it is sufficient to go with us through troubles before death. This is key: Paul had to rely totally, one-hundred percent, on God.

Third, that's when comfort was felt. He said, "And he did rescue us from mortal danger, and he will rescue us again" (1:10). The comfort received gave Paul strength to deal with the immediate trouble but even further, it began to deepen his confidence in God to deal with trouble in his future! That's an important fact for all of us.

Now here's the fourth thing we learn about the cycle of comfort. Not only did the comfort come from God (the Father, the Son, the Holy Spirit), it came when Paul relied totally on God. And comfort did come, God did not let Paul down. When he had that comfort from God, he could comfort others with the same comfort he had received. So, to share in suffering would ultimately mean to share in comfort.

Finally, the principle of comfort has no boundary, it is unlimited. The more suffering, the more showering with comfort, with the ultimate result of thanksgiving to God for how He has comforted and how you were able to comfort others with the comfort you received.

The cycle would look like this: (Note the chart below)

God is the source of the best comfort and comes with no strings attached

We must rely on Him alone for comfort

Comfort does come

Comfort can be extended to others when recognized by you as being received from God

More suffering brings more comfort and thanksgiving is given back to God

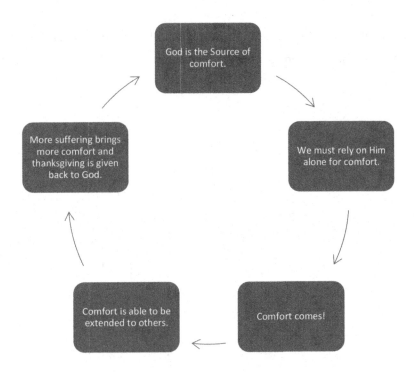

Comfort is given when crisis happens. It helps us to have hope amidst turmoil and allows us to think beyond that which has captured our focus. It takes effort for comfort to be given. It is not coming alongside like Job's friends and making assumptions or accusations. There is no comfort when that happens. Comfort brings peace to our heats and glory to God.

Key Takeaway: Comfort begins with God, is extended to us and through us to others, and then is our reason for thanksgiving and glory back to God.

Applications:

How good is your ability to comfort others? How could you make it better?

Knowing that all children are unique, what are the best ways to comfort each of your children?

How could your church develop people who know how to comfort and then enlist them to comfort others inside and outside the church body?

Companionship Principle

Solomon was a man on a lifelong journey to find the wisdom in everything. He found it through learning and observing people. In Ecclesiastes, which is a somewhat dark book, this is one of the most positive affirmations he made: "Two people are better off than one, for they can help each other succeed" (Eccl. 4:9). Solomon illustrated this truth in three concise ways:

1. "If one person falls, the other can reach out and help. But someone who falls alone is in real trouble."
2. "Likewise, two people lying close together can keep each other warm. But how can one be warm alone?"
3. "A person standing alone can be attacked and defeated, but two can stand back-to-back and conquer. Three are even better, for a triple-braided cord is not easily broken" (Eccl. 4:10-12).

This speaks to the way God has made us in His own image. God the Father, God the Son, and God the Holy Spirit are three persons in the Trinity that live in community and operate out of the same essence, attributes, and nature. God has also put the desire for community within us. He saw Adam, the first man, in the Garden of Eden and said "it is not good for the man to be alone. I will make a helper who is just right for him" (Genesis 2:18). So God created Eve and she became Adam's companion.

However, the realization of community goes deeper than a husband and wife relationship, although that is a true expression of unity and community. The same can apply to brothers, sisters, and others connected in deep friendship. They look out for each other on their journey through life. They keep each other from pitfalls with warnings and broad observance of the road they are traveling.

They stay warm together whether it is temperature related or attitude of the heart related. The one alone can think selfishly, greedily, and narrowly while the two together think beyond self and encourage each to be better than they are alone.

They also can be more effective in battle, whether that is actual hand to hand combat or it is mental struggles to overcome selfishness and self-talk that destroys. Accountability is a positive aid to those who are in companionship; someone to ask them the hard questions about their life.

How can we translate these three comparisons of one alone and one in community? It is enough to say that each of us needs another to walk with us through life. Sometimes that is a spouse, but other times it is a close friend. We need someone to bounce things off of, one to express confidentially our inner feelings to and still know that we are accepted. Compare aloneness to laughter together, success through struggles, and growth through a challenge. Consider the bond that is made by men in war. They live and die together and it is normal for them to find no other friendship that will be as strong.

David and Jonathan are one of the clearest examples of this. David was the second King of Israel. Although anointed by Samuel at sixteen, he had not yet ascended to the throne. It was presently in the hands of Saul, the first King of Israel. Saul's son, Jonathan, was the heir apparent but Jonathan's heart was knit with David's, possibly from the time of David's killing of Goliath.

Jonathan deferred to David, even though it would mean his loss of the crown. David recognized the great sacrifice that Jonathan made to be his friend and respected and admired him for his deference. This proved to go beyond the two of them, for after all of Saul's family was killed, there remained one grandson, whom David took care of because of a vow he made to Jonathan. His name was Mephibosheth. David showed him kindness for Jonathan's sake and he ate at the king's table regularly.

Good friends help us to do what is right. They challenge our thinking. They encourage our growth. And, just think how productive life is when you have others beside you!

We come into the world dependent on our parents and they keep instilling in us the need to be independent. Then, we get to independence and we are alone, and that is not good. The step beyond independence is interdependence. That is the place where we develop companionship with God and others which leads to community.

Key Takeaway: Being independent and alone is not an end all. In fact, it is counterproductive to an excellent life. Companionship that grows into deep admiration and respect going both ways will enhance and expand your life.

Applications:

How can you enlarge your connection to a friend in hopes that your companionship will grow into one to last for the rest of life's journey?

How can you influence your children to pick their friends carefully and hold on to them for the long haul of life?

How can your church foster the development of companionship among students, singles, and married couples of all ages?

Comparison Principle

Measuring your life by the lives of others can get you into trouble. There are some assumptions that are made when you do this. One, the actions you take in comparing with another will help you be more liked. Two, your measuring is equal, however it is their exterior with your interior and that is not a proper equation. Three, some people are better than others and you got the short stick.

Humans have a DNA that is particular to them. No fingerprint or iris of the eye is the same. Our similarities may cause us to think that we are not unique, but God has endowed us with uniqueness beyond the likenesses, and His purpose is for us to have our own special way to be the best we can be and contribute positively to the world.

There were leaders in the Corinthian church that were disparaging the Apostle Paul. They said of him that his letters were "demanding and forceful, but in person he is weak, and his speeches are worthless" (2 Corinthians 10:9). They sought to lift themselves up in the eyes of the Corinthian believers by belittling Paul and comparing themselves with those in their little circle which all seemed to be better than Paul.

He wrote to them cynically saying, "We wouldn't dare say that we are as wonderful as these other men who tell you how important they are! But they are only comparing themselves with each other, using themselves as the standard of measurement. How ignorant!" (2 Corinthians 10:12).

There will always be those who push themselves forward as a standard to live by. They say they are the best, better than you, or anyone else. They look at their abilities, giftings and accomplishments and feel they exceed others. They are kidding themselves. Every human being has cracks in their armor.

There is no standard of measurement, other than that of being like Christ, because we are all unique. Paul said they were unwise because any measurement to a person other than Christ will continually change, based on that person's development. In addition, this can be measuring your body with their body and DNA is the source of both, so not much room for change there. Or it deals with skills, strengths, knowledge, or presence and that is more personalized with their whole development.

You can't make your legs longer, your hair thicker, your nose smaller, or your strengths the same as theirs. Whoever you are comparing yourself to, like friends, movie stars, politicians, or leaders; they are also measuring their lives against others and so it seems everybody is unsatisfied with their own DNA, abilities, and strengths.

There is concern for those who do this, that they might be dissatisfied with the way God uniquely made them, and that becomes the basis for envy, jealousy, or idolatry of others. This is not helping them to make their own personal mark on humanity. They are so focused on self that they are blinded to the weaknesses of the ones they are comparing to.

There is a better way. The Bible shows us the interior of the human heart. It reveals the inward thoughts and intents of individuals. It allows us to compare our interior with the interior of other men and women who have passed before us; people who were kings, queens, prophets, and warriors. This is the only way to compare properly. What we find are individuals who have feelings, actions, and attitudes like ours and we realize that God is the only one who has a solution for the darkness in each heart.

It's time to put away the posters and praise for other men and women, who we only know by their outside appearance, and seek to conform ourselves to the one and only perfect man, Jesus Christ. The way to do that is to saturate ourselves with the Scriptures that reveal both him and the inside of us. Then engage with the Holy Spirit, who helps us "become like his Son" (Romans 8:29).

Are you measuring your life on the basis of others or by the true standard that doesn't change, Jesus Christ, as revealed in the Word of God? Seeking to be like someone else causes us to miss the opportunity of uniqueness that God can use in His own special way.

Key Takeaway: Measuring or comparing yourself with others cannot be done equally, for we may know ourselves inside and out, but we only know the exterior of others that we use as a measuring stick. It is best to measure ourselves against Christ and acknowledge how his sacrifice has made us better and more able to help the church and the world around us.

Applications:

What person are you using as your measuring stick for yourself?

How can you help your children see that trying to be like someone else causes you to miss the opportunity to be the real you?

What could a church do to promote the uniqueness of every believer?

Confronting Principle

The Apostle Peter traveled to Antioch where Paul confronting him for his behavior. He had no problem eating with Gentile believers who were not circumcised. "But afterward, when some friends of James came, Peter wouldn't eat with the Gentiles anymore. He was afraid of criticism from these people who insisted on the necessity of circumcision. As a result, other Jewish Christians followed Peter's hypocrisy, and even Barnabas was led astray by their hypocrisy" (Galatians 2:12-13).

Paul confronted Peter with this obvious dubious behavior of shunning Gentile believers under the pressure of Jews that were steeped in their legalism. Not only that, but other Jewish Christians, even Barnabas who had traveled with Paul, had alienated the Gentile Christians. The discussion was about people being made right by faith and not by obeying the law. He discussed this from 2:14-21. Peter was called out by Paul for not living the same way with the Gentiles as he did with the Jews.

In another example, the Apostle Paul and Barnabas, a responsible Jerusalem leader in the church, traveled on the first missionary journey from the city of Antioch to the island of Cyprus. They went from town to town across the island to the port of Paphos where the governor became a believer. From there they crossed the water to Perga and Pamphylia in today's southwestern Turkey.

Their story includes the following statement. "There [at Pamphylia] John Mark left them and returned to Jerusalem" (Acts 13:13). Nowhere in

Scripture does it say why Mark left. But it caused a problem later between Paul and Barnabas.

They traveled to several more cities before returning to Jerusalem and Antioch. After some time, Paul wanted to go back to the cities to see how the new believers were doing. Barnabas agreed and suggested they take John Mark with them again. "Paul disagreed strongly, since John Mark had deserted them in Pamphylia and had not continued with them in their work. Their disagreement was so sharp that they separated. Barnabas took John Mark with him and sailed to Cyprus. Paul chose Silas and went toward Syria, and as they left, the believers entrusted him to the Lord's gracious care" (Acts 15:38-40). Both teams had successful journeys and the new believers were encouraged. I guess you could say they kept their distance; one traveling southwest and the other traveling north.

Several years later, we encounter a short statement to Timothy in the writing of Paul, who is now in Rome awaiting his trial. It reads, "Only Luke is with me. Bring Mark with you when you come, for he will be helpful to me in my ministry" (2 Timothy 4:11). Barnabas, Paul and John Mark had dealt with their differences and Paul was not one to keep a grudge, so he encouraged Timothy to bring John Mark to him and confirmed that he could be trusted now.

It is difficult to stand face to face with another person and speak to them about their life. You can feel like this is overstepping a boundary or you could ask yourself how you are any better than them. It can bring real angst to a heart.

However, if you are their friend, and you care about them and believe their actions are moving them away from health and wholeness, wouldn't you want to help them? That is the essence of the last two verses written in the book of James. He wrote, "My dear brothers and sisters, if someone among you wanders away from the truth and is brought back, you can be sure that whoever brings the sinner back will save that person from death and bring about the forgiveness of many sins" (James 5:19-20).

"Brothers and sisters" are believers. To "wander away from the truth" is to sin. God has not stepped aside, but the person doing the wandering has. James says we need to be ready to confront wrong actions in other believers with the pure purpose of drawing them back from the discipline of God.

Fortunately, Jesus provided a process for confrontation in Matthew 18. He begins with a parable about a lost sheep and what the shepherd should do. He should go after the sheep and then rejoice when he finds it. Jesus goes on to say, "it is not my heavenly Father's will that even one of these little ones should perish" (Matt. 18:14). This is setting the stage for what he will next say about confrontation.

"If another believer sins against you" (18:15-17) is the way he starts. Their needs to be a legitimate sin involved, and if there is, then there is a possibly three-step process to resolve that hurt. One, go privately and point out the offence. If the person listens and confesses it, you have won that person back. Two, if you are unsuccessful, take one or two others with you and go back again, so that your words can be verified as desiring reconciliation and his words also can be verified. Three, if they still refuse to listen, take the case to the church. This connects with the James passage we are considering, also.

The confrontation that takes place has a good result if the person being confronted is willing to change. If so, then he is saved from physical death because both confronter and the one confronted have already been saved from eternal death. And in the James passage, to "bring about the forgiveness of many sins" means to guarantee present sins are remembered no more.

When we look at the confrontations represented above, we can see that they were strong, had a logical development, and had the best interest of all parties involved, and were resolvable. That's the way it should be.

Back to our initial story of Paul, Barnabas, and Mark. These were all big personalities in the Antioch church at that time. Yet what happened, even among the strongest of men, was division. We can see that there was a ripple affect also to more than just the central parties that included all the church. Something to be very careful about. However, God did use this problem situation to advance the gospel. Here He sent two mission trips out when there was only one planned. He also clarified rules for Gentiles with Peter's misstep by incorporating Gentiles back into the main body of the church, and in our James passage the sinner repented and sins were remembered no more. All to the glory of God.

Sometimes our care for one another in the body of Christ has to go to the place of confronting, and when it does, we have to recognize that it could be us in that position, too. Our humility in confrontation and our sensitivity to God in that process can reap good rewards for the person we are confronting.

Here are some further helps for the confronting process. Understand first that when confronting or being confronted there are three actions you do not want to take:

- Respond with physical or verbal abuse
- Blame others for what has happened
- Keep how you really feel inside you

You can share in a less offensive way which seems to not indicate you are judging them:

- You say…."Here's what I observed………" (explain what you have seen but do not make any judgment statements about it)
- You say…."That makes me feel" (good to keep it focused on you)
- You say…."Because I interpret that to mean……….." (this is what I am thinking)
- You ask…."Is that true?" (stop talking and let them talk about what you have just said, keep quiet, only using "uh huh," "okay," or "hmm"

- If their answer is "no, that is not true" then you can ask the following question,

  "Then how should I interpret the facts or actions I have differently?" OR

  "Then help me to re-interpret what I have seen / heard / experienced so that I can feel differently."

This response puts you both on a path to dialogue and expression of true feelings. The most important action is to be a good listener and ask questions about any words you feel might have different definitions for them than they do for you.

- Who would you like to use this confrontation process with?
- How would you begin your time with them?
- What would be your objective in the confrontation?
- What would be a reasonable positive result?

Key Takeaway: Confronting is an essential part of keeping harmony in the church. To ignore sinful acts is not living by Biblical standards. Hopefully, in addressing sin the situation can help all that are involved; to clear consciences, build guidelines in murky issues, and bring glory to God.

Applications:

How can you approach a believer in love who is wandering from the truth?

What happens in your family when confronting a child or an adult is necessary?

How can a church teach confrontation as a blessing in the church?

Encouragement Principle

At times, all of us need help with some encouragement. We may not even know what that would look like, but when it comes, we will certainly recognize and appreciate it. Encouragement is the act of inspiring another courageously to gain spirit and hope.

Barnabas' real name was Joseph, but he was called Barnabas as a nickname which means "Son of Encouragement" (Acts 4:36). This was probably because those around him saw that he was always encouraging others. Here's an example of that in Barnabas' life concerning Saul, who would later be spoken of as Paul.

After Saul's meeting with Christ on the road to Damascus and after his eyes regained their sight with the help from Ananias and God (Acts 9:17), Paul began preaching Jesus as the Messiah in the synagogues of Damascus. But some Jews plotted to kill him and waited at the gates to capture him. He was lowered in a basket through a window in the city wall and disappeared for a while to Arabia. Then he returned to the city of Damascus (Galatians 1:16-17) after what could have been several years.

Three years later, Saul traveled from Damacus to Jerusalem by himself to speak to the leaders of the Jerusalem church. But the believers were afraid of him until Barnabas showed up, introducing him to the apostles, and speaking high praise about Saul's boldness in preaching about Christ (Acts 9:27). That opened the door for Saul to minister with the apostles and preach all over Jerusalem. But again, some Jews try to kill him, so the believers escorted Paul to Caesarea and he sets sail for his home town of Tarsus (9:26-30).

Barnabas, a leader in the Jerusalem church, was dispatched to Antioch to obtain information about the growth of the number of Gentile believers in the church which was a matter of concern to the mostly Jewish church at that time. He listened to the leaders about this door that the Holy Spirit had opened, was filled with joy, and encouraged the believers to stay true to the Lord (11:22-24).

But note this in the text, "Then Barnabas went on to Tarsus to look for Saul. When he found him, he brought him back to Antioch. Both of them stayed there working in the church for a full year" (11:25-26).

A famine arose and hit Judea hard, so the church at Antioch of Syria raised a love offering to give to the elders of the church to aid the people in Jerusalem. They entrusted it to Barnabas and Saul who traveled together to Jerusalem (11:29-30). "When Barnabas and Saul had finished their mission to Jerusalem, they returned to Antioch" (12:25).

In the midst of their continued teaching there, the Holy Spirit said, "Dedicate Barnabas and Saul for the special work to which I have called them" (13:2). So, Barnabas and Saul were sent on their first missionary journey (13:3-5) returning after much ministry and persecution to report to the church at Antioch (14:27).

Barnabas is identified as "a good man, full of the Holy Spirit, and strong in faith" (11:24). He was definitely an encourager because he sought out Saul in Jerusalem, spoke up for him, and relieved the fear of the people concerning Saul. Barnabas again sought out Saul at Tarsus and encouraged him to teach at Antioch and they also traveled together on the first missionary journey (Acts 13:2-4).

The Bible is full of other encouraging moments and the challenge to all of us is to "encourage one another and build each other up" (1 Thess. 5:11; Heb. 10:25). In the Old Testament, Jonathan's friendship was an encouragement to David as he was hunted by King Saul. That story can be found in 1 Samuel 20.

Paul wrote to the Roman church before he traveled there with the purpose "to encourage you in your faith, but I also want to be encouraged by yours" (Romans 1:12). There was the possibility of a reciprocal opportunity to be of encouragement to each other.

As Paul traveled on his three missionary journeys, birthing churches in every city, he made encouragement a part of his daily activity with all the believers (Acts 20:1-2; 14:22; 1 Thess. 2:12)

Encouragement can happen in the midst of a message to people (Acts 13:45; 15:32; 1 Cor. 14:3), encouragement can help believers find the proper actions to do, as in the churches at Corinth and Antioch (2 Cor. 7:13; Acts 15:31), encouraging words about the resurrection of the dead and the living can help those in sorrow (1 Thess. 4:18), and encouragement can be offered from the Scriptures (Romans 15:3).

We see that God is also an encourager and gave this spiritual gift to certain individuals, among whom was probably Barnabas, to aid believers in their daily faith (Rom. 12:8; 15:5; 1 Peter 5:12; Heb. 12:5). Another blessing that encouragement brings with it is joy, as expressed by Paul in verses 4-7 of the short book of Philemon.

Here's what we can learn about being an encourager from Barnabas and other Scriptures:

- An encourager stays involved with you, but does not pester.
- They take chances catching up to you to encourage you.
- They are not passive in their steps, but come forward when they need to.
- They go out of their way to encourage.
- Sometimes they are with you for an extended period of time.
- Encouragement can have a reciprocal effect by touching you back and giving you joy.

- Encouragement doesn't always have to be directed at you, it could be on behalf of you, as it was in Jerusalem when Barnabas put his stamp of approval on Saul.
- Encouraging may be one of your spiritual gifts.

Whether through the use of Scripture, an act of love, a statement of comfort concerning the future, or a word of truth to a weary life, encouragement is an important part of the DNA of believers in community.

Key Takeaway: Lifting the soul and spirit of another through encouragement is a gift for some and a responsibility for all. It strengthens others to be confident and stand firm in their faith, and creates the byproduct of a joy that is unrelated to their circumstances and aids them in their journey through life.

Applications:
How could you become a better encourager of others?

What are words you say and actions you do that encourage the members of your family?

How could your church find those with the spiritual gift of encouragement and deploy them, and also emphasize the importance of everyone being an encourager, too?

Fasting Principle (Corporate)

Esther's rise to Queen of Persia and Media was not an accident, as God would use her in the deliverance of the Jewish people from extinction. Mordecai, her uncle, had cared for her since her parent's death, but little did they know she would be chosen to become the new queen after the present queen, Vashti, disobeyed the King in front of a crowd. Esther entered a powerful realm with many undercurrents.

Haman was one, an evil man who rose in this government until he was the most powerful official in the empire outside of the king. He despised Mordecai because he would not show him honor when he passed. So Haman decided not only to kill Mordecai but all his people, the Jews. His plot developed and a decree was issued with the king's name on it that the Jews be destroyed on a specific date. Haman motivated the killers by declaring that the property of the dead Jews was to be given to them.

When everyone in the kingdom heard of this new decree, there was "great mourning among the Jews. They fasted, wept, and wailed, and many people lay in burlap and ashes" (Esther 4:3). Mordecai and Esther worked on a plan to reveal Haman's diabolical plan and it worked. Haman was killed by the king, but his decree could not be dissolved. So, they created a new decree that the Jews could fight back. Because of that change, those who sought to kill them were instead killed and success was achieved in the saving of the Jews. This is the illustration of fasting for deliverance from death.

It's been a long time since I have seen, read or heard about a church, a city, or a nation proclaiming a fast for at least one day. How about you? If you were to offer fasting as a suggested action concerning a present situation, how do you think people would respond?

In the Conduct area of Living a Principled Life, we wrote about individual fasting. We explained it's need, process, and results. Here we are suggesting some adjustments for corporate settings.

Let's understand that fasting has always been one of the Spiritual Disciplines and enacted many times through the centuries of Christendom. These Disciplines were designed to further the development of Christian maturity and to align people with the will of God.

Let's start by acknowledging fasting as a possible action to aid in any present situations and by reviewing some of the other corporate illustrations presented in the Bible.

Fasting related to war: The Israelites fasted in regards to knowing the will of God in a war against the Benjamites, one of their own tribes. In the time of the Judges, the Benjamites had gone off the rails. At Gibeah, one of their main towns, a group of men abused the wife of a traveling Levite who spent the night there. He was so distraught that he sent a piece of his wife's body to all the other tribes in Israel to reveal the "terrible and shameful crime" (Judges 20:6) of the Benjamites. She must have been severely bruised on every part of her body. They were shocked and united against the Benjamites but the tribe was hard-hearted and fought back. Three battles took place at Gibeah. The Benjamites killed 22,000 soldiers of Israel in the first. The next day they fought and 18,000 more soldiers of Israel perished. That caused Israel to weep, fast again, and present offerings to God. They asked if they should fight again and God said yes, so the next day they rallied and killed 25,000 men of Benjamin to win the war.

Fasting for restoration from a plague: Three hundred years before Israel would go into captivity the people were deep into rebellion and sin. So God allowed a plague of cutting, swarming, hopping, and stripping locusts to destroy their crops. The prophet Joel declared, "Announce a time of fasting; call the people together for a solemn meeting" (Joel 1:14). He called for a fast as he explained this plague was the Lord's chastening. He told the people, "Turn to me [the Lord] now, while there is time. Give me your hearts. Come with fasting, weeping, and mourning"…"Blow the ram's horn in Jerusalem! Announce a time of fasting; call the people together for a solemn meeting" (2:12, 15). Let them pray, "Spare your people, Lord!" (2:17). The Lord responded with promises of restoration and the pouring out of His Spirit.

Fasting because of idolatry: Defeating Israel, the Philistines in 1 Samuel 4:3-11 captured the Ark of the Covenant of Israel. They kept it for seven months and, as a result, deadly tumors broke out on the people of each of the Philistine's leading cities where it was brought. Finally, they placed the Ark on a cart led by two cows and sent it, without a driver, down the road toward Israel. It was found and taken to Kiriath-jearim where it would remain for twenty years, because the people of Israel were still mired in idolatry. Samuel called them to Mizpah, a location at which the people of Israel often conferenced, to come back to the Lord which did happen after they got "rid of their foreign gods and images of Ashtoreth" (1 Samuel 7:3). They "went without food all day [fasted] and confessed that they had sinned against the Lord." (7:6)

Fasting due to sin: Having completed the work of rebuilding the walls of Jerusalem after returning from the seventy years of captivity, the people of Israel came together to listen to Ezra read the book of the Law of Moses. They had not heard it in a long time and did not know what it all meant, so the Levites explained it to them. This led to a reinstituting of the Feast of Tabernacles to celebrate Israel's wandering in the wilderness and God's provision for them. This was to be a joyous occasion of deliverance but all the people mourned and wept!

So, Nehemiah sent them away stating, "celebrate with a feast of rich foods and sweet drinks, and share gifts of food with people who have nothing prepared" (Nehemiah 8:10). They were all called back together to hear the book of the Law of Moses read each day until the end of the seven-day Festival. The eighth day was to be a "solemn assembly" required by the Law, so they fasted and dressed in burlap and sprinkled dust on their heads. After hearing the Law read for three hours, the people "confessed their sins and worshiped the Lord their God" for three hours (Nehemiah 9:3). They ended this time standing and praising the Lord.

Fasting for a city: Jonah endured the raging Mediterranean Sea and a three-day ride in the belly of a giant fish in order to obey God. He went to Nineveh the capital city of Assyria, and preached the message that, "Forty days from now Nineveh will be destroyed" (Jonah 3:4)! To his disappointment, the people of Nineveh and their King participated in a fast. It was declared to be observed by the whole city even stating that the animals must not eat also. Garments of mourning were worn, earnest prayers to God were lifted, and evil ways were turned from. Because of this, God did not carry out their destruction and the city prospered for one-hundred and fifty more years until a new prophet, Nahum, warned of their impending fall. This time it did happen.

Fasting related to Missionaries: The church at Antioch was involved in fasting, worshiping, and listening for God to speak about sending out missionaries. "So after more fasting and prayer, the men laid their hands on them [Barnabas and Paul] and sent them on their way" (Acts 13:2-3). This would be the beginning of three missionary journeys for Paul and Barnabas and they would repeat this process often.

Fasting related to appointing leaders in the church: As Paul and Barnabas traveled on their missionary journeys their normal process of establishing elders required prayer and fasting by each church. The New Testament church of Antioch of Pisidia was encouraged by Paul and Barnabas to pray and fast as they turned "the elders over to the care of the Lord, in whom they had put their trust" (Acts 14:23). They wanted to have elders that would be wise and lead with God's will in mind at all times.

The major objective of corporate fasting was to draw the group, church, or nation back to God. It was to seek His will in determining who would be in positions of leadership and was also done to purify the people whether group, church or nation.

We have recognized several results of fasting above; a city or people spared from destruction, a body of believers obtaining leadership and missionaries, and the removal of idolatry and the reinvigoration of worship to the one true God.

Key Takeaway: Fasting should be a regular occurrence not only by sincere individual believers but by corporate bodies that are desirous of living under the direction of Jesus Christ the Lord and God the Spirit, the one who provides unity among groups of believers.

Applications:

What could you do as an individual to support the discipline of fasting in spiritual groups?

How could you, as a parent, implement regular fasting in your home?

As a church, at what opportunities do you offer fasting for your congregation?

Fellowship Principle

The class at church invited everyone to bring a dish for the potluck. They felt this would be a great time of fellowship. Little did they know that this was a loose meaning of the word. We have surrendered its usage to no more than a meal with beans, hamburgers, salad, and dessert. That does not meet the true sense of this valued word. Christian fellowship requires hard work, lots of patience, and lots of forgiveness. It is a demanding discipline to be learned and practiced.

The Bible says much about a vertical fellowship between us and God (1 Corinthians 1:9; 2 Corinthians 13:14; Philippians 2:1; 1 John 1:3, 6), but this is not the emphasis here. We are focused on the horizontal relationship between two or more believers. However, for there to be true Christian fellowship both the horizontal and the vertical will be present.

Jesus pictured many examples of the true nature of fellowship. No class of people were off limits to him, whether Jewish tax collectors, like Zacchaeus, who were hated by their own people, or prostitutes, or diseased or impoverished individuals, or intellectual leaders of the nation like Nicodemus. Jesus sought to fellowship with them all as they came to know God personally in homes, Synagogues, and in the city (Mark 2:15-16).

He exampled the act of fellowship by being with the disciples in all kinds of situations and always willing to talk about what he had said and what he was doing (Mark 3:14-15). He also fellowshipped with them in prayer, sometimes longer than they could stay awake for.

Fellowship is one of the two English words, along with communion, used in Scripture to translate the Greek word koinonia. The basic meaning of this word conveys the idea of participation. But, the definition of fellowship goes much deeper in Scripture to include, the observable acts done together by the early Christians, the impressions and expressions of unity that were created by acts done together, and it also occurred in relation to abstract ideas or experiences.

This word is initially used on the day the Church began, "All the believers devoted themselves to the apostles' teaching, and to fellowship, and to sharing in meals (including the Lord's Supper), and to prayer" (Acts 2:42). Fellowship is listed as one of the four actions new believers devoted themselves to along with the apostle' teaching, meals and prayer. This passage reveals that koinonia or the word fellowship was possible when these believers gathered together and because of its equal value with the other three actions listed in the passage, it leads us to believe that it was distinctly different from those three, having a unique meaning.

Possibly, this may relate to the uniting of their goods in the verses immediately following, but we believe this word koinonia is also being used to explain the interchange of spiritual experiences that were going on when these believers came together. They might be in fellowship about how they shared their faith or were asking for prayer related to unbelievers they desired to come to Christ, or about decisions they had to make, or friends or family that were ill and in need of curing. This could all be considered fellowship.

The following verses illustrate acts done in the New Testament giving us the impression and expression of unity:

- The Lord's Supper –The ordinance of the Lord's Supper is identified as "communion" in our churches and constitutes a participation with others in a mutual remembrance of the Lord on the cross. By partaking of the elements, the participants were linked together in unity, one with another and all with Christ (1

Corinthians 11:33). True fellowship would involve an examining of self as noted in the Supper (11:38).

Acts done in the New Testament identified as fellowship:

- Communal living – Acts 2:44-47 Having all things common to the cause of Christ, but note in the passage that they still had their own homes, so the "all things" may be in regards to their unselfish attitude about the things they personally possessed, vs 45.
- Contributions to the church for dispersal to needy persons, as seen in Phil. 4:15. There is clearly a sense of participation already present in the word and now there seems to be a sense of sharing and self-sacrifice indicated by the word koinonia as used here and in other references to financial support.
- Cooperation of Paul and others – The aid given to Paul by the Philippians created a partnership in his work (Phil. 1:5 "partnership").

Abstract ideas discussed in the New Testament related to the word fellowship:

- Do not have fellowship with the worthless deeds of darkness (Eph. 5:11). There is a command to not partner or participate in deeds of darkness. This is a fellowship that leads downward, not upward, and does not include a vertical connection with God.
- The fellowship of sharing in Christ's sufferings. The true believer has fellowship in the implications of the sufferings of Christ (Phil. 3:10; 1Pet. 4:13), the sufferings of the apostles (2 Cor. 1:7), and the sufferings of others (Heb. 10:33 "you stood side by side"). There is a connection between your suffering and Christ's suffering. It goes beyond His cross experience to the sufferings by Jesus before the cross where He acted righteously and paid the consequence

for it from evil people. He was doing good and being persecuted for it. This is how the sufferings of Christ equate to your suffering (Col. 1:24).

Experiences that happen in the New Testament identified as fellowship, and are hard to define but rather are understood as part of the Trinity's union or the mystical union with others in Christ:

- Fellowship between the Father and the Son (Matt. 11:25-27; Luke 10:21-22; John 14-15)
- Fellowship with the Spirit (Phil. 2:1; 2Cor. 13:14).
- Believer's fellowship with God (1 John 1:3; compare to John 14:6,23,26; 1Cor. 1:9; 13:14).
- Believer's fellowship with believers. A dynamic interdependence is seen here as you are "living in the light, as God is in the light" (1John 1:7).

Also, the idea of acceptance can be implied by its usage in the Scriptures concerning financial help. Paul viewed the acceptance of the contributions sent by the Gentile churches to the Jerusalem church, probably mostly if not all Jews, as an expression of acceptance by them of Gentile believers and their helpful gift. They could have refused the funds because they still were struggling with Gentiles as brothers in faith, but they did not. Thus, their acceptance and gratitude for the money created fellowship between them and their previously estranged Gentile counterparts. An interesting sidelight is that they are identified as having fellowship with them although the givers and the receivers were in different cities and only the messengers participated in both ends of the transaction.

Unity in the fellowship of the early church was not based upon uniformity of thought and practice, except where limits of immorality or rejection of the confession of Christ were involved. Fellowship of one with whom you disagreed is illustrated by Paul and Barnabas and their falling out in Acts 15:36-41 that was reconciled. It is unlikely that they would have left for different ministry destinations having still held bitterness in their hearts, but they did disagree on Mark's worthiness for ministry. It also goes beyond church settings into the home, as a believing wife was exhorted to remain married to an unbelieving husband as long as he was content to dwell with her (1Cor. 7:12-16), i.e., able to feel that fellowship or communion existed between them on some issues.

In the twenty-first century, there seems to be of necessity a point of connection between people when they engage in what we term as fellowship. The words and concepts that best express the idea of koinonia in and among those in the church are:

- Participation: To participate together in some spiritual action.
- Sacrifice: To be able to share or sacrifice as a group for the good of others.
- Common spiritual task: to be brought into relationship with another through Christ in a common task.
- Common spiritual experience: to deepen in friendship/fellowship by having spiritual experiences together.
- Unity on an issue: to have a strong tie of unity on one issue without necessarily being in total agreement on everything the other believed or did.
- Worshipping together: To commune together with other believers in a holy aspect of worship.

All said, the church could do well to elevate the term fellowship to a higher level than presently exists. We have participation in a global endeavor that draws others into fellowship and connects all to our Heavenly Father and Lord Jesus Christ through the Spirit who dwells within us.

Key Takeaway: Fellowship is participation with other believers in endeavors that are prompted by the Spirit and endowed with His presence.

It includes worship, giving, praying, eating, and sharing God's Word within the body. This fellowship brings us closer to others and to God.

Applications:

How could you become more involved in the various areas of fellowship we have discussed?

How could you communicate the spirit of fellowship with your family and extended family?

What could your church do that would expand the ability of its participants to fellowship together in many more ways?

Forgiveness Principle

Forgiveness, though sometimes hard to do, brings relief to the mental, emotional, and spiritual parts of our lives. It is God's invention. He made a way to forgive. It is coming to terms with a world where people are unfair to each other and hurt each other on a regular basis. It's unnatural at first because our nature seeks revenge rather than reconciliation. One might say, "If I forgive them, then they won't get what's coming to them!" We want people to pay for what they've done; for everything to be fair. But we know and tell our children when they say, "That's not fair!" to get over it because "life's not fair."

Forgiveness is love's permission to break the natural rules; to take exception to the revenge of an eye for an eye and a tooth for a tooth. One Christian leader said, "Forgiveness is surrendering my right to hurt you back if you hurt me."

King Solomon, in all his wisdom, reflected on forgiveness when he said, "Love prospers when a fault is forgiven, but dwelling on it separates close friends" (Proverb 17:9). A fault forgiven allows love to expand and thrive, but a fault dwelt on separates friends. It creates a rift or chasm, and a black spot on the heart. The writer of Hebrews penned a powerful verse, "Look after each other so that none of you fails to receive the grace of God. Watch out that no poisonous root of bitterness grows up to trouble you, corrupting many" (Hebrews 12:15). Notice that the root of bitterness that grows is poisonous, troubles you, and corrupts many others around you, if not dealt with.

Now before we go any further, let's see what forgiveness is not. It is not forgetting, because if we forget we cannot forgive. Burying it so deep that we never think about it means we are not processing it and that is more denial than forgetting. Secondly, it is not excusing or justifying. We excuse a person when we understand they are not to blame for what has happened. We forgive a person for the things we blame them for. Excusing is the easy way out and brings no comfort to the heart. Finally, forgiveness is not accepting a person's hurtful actions. Contrary, we accept a person for the good they do to us, while we forgive a person for the bad they do to us.

So what are the alternatives to forgiveness?

- Deny that the action ever happened or you have any responsibility for the action. If we deny that it is even an issue then there is no need to forgive. But we know that in most cases both people involved have responsibility and we can't deny our guiltiness. If we do, we end up suppressing or repressing it.
- Blame of others or ourselves totally. Blame a spouse or a parent for the fact that things turned out badly. Our environment made us do it. Or blame ourselves for the hurt that was imposed on us, after all we were the victim.
- Declare that there is no remedy. This makes it a standoff, a tie with no way to break it. But forgiveness is the remedy, even though it's not the natural solution we expected or wanted.
- Stew in our juices. We can maintain the hurt and even water it and certainly it will grow into bitterness. But who wants that kind of plant? What you do when you stew is tie yourself, in a negative emotional way, to the offender, like hanging the proverbial mill stone around your neck. Good luck with that.

Consider the consequences to your growth if you pick one of these as your alternative to forgiveness and also consider the unintended consequences you will be imposing on others.

Now we know that there are three different persons who can give forgiveness. One is God, who offers all people forgiveness through His Son, Jesus Christ's work. Two is others; a spouse, children, parents, employer or fellow workers; really every person outside of yourself. And three, is you, allowing forgiveness to yourself.

How will forgiveness help? Holding on to bitterness and unforgiveness creates problems physically with our health, countenance and spirit. Muscles, nerves, and organs interconnect and reveal our state of being. David penned this psalm after his adultery with Bathsheba and his murder of her husband, Uriah, "My health is broken because of my sins. My guilt overwhelms me—it is a burden too heavy to bear. My wounds fester and stink because of my foolish sins. I am bent over and racked with pain. All day long I walk around filled with grief. A raging fever burns within me, and my health is broken. I am exhausted and completely crushed. My groans come from an anguished heart" (Psalm 38:3b-8).

Even as far back as Cain, the son of Adam and Eve, after he killed his brother, Abel, God spoke to him because He could see that his countenance was downcast. He offer a solution, but Cain would not accept it (Genesis 4:6).

It creates emotional instability. Bitterness, which is hurt meditated on, leads to anger and depression. It is a continual acidic drain; a dripping faucet which can bring about a surprising end because failure to forgive causes us to become like the object of our bitterness. Remember the verse in Hebrews 12 stated before. A root of bitterness turns you sour.

Unforgiveness and the bitterness it grows can cause us to disconnect with people; close off our life in order to defend our right to be bitter. It can cause us to dig a deep hole with the shovel you provided for yourself, that's a grave.

And finally, unforgiveness turns you away from God. It blinds you from seeing and feeling His love and plan for you. It makes you aware that you don't have control and must recognize God's ability to deal with the sins and the hurts committed against you. You have the power to release others, to turn your "right" over to God, and to trust Him to exact a penalty in His timing, not yours.

How then can you find direction to forgiveness? You must realize that the alternatives to forgiveness are not beneficial to your ongoing health and growth. They choke off the best for your life. They create future roadblocks on the highway of life. Second, you must view the standard setter. In the Sermon on the Mount, Jesus gave you the Lord's Prayer. It is a concise prayer that involves you, others and God. In it he prayed, "forgive us as we have forgiven others" (Matthew 6:12). We live among a creation that forgives; the land forgives, the forest forgives, animals forgive, and so should we.

Next, be honest and accountable for your part in any wrong doing. It is impossible to accept forgiveness from God, to forgive ourselves, or give it to others unless we are honest and accountable; accountable in our contribution to the problem, our dysfunctions, our selfishness, or our manipulations in the issue.

That means we need to seek forgiveness for our part. Verbalize that to the other person, relating your attitudes and actions that promoted the issue. Don't say, "I'm sorry." Say instead, "This is what I have done that was wrong; will you forgive me for that?" They can respond one of three ways: "yes I forgive you," "no I won't forgive you," or "I need to think on this before I answer you." It really doesn't matter how they respond; it just matters that you confessed your part and asked for forgiveness.

Also, here's an interesting way to tie this up. Determine to forgive them for their part irrespective of their response. But, don't say "I forgive you" if they have not yet admitted they did something wrong. They won't accept that forgiveness. What you can do as you move forward, after all the above, is to not forget about what happened as much as release the pain in remembering.

We all need forgiveness because we all sin; it may be against yourself or another, but all sin is primarily against God. In Psalm 130, the writer cries out to God because of the depths in which he finds himself. He identifies these depths as the result of sin, but also identifies God as full of forgiveness, so he waits for the Lord to cleanse him. The benefit of the forgiveness he receives from God is threefold:

1. He is refreshed and relieved. His conscience is cleared and there is peace in his heart.

2. He is restored to a relationship with God. He reverences God because of His forgiveness. He says, "with you there is forgiveness, therefore you are feared" (Psalm 130:4). God is respected, not only because He can discipline because of sin, but also because He can forgive.

3. He brings hope to others who are also willing to seek forgiveness. He says in verse 7-8, "O Israel, put your hope in the Lord, for with the Lord is unfailing love and with him is full redemption. He himself will redeem Israel from all their sins."

We think no one will care, but what we fail to realize is that everyone is desirous of forgiveness. Everyone is dealing with a conscience that continues to assail them for their wrongdoing. They are in need of forgiveness and we can bring that hope to them.

Key Takeaway: The benefit of forgiveness is not just for you, it is for others, too. Understanding that you can be a testimony of hope to others because you speak of God's forgiveness helps you to do just that; speak of the forgiveness that you have been given by Him.

Applications:

What has God forgiven you for and how could you share that with others?

How can you teach the art of forgiveness to your children and your spouse?

What can your church do to emphasize the need for forgiveness within the body?

Harmony Principle

We often think of harmony in relationship to music. We have a melody and then other notes travel along beside it and expand its consonance. We can also view it as a virtue in the life of a family, a city, a nation, or a church. Harmony keeps things growing, moving forward, brings a sense of confidence, and, when present, makes it easier to get things done.

King David understood the blessing of harmony. After the death of King Saul, David became King, reigning from Hebron for seven years, not Jerusalem. Abner remained faithful to Saul's kingship setting up Ish-bosheth, Saul's son as king before the house of Saul acknowledged David's leadership and Israel became united again.

He wrote a short psalm to example what harmony was like. "How wonderful and pleasant it is when brothers live together in harmony" (Psalm 133:1). Then David identified it "as precious as the anointing oil" and "as refreshing as the dew of Mount Hermon" (133:2-3). Anointing oil was used to anoint the kings of Israel, the High Priests and specific items used in the Tabernacle. The anointing oil poured over the head of the High Priest flowed down onto his beard and the sacred garments he wore unifying the man and his mission. It gave off a wonderful fragrance and reflected on their consecration and the blessing of God upon them.

The dew falling on Mount Hermon came noiselessly and even invisibly. It was pervasive, and proved invigorating and refreshing for the vegetation on the mountain. It was not done by man but by God who cares for all under heaven.

What David was illustrating was that harmony had a positive influence. Within a family, city, nation, or church, harmony united them as one. It dissipated discord and diluted animosity. It refreshed their joyfulness and caused a sweet fragrance to waft out from them as a testimony to unity as they became gentle towards each other.

In his first letter to the Corinthian believers Paul said, "Some members of Chloe's household have told me about your quarrels" (1 Corinthians 1:11). They had fallen into factions that lifted up particular leaders rather than Jesus Christ. Paul said to them, "I appeal to you...to live in harmony with each other. Let there be no divisions in the church. Rather, be of one mind, united in thought and purpose" (1 Corinthians 1:10). Also, Paul said to another church, "live in complete harmony with each other" (Romans 12:16; 15:5).

You know when you have harmony and you know when you don't. It is not something you just conjure up. Harmony happens when each person lives a life of goodness, peace and joy. In Romans, Paul ended his emphasis on harmony by saying, "so then, let us aim for harmony in the church and try to build each other up" (Romans14:19). Silence is not harmony.

Harmony is the result of many influences which include: encouragement, shared vision, respect for each other, a desire to move forward positively, the patience not to speak evil of others, and the desire to recognize all people as somewhat broken.

Paul speaking to a divided church emphasized the message that the body of Christ is to have unity and that, "extra honor and care are given to those parts that have less dignity. This makes for harmony among the members, so that all the members care for each other" (1 Corinthians 12:24b-25). No matter what the level a person is at, there is respect above them and below them and that extends harmony to the whole.

Harmony is a good, proper, and fitting promoter of happiness and a diffuser of good influence in any community and beyond. Our nation needs harmony. Our families need it too! When harmony exists in families, then cities, churches, and the nation will have a calming, caring, and curing presence in them.

Key Takeaway: Harmony is a necessary ingredient to a well-balanced family, church, city, state and nation. It reveals a deference to humility, a determination to stay united, and a deterrent to factions and selfishness.

Applications:

What could you do to have harmony within yourself and with those around you?

What would it take by you as a parent to maintain harmony in your home?

How could your church remind its people of the duty to be harmonious?

Impartiality Principle

Keeping ourselves neutral in relation to judging others is difficult. God said, "Always judge people fairly" (Leviticus 19:15b). We dislike it when we feel we are judged unfairly. We want justice, but justice begins in the heart and is based on cold, hard, substantiated facts. Earlier in this verse, unfairness was explained when Moses said, "Do not twist justice in legal matters by favoring the poor or being partial to the rich and powerful" (19:15a). Favoritism perverts' justice.

In God's Temple service, whether as a priest or as a worship leader in their specific division of the Levite clan, all were randomly chosen by lot as to when they would serve at the Temple. There were no bribes for special weeks; no one was given special treatment. The selfishness of sin did not enter into any choice. Note these statements:

- "The families of the oldest brother were treated the same as those of the youngest" (1Chron. 24:31).
- "Young and old alike, teacher as well as student, cast lots for their duties" (1Chron.25:8). God was no respecter of persons.

When Jesus looked at people, he saw them all the same. Some had power or position or both. Others were terminally ill. He saw Matthew, a tax collector, the same way he saw the Pharisees and Sadducees. He viewed women like Mary and Martha the same as Peter, James, and John.

The spies of the Sanhedrin came to him and said, "Teacher, we know that you speak and teach what is right, and that you do not show partiality but teach the way of God in accordance with the truth" (Luke 20:21). Obviously, Jesus dealt impartially and truthfully with all persons, spent time in all the class levels and charged them all with the same message.

Preferential treatment of one above another was not a part of God's creation; all are unique yet treated the same. He gifts us differently and recognizes our individuality but without the preference of one above another. James speaks to this with the statement, "don't show favoritism" (James 2:1). He said discrimination based on beauty of body or the benefit of external circumstances that gave them wealth, power, or influence did not meet God's standard of impartiality.

He went on to say that believers within the church gave well-dressed and jewelry-laden persons the best seats and special attention, while the poor were told to "stand over there, or else sit on the floor" (James 2:3). Favoritism based on a person's more or less of something temporal was discrimination and partiality guided by evil motives was declared wrong.

Both the rich and the poor believed the message of the gospel, recognized the same Savior and together would inherit the same eternity in heaven. So, they were brothers, neither saved on the basis of any external criteria. James desired that all the people of God act like God does by not showing favoritism.

However, understand that respect was due to aged persons, to certain callings, and to those with special gifts or graces. This respect was not given for their sakes but for God who made them. It allowed them to have positions of honor but the glory always going to God, not to the person.

Favoritism, or partiality, appears many times in the Scriptures. In fact, over thirty passages discuss it in areas of legal justice, religious law, family law, national and relational settings, and classes. Even Paul gave notice to his readers to be impartial about obeying his instructions.

Genesis to Deuteronomy, Job, Psalms, Proverbs emphasizes impartiality, along with Isaiah, the first major prophet, Malachi, the last minor prophet, and the New Testament. God lifts Himself up as the best example of one who is impartial and who does not show favoritism.

With this amount of evidence, why do we still treat some people better than others in our churches? Why do we talk with some and ignore others? We are guilty of favoritism on a regular basis. We act like unbelievers in this regard. We do it because we don't see people in the same light. We see classes. We see gifted and non-gifted. We see intelligent and ignorant. We are misguided in our view of others.

So how does it play out in your life with family members and work associates? Whom do you prefer above others? When you look at those around you, could you say that you do or do not abide by God's standard of impartiality?

With those questions personally addressed, then how can you excel at being impartial to persons of other ethnicities, to those who have wealth or lack it, have different likes and dislikes than you, and possibly even differ in political views? Some suggestions:

1. Never assume you know everything about any person or any situation.
2. Find out the facts, not just the story.
3. Gather input from others.
4. Pray to God for clarity, wisdom, and grace.
5. Understand that differences don't make one person wrong and the other right.

Key Takeaway: "Showing partiality is never good, yet some will do wrong for a mere piece of bread" (Proverbs 28:21). Seeing people, the way God the Father and Jesus Christ see them is the first step toward impartiality. Daily following the five suggestions above is the second step toward an impartial view of all. What do you think would be the third and fourth steps?

Richard C. Matteson

Applications:

What will it take for you to push favoritism to the side and honestly address all people impartially?

How could you, as a parent, teach impartiality/no favoritism to your children?

How could a church make impartiality a key principle in everyone's actions?

Kindness Principle

Who is the kindest person you know? Let that question resonate with you for a moment.

You probably have a mental picture of someone and identify them as kind because of their conversation with you and others. They didn't raise their voice, they kept a smile on their face, and they were enjoyable to be with because they weren't boastful about themselves. They seemed honestly interested in you, kept looking at you in a kind way, and were curious about you as shown by the questions they asked.

Kindness is a pervading and penetrating of the whole nature with the desire to enfold rather than scold. It is a mellowing of all that is within you which would otherwise be harsh and stern. It is the quality of the mind and emotions that expresses an inner attitude of care. It is not something that flows out of the old self, which is selfishly focused. Kindness is a fruit of the Spirit and the new nature placed within us when we believed.

It was evident in Jesus Christ's life. He cared for children, for women, for those facing deep struggles with disease, for men and family issues, for hunger and death issues just to name a few. Paul in referencing his desires for the Corinthian church used Christ as an illustration of how he wanted to be with the church when he said, "I appeal to you with the gentleness and kindness of Christ" (2 Corinthians 10:1).

Paul was once, in his natural state, angry and acted like an enraged man, eager to find Christians and destroy them. He went from house to house dragging out believers, sentencing them to death, and he felt good about this in his warped mind. We could call him the Hitler of his generation. But after meeting Christ and being changed, he was a different person. The Spirit had brought kindness to his heart.

He helps us picture the actions of kindness by using two examples when he reflected upon time spent with the Thessalonian church. He said, "we were like a mother feeding and caring for her own children. We loved you so much that we shared with you not only God's Good News but our own lives, too" (1 Thessalonians 2:7b-8). And, just a little later he said, "you know that we treated each of you as a father treats his own children. We pleaded with you, encouraged you, and urged you to live your lives in a way that God would consider worthy" (2:11-12).

To put this in the context of a good mother and father provides strikingly clear images for us. A mother does not do her work expecting perpetual thanks. She steadfastly provided food for her children and further cared for each of them. She allowed her time to be controlled by them and played with them, walked with them, talked with them. She is totally involved and they know her love by her actions and words.

And then the father illustration has another whole set of words to describe his actions with the children. They are different from the mother's because the father has a different role. He is focused on developing the children, moving them on to maturity. He knows the mother's responsibility is being carried out well and that allows him to extend his influence in a different direction. He is seen exhorting or pleading with them. He is like a dad in the stands of his son's little league baseball game, shouting and cheering his son as he comes up to bat. Then Paul used the words encourage or comfort. These are shown from the baseball stands when his son struck out, telling him he'll do better the next time. And finally, he is urging or charging his children. He is urged his son in his baseball efforts to keep on playing, don't give up, you'll get the hang of it. These are illustrations of kindness.

Now, here is the wider view. What we have talked about above, relates to the church and the family, but is there a larger view of kindness in action? Yes there is. "If you are kind only to your friends, how are you different than anyone else" (Matthew 5:47)? We are certainly kind to our friends and want them to be kind to us. But what about exhibiting kindness to unbelievers, those who are not friends and possibly even enemies? Can you be kind to them? The way you exhibit kindness to friends and family ought to be the way you are with everyone else. "Love your enemies! Pray for those who persecute you! In that way, you will be acting as true children of your Father in heaven. For He gives His sunlight to both the evil and the good, and He sends rain on the just and the unjust alike" (5:44).

That's maybe a real challenge for you to wrap your head around but think about it this way. As we have said before, kindness is a fruit of the Spirit, so it will come out of a believer naturally if they are yielded to the Spirit and submitted to the Lord. So, it won't be something you have to conjure up, it will be there when needed.

All of this being said, how can you enhance the fruit of kindness in your life? Here are some practical suggestions:

- Practice – Take time to be kind every day with friends, at work, at church, and with your so-called enemies.
- Break the paradigm – In your head you are thinking you cannot be kind, but need to be harsh or strong to let them know who's right. Strike that thought pattern when it pops up.
- Continue – Let kindness exude from you all the time, even when you are in pain physically, emotionally, or spiritually. Don't let the pain dictate how you are to respond. Be above that.
- Pray that God will give you opportunities to be kind – He can fill you with kindness and soften your responses to the world.
- Examine – Meditate on Jesus' life situations and how he responded in kindness.

Key Takeaway: Put on kindness like you would a coat; cover yourself with it. Your kindness should show every consideration to all people. Meditate on the five actions of kindness noted in the pictures of a mother's and father's relationship to their children. And remember, "Your kindness will reward you, but your cruelty will destroy you" (Proverbs 11:17).

Applications:

What did it feel like the last time someone exhibited kindness to you?

How can you teach your family members about kindness, and talk about the times they have exhibited kindness to others?

How could your church do a better job of teaching this to everyone in the congregation?

Love Principle

"What the World Needs Now is Love Sweet Love" was recorded by Jackie Deshannon in 1965. We think we know what kind of love she was singing about, because it's in the lyrics, that she believed there was too little of it and everyone was not experiencing it. Its curious phrase, Love Sweet Love, presents only one side of love. Love is multifaceted and so deep and wide that we cannot fully understand it.

We can disagree with her conclusion, that there's too little of it and everyone hasn't experienced it. God's love has always been present and is the most massive love that anyone could ever experience. A testimony to that is this verse, "For God loved the world so much that He gave His one and only son, so that everyone who believes in him will not perish but have eternal life" (John 3:16). Note that the measure of that love is "so much," which is an indeterminable amount. It was sacrificial, like love is supposed to be. And everyone could obtain it with no regulations on how rich or poor you were, what color your skin was, or what national or ethnic group you came from. You also will be surrounded by His love for all eternity.

Before we get too much further, let's understand that there are three Greek words translated into English that become our word love. One, eros or erotic love, describes physical love and is not used in the Bible. Two, phileo love, a brotherly type of love used in the Bible. Three, agape love, used often in the Bible and which speaks of a love related to the spirit of a person's heart which desires only the highest good for another.

So, Jesus was sent into the world and established a new commandment for his disciples to put into action, "Love each other in the same way I have loved you. There is no greater love than to lay down one's life for one's friends" (John 15:12-13). The Ten Commandments of the Old Testament stressed loving God, honor for parents, and several "must nots" about neighbor relationships. But Jesus' own commandment challenged believers to love each other in the sacrificial way that he would example by his sacrifice on the cross. These verses use the word agape and emphasize the "so much" love of the Father.

Let's take a moment and examine Jesus as he exhibits agape love to others. Here are ten examples, out of many, of his love put into action for people:

- A divorced woman at a well in Samaria, John 4:7-42 --- Salvation
- A crippled man around the Pool of Bethesda, John 5:1-9 --- Healing
- A woman with an incurable disease that touched his garment, Matt 9:20-22 ---Relief
- A Pharisee looking for answers from Jesus, John 3:1-21 --- Belief
- A love for his own mother by appointing the disciple John to take care of her after he died, John 19:25-27 --- Protection
- A criminal hanging next to Christ on his own cross, Luke 23:32-33, 40-43 Forgiveness
- A child, when Jesus said, "Let the children come to me," Luke 18:16-17 --- Impartiality
- A disappointed disciple, Peter, when Jesus spent personal time to challenge, John 21:15-18 --- Encouragement
- A tax collector, Zacchaeus, who dined one night with Jesus, Luke 19:2-8 --- New Life
- A widow whose only son was raised from the dead, Luke 7:11-15 --- Life and Help

The story goes that there was a psychological experiment in a hospital in Europe many years ago. Newly born babies were placed in two different areas. They both had food, water and other needs taken care of, but in one of the two areas, nurses were instructed to not pick up the babies or show any kind of affection toward them. The other area got hugs and kisses. Over the period of the experiment, it became evident that the children denied any touch or expressions of love wasted away. What a terrible thing to do to babies, but what an obvious truth that love is necessary to live.

So, what is the purpose of love? It strongly unites people and infuses them with feelings of belonging and dedication to each other. It is an example to the rest of the world of what God did for us and draws them to come join. And, it causes obedience and other right responses in living.

Where does that love come from? In writing to Timothy, Paul identified the purpose of his instructions to all believers that they be filled with love, and then he located the source of that love, out "from a pure heart, a clear conscience, and genuine faith" (1 Timothy 1:5). Purity is being clear of any offending attitudes and actions, blamelessness is being free of guilt, and sincere faith is living an unhypocritical life. Love is built on these essential piers so it can flow out to others through us. And we know beyond all doubt that God is the rock below the piers, for He has, does, and will always love us.

Where is love best revealed? One place to start is in the writing of Paul to the Corinthian church, who were entangled in many sinful acts, most of which divided the church into factions and created hostility within its walls. He listed fifteen powerful words in chapter thirteen that specifically describe the actions of love. You could spend hours reviewing and discussing them and developing a gameplan to make them evident in your life.

Considering love as an important principle in expressions of community, such as small groups, congregational meetings, home meetings, and more, means living life as a clean vessel able to allow God's love to flow out to those around you and even to those who are beyond the walls of your church.

Key Takeaway: Love is a big subject and not to be ignored. It requires a clean life, a clear mind and heart, and diligence in actions every day. It is the basis for other fruits of the Spirit identified in Galatians 5:22-23. If you don't have it, then you will waste away.

Applications:

What are some actions you could take to enhance the expression of your love?

How could you, as a parent, deepen your children's understanding of real love rather than that which is advertised in the world?

As a church, what could you do that would better express love to your attenders and to the city in which you live and worship?

Mercy Principle

Jesus was asked by an expert in Jewish law the question, "Who is my neighbor" (Luke 10:29)? He responded with the story of a Samaritan who extended mercy to a man left by robbers on the side of the road. This was a person who acted out of the ordinary for someone in need.

Samaritans were looked down upon because of their intermarriage with Gentiles during the Assyrian captivity. Their allegiances flip flopped between Judah and rising empires. Because of this, Samaritans were denied by Zerubbabel the privilege of working to rebuild Jerusalem and its Temple. Plus, Jews felt the Samaritans were half-breeds, not worthy of worshiping God at their Temple. That's why the disciples seemed surprised as John records the necessity of Jesus traveling through Samaria, "He had to go through Samaria on the way" back to Galilee (John 4:4).

Every other Jerusalem Jew would take a longer route to get to Galilee just so they could avoid Samaritans. Why did he have to go through Samaria? John 4:6-41 clearly gives us the reason. A Samaritan woman would be at Jacob's well outside of Sychar and Jesus needed to talk with her. Their discussion led her to believe in Jesus as the Messiah, the same as the disciples, and her witness in the city led Jesus to stay there for two days, sharing the good news with Samaritans and many believed in him. We never hear much from the disciples about this detour. They were learning about mercy, too.

This good Samaritan came upon a man lying beside the road very near to death. Previously, two other men, a priest and a Levite of the Jewish faith, who worked at the Temple in Jerusalem, passed by but made no effort to help the dying man. However, the Samaritan "took pity on him…, bandaged his wounds, pouring on oil and wine. Then, he put the man on his own donkey, took him to an inn and took care of him," paying the bill and requesting the innkeeper to look after him until he could return (Luke 10:30-37).

Jesus asked the expert in the Law, "of the three men who met the dying stranger, which one was his neighbor?" The expert responded, "the one who had mercy on him" (10:37). Jesus expanded the meaning of neighbor beyond proximity, location or any other commonality to a term of connection with a person at a certain point in time. It became more about being one who extends mercy to someone you don't know or have any affiliation with.

God is the greatest example of one who extends mercy. He is "so rich in mercy…He loved us so much…even though we were dead because of our sins, He gave us life…" (Ephesians 2:4-5). Even more, Micah said, "Where is another God like you, who pardons the guilt of the remnant, overlooking the sins of His special people? You will not stay angry with your people forever, but you delight in showing unfailing love" (Micah 7:18). God delights to show mercy. Good for us.

Zechariah's word from the Lord was, "Judge fairly, and show mercy and kindness to one another" (Zechariah 7:9). In other words, do not begrudgingly show mercy, but extend it lovingly, graciously, and with compassion.

Mercy seems to be a lost art. We are all focused on ourselves and like the priest and the Levite, we pass by opportunities to extend it regularly. Mercy brings reward either here on earth or in heaven. What mercy have you shown to someone lately? Or more clearly said, when was the last time you did something out of the ordinary for someone in need? Do you delight when you show mercy? It's important to keep mercy top of mind daily.

Key Takeaway: "The Lord has told you what is good, and this is what He requires of you: to do what is right, to love mercy, and to walk humbly with your God" (Micah 6:8).

Applications:

What would make you a person who offers mercy on a regular basis?

How can you make mercy a part of the fabric of your home?

What would it take for your church to be called a place of mercy?

Prayer Principle

Jesus was always talking with his Father and on one occasion, after a season of prayer, his disciples came to him and asked, "Lord, teach us to pray, just as John taught his disciples" (Luke 11:1). This tells us several things. One, Jesus was an example of a prayer warrior. Two, John the Baptizer taught his followers to pray and there was a good response to it. Three, the disciples, for the most part simple men, were asking to improve their lives by learning how to pray more effectively.

Most of us struggle to have an effective prayer life. And many would request the same thing the disciples did. But it ends up being more a desire than a reality. We are so busy and connected heavily to the physical rather than the spiritual realm. God seems to be on a faulty telephone line. Most of the time, we can receive by reading His Word and listening to the promptings of the Holy Spirit, but God has a hard time hearing us. We don't speak up, we are cut off, or we fail to dial correctly.

Most of us have seen answers to prayer. We have sung songs about prayer but that has not made us pray more often and more sincerely. Why? What is it about this particular spiritual exercise that doesn't capture us? Why are we not motivated to stay on our knees more often and pray about routine and normal matters of life? Why is it that our prayers pick up tempo only when we are under siege or desire something of God? We all need to connect with God in prayer and grow stronger because of time spent with Him. We need to first understand prayer.

Prayer is a spiritual exercise which is harder to maintain than studying

God's Word, attending church, partaking of the Lord's Supper, or being baptized, or at least we think so. But it is no different than the exercise of our physical body to keep us fit and trim. Spiritual muscles are only developed by repetition over time and with planned effort.

Elijah prayed great prayers to bring down the fire of God, (1 Kings 18:16-46). Jesus prayed in the garden before His crucifixion and sweat as it were great drops of blood. But the disciples had not learned their lesson and couldn't keep their eyes open and pray with Jesus. The story of this failure to pray is written in each of the gospels: Matt. 26:36-46; Mark 14:32-42; Luke 22:39-46; John 17.

Prayer is work. The more you look into books on prayer, the more you realize that there is no secret to prayer. There is not a special phrase, right terminology, exalted beginning, correct final phrase, or even a particular position or volume to right prayer. It is just hard work.

Further, prayer is a communication of the heart. It doesn't just come out of the mind, but the emotions, too. It is a vehicle to express our inner feelings to a loving heavenly Father. It's a private exercise according to Matthew 6:5-9, and it's not what you say, but where your heart attitude is, that makes it effective.

God doesn't need your prayers to accomplish His will. There is sufficient power within the Trinity to carry out anything they want to do. God isn't hampered because we don't speak to Him. But He does want us to be empowered, to pray in accordance with His will, and to have a part in seeing answered prayer.

Beyond all that, prayer is a miracle. That would be defined as a happening or event that is not governed or subject to the laws of space and time. We pray for an event which will happen in the future; for the right marriage partner, the right decision in a job, for protection in travel and to have a healthy body. It is a miracle to see those prayers answered.

We pray for those halfway around the world and it seems impossible to affect change this way, but change does happen. We pray for individuals whose language we don't speak, whose location can't be pinpointed and whose faces we have never seen.

It can be dramatic as we pray for a person to be taken home to heaven because their body is worn out or full of disease and God answers. We pray for change in a person's heart and intimate change occurs at the hand of God.

During Stephen's stoning in Acts 7, he prayed "Lord receive my spirit, and do not hold this sin against them." When a decision was needed for a new twelfth disciple to replace Judas, the disciples prayed. When there was an obvious need for some deacons to be chosen to take care of the widows in the Jerusalem church, the church body prayed. When Paul and Barnabas were set aside for missionary work, the church at Antioch prayed. And, on the second missionary journey Paul and Silas prayed inside a jail after they were flogged (Acts 16:25).

When friends are in need, we can pray. Prayer was an important part of the release of Peter and John from the Sanhedrin. They returned to the believers and "lifted their voices together in prayer to God" (Acts 4:23) for that answered prayer. The result was after they had prayed, the meeting place shook, and they were all filled with the Holy Spirit. Then they preached the word of God with boldness, there was a divine unity among them, they shared everything together, and there was great blessing.

And sometimes, God answers prayer so quickly it produces some short-lived disbelief. Consider Peter in prison while many gathered to pray for him at Mary's home. Peter is released, returned to them, and knocked on the door. Rhoda came to the door to open it but when she heard Peter's voice, she bolted back into the house to tell the good news, leaving Peter still at the gate. Their disbelief turned to amazement when the door was opened (Acts 12:13).

Basically, prayer is the backbone of the Christian life. Would you try to live life without a backbone? No, you couldn't. At key times prayer will allow you to be a part of God's bigger plan but He also wants us to regularly commune with Him, as He did with Enoch, Adam, and many others through the centuries.

The invitation is always there for an individual, family, group, or church to pray. God is never asleep and has His ears attuned to a time when you will talk with Him. The psalmist said, "Here me as I pray, O Lord. Be merciful and answer me! My heart has heard you say, 'Come and talk with me.' And my heart responds, 'Lord, I am coming'" (Psalm 27:7-8).

Key Takeaway: Prayer is important, much more than we even think. It is our hot line to heaven and our ability to have intimate conversations with our Heavenly Father, who is there for us all the time. It has proven to be one of the most powerful weapons that a believer has for the glory of God.

Applications:

What would increase your ability to be more of a prayer warrior?

How can you give prayer in your family a more central place?

How could your church better emphasize prayer?

Reconciliation Principle

The pastor stepped to the podium and introduced the missionary visitor. But he was not introducing him to the congregation to hear him preach from the Bible. He was about to shock the church with a sad story.

It seems this missionary was involved in an extra-marital affair on the mission field. It was discovered and dealt with, but it was felt that the missionary needed to address it with his sending church. They had committed to this missionary couple and their ministry; to pray for them, their work, and financially support them. There was no way he could cover this up from this church.

So the missionary and his wife were brought home and now he was standing before the congregation to share a statement of confession. His words were few, but necessary. He had sinned grievously against God and this church, but also against his wife, family, and the other woman. His wrong doing was massive in his life and in his ministry.

The congregation was very quiet, some were shocked and saddened by the revelation. It was a wakeup moment for others. There's no telling how much impact that day had on the church. It sent a clear message of what God expects from His children. There would be some changes in other lives due to the honesty and humility exampled that morning. This story took place in a church in Dallas, Texas in the 1980's.

Reconciliation is not easy. It takes work, understanding, willingness, and patience on the part of the both parties. It deals with hurt persons and the offending person.

How can you continue to make sacrifices when you know there is someone who has something against you? The question every Jew needed to answer before he offered a sacrifice at the Temple.

The right answer in the words of Scripture was, "Offer sacrifices in the right spirit" (Psalm 4:5). "If you are presenting a sacrifice at the altar in the Temple and you suddenly remember that someone has something against you, leave your sacrifice there at the altar. Go and be reconciled to that person. Then come and offer your sacrifice to God" (Matthew 5:23-24).

Being reconciled with another person was more important to God than your sacrifice. In the time of these verses, the Old Testament Temple was the place you brought your animal sacrifices for sins. God wanted you to be in a right spirit when you offered your sacrifices to Him. But even then, the psalmist spoke about something more than animal sacrifice. He said, "The sacrifice you [God] desire is a broken spirit. You will not reject a broken and repentant heart, O God" (Psalm 51:17).

God has defined a right spirit as a broken and repentant heart, and He wanted then, as He does now, for the heart to be right before the sacrifice was given.

Resolving hurt you have received and hurt you have caused is how you obtaining a clear conscience. That is the ability in reviewing your life to determine that there is nothing you have done to offend or hurt anyone that you haven't been willing to go and confess your wrong and seek forgiveness. If you think this is something you wanted to do, how would you go about it?

First, you have to clearly understand what the wrong is to gain perspective on how you hurt someone or how you were hurt by someone else. It helps to write down your thoughts and organize them until you are clear on what happened.

Second, pray over you written thoughts and ask God for the opportunity to clear it up and to be humble throughout the process.

Third, write out what you want to say in one brief paragraph. In the case of being the one who hurt another, set a time to speak with them by phone or in person. Then call or meet with them and say, "I have something I need to say to you. Could you listen to it fully before you speak?"

Then share your brief paragraph followed by the words, "I feel I have hurt you and am asking if you will forgive me?" Then allow the person time to think before they respond. It is key to ask, "will you forgive me?" and not say, "I'm sorry" or "I apologize," because neither of these statements are a question that requires a response, which is what you are looking for.

There are possibly only three responses to this request for forgiveness: one, "No, I will not forgive you!" Two, "Yes, I forgive you." And three, "I need time to think about this."

However they choose to respond doesn't matter, for it is the act of asking that frees you from a guilty conscience. Their response is their issue, not yours.

In the matter of being hurt by someone else, first, evaluate if it really is a valid hurt and then if it is, go to them and share the brief story of the incident. You might say, "I was hurt by what you did."

Here you must give them time to respond. They may deny their involvement, recognize for the first time what they did to you and ask for your forgiveness, or blame it all on you and walk away. However they respond, you have done what was necessary to do and freed your conscience from the incident.

To expand on what we have said about individual to individual, Jesus gave us a process to reconcile with those who have hurt us that could involve your church community. We have mentioned it in the confrontation principle, but bears repeating.

What is the process to be reconciled to another person? It's described in Matthew 18:15-17 and is a powerful process which does demand humility, keeping away from blame, or being angry. You are clearly and calmly seeking forgiveness or requesting it from them. Jesus said,

1. "If another believer sins against you, go privately and point out the offense. If the other person listens and confesses it, you have won that person back."

2. "But if you are unsuccessful, take one or two others with you and go back again, so that everything you say may be confirmed by two or three witnesses." This is where the church can help you do the right thing and support you not only with encouragement but with other friends to go with you.

3. "If the person still refuses to listen, take your case to the church. Then if he or she won't accept that decision, treat that person as a pagan or a corrupt tax collector" (Matthew 18:15-17). Here is the second step of church involvement. The previous witnesses can substantiate your intent to resolve the issue and the other party's unwillingness to agree. The larger venue of the church setting is important for the hurt person, the person who offended, and also for the church members. As we unfolded in the story at the beginning, it did have a purifying affect on those sitting in the service.

Being reconciled to another person does not mean that everything is back to where it was before the hurt occurred. It may mean you aren't around them anymore and that's all right. What it does mean is that both parties have recognized their part in the matter and cleared the air. Forgiveness has been sought and received and hurt has been dealt with. God sees the hearts of both and He is the only one who knows intent. We have to leave it at that.

What you don't want to do is short-circuit the process by lowering the real damage estimate of your hurt by saying, "Thank you, but is was really not that bad." It is important to not let the hurter off the hook. The pain of going through the process means you let them feel it and don't decrease the impact of it.

It is also not necessary to say, "I forgive you," unless they actually ask for forgiveness. Otherwise, you don't know what they are thinking when you say this. They might still not think they did anything wrong and are just going through the process for you.

Be careful how you handle reconciliation. It is a difficult issue and there's nothing simple about it.

Key Takeaway: Reconciliation is a positive action you can take to clear your heart of hurt. Jesus suggested it and we are encouraged to do so. It must be handled with humility on both sides and clear communication. The freedom you receive from reconciliation is beyond description.

Applications:

Who have you hurt or who has hurt you that you have not sought reconciliation with?

How would you teach your children to reconcile?

What would be necessary for your church to help people free themselves from guilt or hurt?

Sharing Principle

On the day of Pentecost, Peter shared a powerful message of who the Messiah was. Thousands believed and were baptized, showing their confirmation to the truth of Christ's life. He was the Messiah.

Then one of the most moving events of the Bible took place. "All the believers met together in one place and shared everything they had. They sold their property and possessions and shared the money with those in need. They worshiped together at the Temple each day, met in homes for the Lord's Supper, and shared their meals with great joy and generosity—all the while praising God and enjoying the goodwill of all the people. And each day the Lord added to their fellowship those who were being saved" (Acts 2:44-47).

They loved to be together, were unselfish about everything, sold property and possessions and shared the money from those sales, too. It was easy for them to worship and meet in homes to share the Lord's Supper and a meal. Their generosity exceeded anything their city had ever seen. And God received the glory and even more were drawn to salvation daily.

Luke, the writer of Acts, wanted to emphasize this so he expanded on this phenomenon of the church in a later chapter by saying, "All the believers were united in heart and mind. And they felt that what they owned was not their own, so they shared everything they had. The apostles testified powerfully to the resurrection of the Lord Jesus, and God's great blessing was upon them all. There were no needy people among them, because those who owned land or houses sold them and brought the money to the apostles to give to those in need" (4:32-35). What a wonderful display of selflessness. United in heart and mind, sharing daily, no needy ones, and gifts regularly given to support these efforts was a picture of a perfected church.

It was also exciting to be a part of this event if you weren't from Jerusalem. One person, Barnabas, from the tribe of Levi came from the island of Cyprus, "sold a field he owned and brought the money to the apostles" (4:37). And the result of all this giving was freedom for the apostles to testify powerfully of Christ's resurrection from the dead and the blessing from God was upon all. It would have been great to be there, to feel the electricity in the air and see perpetual smiles on the faces of those in need and those who were fulfilling that need.

Further, believers were also sharing in devotion "to the apostles' teaching" (2:42). This is a second type of sharing. Passages were read and people listened as Peter and others explained the truth of the Word. In this verse "devoted" can be translated "continuing steadfastly." There was steadfastness in their interest in hearing the Word of God. They were desirous of hearing to obey. This laid the foundation for all that came after.

But there was another sharing that took place in the churches of the first century. Paul encouraged the people in the church of Galatia to "share each other's burdens, and in this way obey the law of Christ" (Galatians 6:2). This "law of Christ" was identified when John recorded Christ saying, "This is my commandment: Love each other in the same way I have loved you" (John 15:12). It was a law/commandment of love that the Galatian church was admonished to keep doing. But Paul went on to drive home this point by writing, "If you think you are too important to help someone, you are only fooling yourself. You are not that important" (Gal. 6:3). What was important was people finding Christ and needs of all being met.

A fourth form of sharing is mentioned in Paul's second letter to the Corinthian church. This group of believers experienced trouble, possibly persecution, and Paul explained the process that took place in God's church related to comfort. "He [God] comforts us in all our troubles so that we can comfort others. When they are troubled, we will be able to give them [share] the same comfort God has given us...For when we ourselves are comforted, we will certainly comfort you. Then you can patiently endure the same things we suffer" (2 Cor. 1:4, 6). The result of being comforted would be to share that comfort with all others to bolster their resolve in the midst of trouble.

Later, as Jerusalem believers were in the battle of their lives against strong persecution, Paul gathered funds to share from many of the churches he had established in what is today's Greece. He writes, "For I can testify that they [Macedonian churches] gave not only what they could afford, but far more. And they did it of their own free will. They begged us again and again for the privilege of sharing in the gift for the believers in Jerusalem. They even did more than we had hoped, for their first action was to give themselves to the Lord and to us, just as God wanted them to do" (2 Corinthians 7:3-5). Here we see sharing with true sacrifice. These churches went beyond what they could afford, of their free will, and much more than Paul thought they could. They were begging to give both themselves and their money to support the first Christian church.

Sharing is an important part of Christian living. There are always many needs in the body of Christ and the gifts of the Spirit are present in believers to help the church, but also we see here a unity of many churches all giving in abundance and being delighted about it. They are living out love in a practical way.

Key Takeaway: The Christian life is a life of sharing and recognizing that God really owns everything anyway. The first believers shared their possessions, the Word of God, their burdens, and shared comfort from each other. Finding needs and fulfilling them is to be a normal action within each church and out from each church.

Applications:

What are the places you would like to share your resources with?

What projects could your family happily give toward?

How could your church reach out to your community and beyond with acts of sharing?

Trusting Principle (Corporate)

The world is in chaos. Wars are ongoing, acts of terrorism happen daily. People divide themselves into factions, by their ethnicity, behind a cause or a person. Trust is hard to maintain and government secrets are placed in leaky buckets that regularly spill out their contents. People are anxious, fearful, tense, worried, and unsettled.

In the midst of all this a phrase from Proverbs, written by Solomon the king who desired the wisdom of God rather than the riches or praise of men, speaks to the unrest in hearts, "Those who trust the Lord will be joyful" (Proverbs 16:20). Trust must be placed in someone higher than each other, more powerful than any, and with the ability to affect the heart of all. That would be God.

Trust is the one thing that changes everything. On the horizontal, it is the glue that connects individuals, teams, and nations throughout the world. If a government, business, or leader does not have trust of the people, there will be confusion. However, if placed at the center of any relationship, it creates confidence and prosperity of life in every way.

On the vertical, Solomon noted that a person with trust in the Lord would be joyful. This key act of the heart towards God raises eyes from the mess that is our world to the Creator of all life. He is not anxious, worried, or unsettled, He is in charge.

This is best illustrated by the Apostle John in his book of Revelation. He started with an introductory chapter which revealed the resurrected

Jesus Christ before him. Then he spent two chapters conveying individual messages from Christ to seven churches in modern western Turkey.

Having addressed the churches, John saw a door standing open in heaven and a voice called to him, "come up here, and I will show you what must happen after this" (Rev. 4:1). What John saw was the throne of God in glorious splendor and everything was calm and everyone was in the midst of worship.

After that vision two chapters long is completed, there is chapter after chapter of horrible revealed events that the world would experience in the future. But notice this, in John's previous vision of heaven there were no emergency meetings going on. God was not wringing his hands, sitting in angst or plotting what to do with His angels. All was quiet and orderly. This suggests that God is the only one who we should place our trust in. He alone knows the past, present and future. He alone is worthy of trust.

When we place it in Him, we are asserting our dependence on Him. We are stating with our trust that we know He loves us, that He is daily around us, and that His will is being accomplished in the world and within us. This attitude, even way of life, removes the negative emotions from our hearts and minds and replaces them with joy. That's right, joy. It is not the circumstantial happiness we so often attribute as joy, but a heart-filled joy resulting from a heart-filled trust.

Trust or mistrust in the life of a child begins in their formative years at home. It then expands to the friendships they make in the teen years, and is confirmed or unconfirmed in the job settings they place themselves. But those are all horizontally related and trust in God is defined, encouraged, and hopefully expanded by community in the church.

Many leaders in our nation have asked for our trust, but do not deserve it. It all comes to naught because it is so temporal in the eternal scheme of things. Placing our trust in God is not a mistake but the only reputable location for it to rest.

King David raised the invitation to the Israelites, which also applies to us, "O my people, trust in Him at all times. Pour out your heart to Him, for God is our refuge" (Psalm 62:8).

Key Takeaway: Trust must not be given unless it has been verified. If a leader today cannot be verified as trustworthy then they are not due your trust. But God can and has verified that He is able to be trusted. He has over four-thousand years of doing what He said He would do, and acting righteously. He is the only one that can be completely trusted.

Applications:

How hard is it for you to trust the Creator with every aspect of your life?

What could you do within your home to build the level of trust among family members?

How can you develop trust with others in your church?

Unity Principle

We need some unity in our nation today. We are divided, separated into factions and perpetuate the lies of jealous people and warring spirits.

In 2017, as elected representatives from our national congress practiced for their annual baseball game to raise money for a worthy cause, another person prepared to open fire on them. His sixty rounds sprayed the field and players, seriously wounding Steve Scalise of Louisiana and four others. Later upon investigation, the police found that the shooter hated Republicans and was taking this opportunity to kill as many as possible.

For one moment, after the reality of evil and death were paraded in front of their faces, the congressional parties united. Then within a week or so, they returned to their corners to divide and destroy again, seemingly dismissing the unity they felt.

David expressed unity with two comparisons. One, "as precious as the anointing oil...poured over Aaron's head that ran down his beard and onto the border of his robe" (Psalm 133:2). The picture here is of the High Priest's head, which God made, and his robe, which man made, being unified together by the covering oil poured on them. The people would watch the anointing of the High Priest and it would unify them as a nation in their worship of their God. It was special and precious because it was not always that way in Israel, due to the fact that there were twelve tribes with leaders and voices who raised their own flags. So unity of spirit in worship was illustrated here.

David secondly compares unity to be "as refreshing as the dew from

Mount Hermon" (133:3), and the dew that falls on the other smaller mountains of Zion. The same dew would refresh both plants and animals no matter on which mountain they dwelt. So illustrated here is unity, refreshed and invigorated by other godly virtues.

Further, true unity allowed for commonalities and differences. Paul wrote to the church at Ephesus on the topic of the body of Christ, meaning the New Testament Church. He said, "Make every effort to keep yourselves united in the Spirit, binding yourselves together with peace. For there is one body and one Spirit, just as you have been called to one glorious hope for the future. There is one Lord, one faith, one baptism, and one God and Father, who is over all and in all and living through all" (Ephesians 4:3-6).

He challenged believers in Ephesus to put in the effort to stay united in the Holy Spirit and the body of Christ and that was possible through keeping the peace. He didn't want to allow the body to be hurt by division. He said this on the basis of the "ones" he identified: one body, one Spirit, one hope, one Lord, one faith, one baptism, and one God and Father. These "ones" stressed unity because there was only one church, Spirit, future, Lord, baptism, and God the Father for all believers. The oneness of these seven would make unity possible and probable with no reason for division. So why create rifts and schisms in the church on earth?

He identified in the verse just previous to this passage what should be the nature of every believer's heart, "Always be humble and gentle. Be patient with each other, making allowance for each other's faults because of your love" (4:2). Their internal attitudes and exterior actions would be such that they contributed to their ability to live unified.

Unity did not have to mean there could not be diversity. Certainly the Holy Spirit is the giver of all spiritual gifts but not everyone has the same gift. The differences were to be a strength, a benefit of each to the whole. The life of the believer was to be humble, gentle, patient and allowing for faults.

Wouldn't it be refreshing and precious to see a unity like that? Discord disrupts, destroys, and kills all the finer elements that can grow under the blessing of true unity. When people's hearts are reflecting the same characteristics, then God can freely bless the church because it is able to reflect His glory and that is when the world sees the difference the church can make. Too often this is not the case, but now that you understand the attitudes and actions essential to unity and understand the seven "ones," maybe it will be easier for you to promote unity.

Key Takeaway: The word community has the word unity in it. We could say it is "common-unity." David stressed the preciousness and the invigorating nature of unity and Paul stressed the internal attitudes and exterior actions which led to unity. This is not something one person can provide for the church, but it is the responsibility of all to live lives that example Christ and unify the body of Christ.

Applications:

What are you doing to create unity?

How does your family exhibit unity?

How does your church exhibit unity?

Working for the Good of Others Principle

It was said in the book of Esther, "Mordecai the Jew was second in rank to King Xerxes, preeminent among the Jews, and held in high esteem by his many fellow Jews, because he worked for the good of his people and spoke up for the welfare of all the Jews" (Esther 10:3). That is the review of Mordecai's story. Here are excerpts of how that came to be:

- Extended Family Good - Mordecai adopted his cousin Esther as his own daughter because her parents had died (Esther 2:7). He took a walk every day near the courtyard of the harem to gain information on Esther's situation after she was taken into the harem of King Xerxes as part of a search for a new queen, and he provided instructions to her (2:11, 19-20).
- Empire Good - Mordecai overheard of a plot to kill the king and passed it on to Queen Esther who shared it with King Xerxes who took care of the plotters (2:21-23).
- Moral Good - Mordecai would not kneel or pay honor to Haman (an evil man bent on the destruction of the Jews) even under the pressure of royal officials (3:2-4).
- Spiritual Good - Mordecai went out into the city to mourn, wailing loudly and bitterly, and fasted at the news of Haman's decree for the annihilation of the Jews (3:13; 4:1-8).
- National Good - Mordecai challenged Esther to get involved for her nation by going to the king to stop this decree (4:12-14).

- Support Good - Mordecai carried out the instructions of Esther to fast for three days while she and her maids did the same, before she went to the king (4:15-17).

- Emotional Good - Mordecai was impacted by four negative events in which he stood strong: captivity, Esther's recruitment into the harem, decree for the annihilation of the Jews, and the threat of death posed by Haman (5:14).

- National and Empire Good - Mordecai received the king's signet ring taken from Haman and began to work to resolve the Jewish death decree (8:2). He created a new order for the Jews to defend themselves against the order of Haman (8:9-11). The people of Susa celebrated the new decree (8:15).

- Power Good - Fear of Mordecai caused all the nobles of provinces, the highest officers, the governors, and royal officials to support the Jews (9:3).

- Legacy Good - Mordecai established the Festival of Purim, a celebration of their victory over their enemies which still takes place in the Jewish culture today (9:26-27).

- Continued to do Good - Mordecai was busy and using his rank of second to King Xerxes to promote good. He was held in high esteem and thus the quote we began with (10:3).

Mordecai was an example of a man concerned for his family, his nation, loyal to his king, and a man with high moral character. And he isn't the only one who continued to work for the good of others. It goes without saying that Jesus was perpetually engaged doing good for people.

Ezra and Nehemiah did good by leading the restoration of the Temple, the city of Jerusalem, and the people of Israel to God. Paul was a witness of Christ, taught and discipled, established churches, wrote letters of encouragement, lived on what he made from making tents, and paid the ultimate price as a testimony to his belief in Jesus Christ.

As believers, it is essential that we are ones who are working for the good of others, too. In fact, this is the mission of each believer to witness to the good that is available in Christ, to be humble, exhibit the fruit of the Spirit, and live a life that represents the Savior who will be the one who says, "Well done, my good and faithful servant" (Matthew 25:23).

Key Takeaway: Working for the good of others is to be a part of every believer's life. Doing good can include giving monetarily, but that is not the extent of it. Good can include lots of different scenarios, but the important thing is doing good. Action should be taken to find opportunities to do good to believers and unbelievers alike.

Applications:
What kind of good things are you doing for others now? What more would you like to do?

Working for the good of others does apply within the family. How are you training your children to work for the good of others by your example and by experiencing it with them?

What is your church actively engaged in that is working for the good of others?

Quotations and Permissions

1. Character: Faithful, Pg. 17: "sow a thought, reap an action..." Attributed to Ralph Waldo Emerson, 1803-1882

2. Character: Honesty, Pg. 25: "Honest is the best policy" Attributed to Edwin Sandys, House of Commons in England, 1589-1626

3. Character: Honesty, Pg. 25: "No legacy is so rich as honesty" William Shakespear, 1564-1616, Act 3, Scene 5 of "All's well that Ends Well" noted in Bartleby Research.

4. Conduct: Compassion, Pg. 79: Words of song, *O To be like thee*, written by Thomas Chisholm 1897

5. Conduct: Courage, Pg. 89: Melanie Greenberg, Ph.D, Article: The Six Attributes of Courage. Psychology Today, August 23, 2012, The Mindful Self Express

6. Conduct: Thankfulness, Pg.157: *Exposition of the Psalms* by Herbert C. Leupold, copyright © 1959, 1987. Baker Books, a division of Baker Publishing Group. 394

7. Confidence: Discipline, Pg. 186: *Exposition of the Psalms* by Herbert C. Leupold, copyright © 1959, 1987. Baker Books, a division of Baker Publishing Group. 319

8. Confidence: Discretion, Pg. 189: William Shakespear, Henry IV Play, Act V, Scene 4, Part 1 "better part of valor"

9. Confidence: Providential, Pg. 227: The Red Sea Rules, Robert J. Morgan, W Publishing Group, Copyright 2001, 2014 by Robert J. Morgan, pgs. 98-99.

10. Community: Belonging, Pg. 256: Taken from The Search to Belong by Joseph R. Myers, Copyright © 2003 by Joseph R. Myers. Used by permission of Zondervan. www.zondervan.com, pgs.11-18.

11. Repentance Chart, Pg. 122: Used by permission of Life Action Ministries, www.LifeActionMinistries.org, Ignite Report, 8/2009

Printed in the United States
by Baker & Taylor Publisher Services